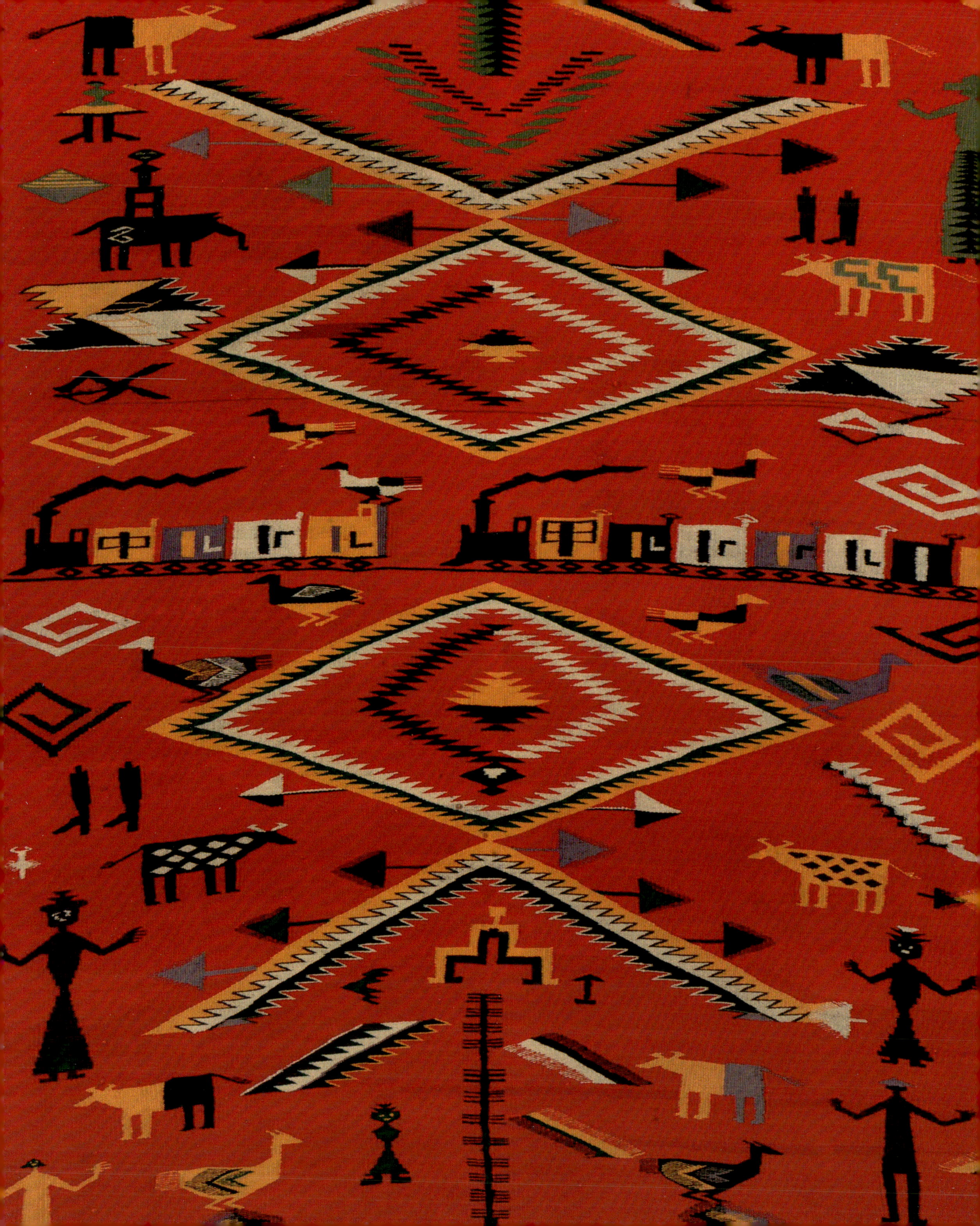

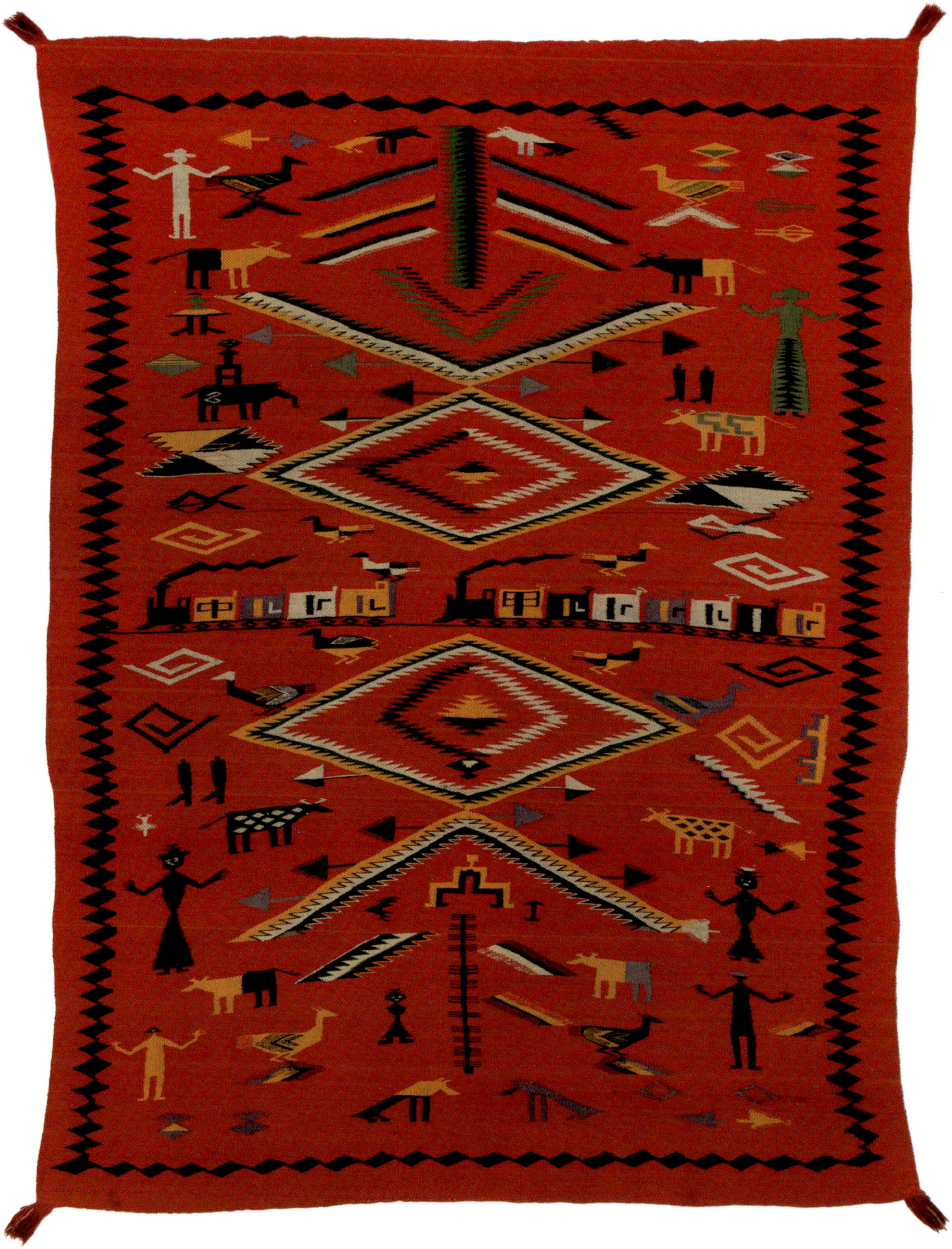

Pictorial blanket, c. 1885. Artist once known (Diné). Germantown wool yarn, cotton string, handspun wool, bayeta. 84 × 66 ½ inches. Museum of Indian Arts and Culture/Laboratory of Anthropology, gift of Mrs. Philip B. Stewart, 9316/12. Photograph by Addison Doty.

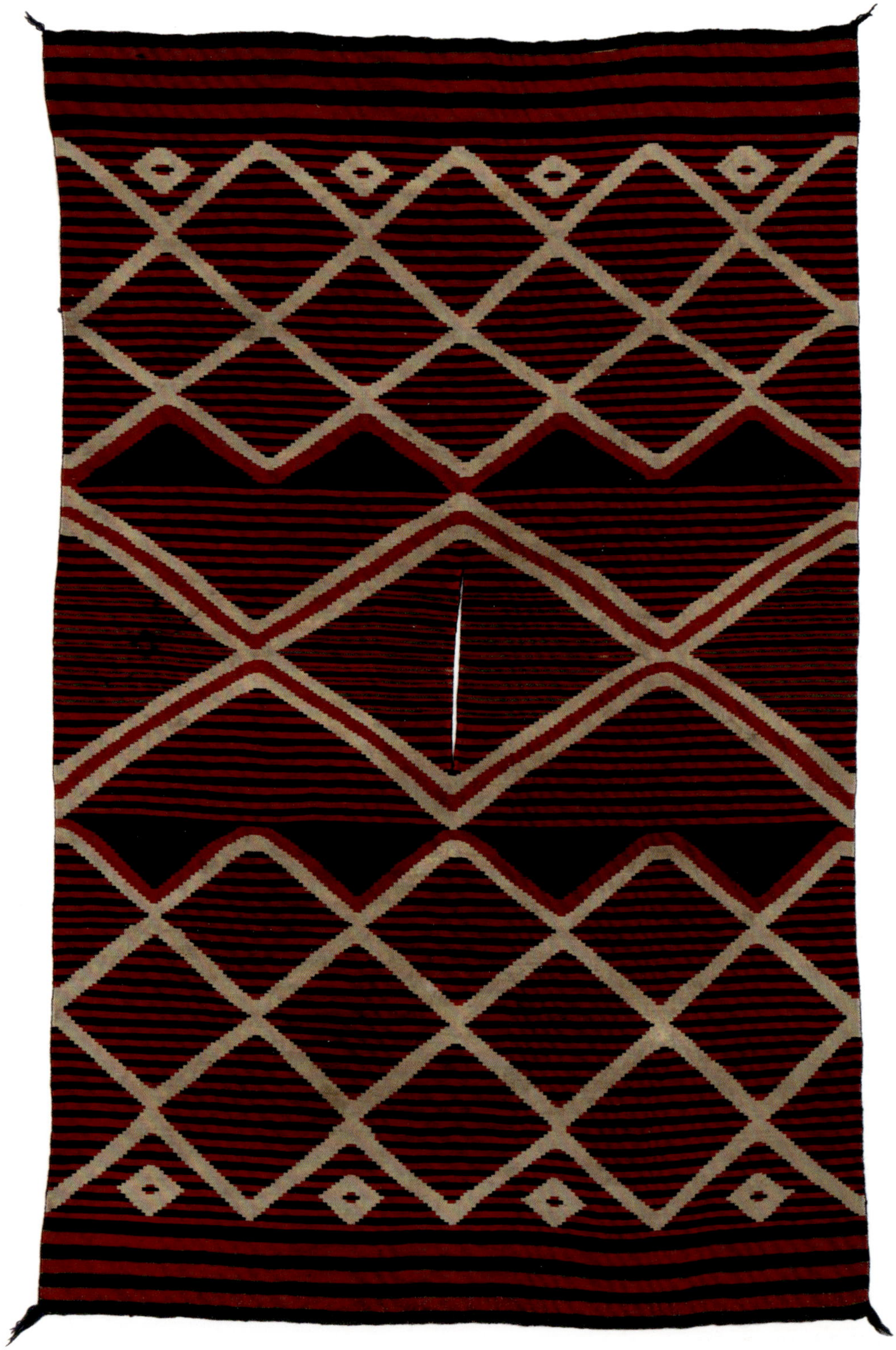

Poncho blanket, c. 1840–1860. Artist once known (Diné). Handspun churro yarn, lac dye, indigo dye, bayeta, vegetal dye. 81½ × 54½ inches. Museum of Indian Arts and Culture/Laboratory of Anthropology, H. C. Yontz Collection, courtesy of John and Linda Comstock and the Abigail Van Vleck Charitable Trust, 9051/12. Photograph by Addison Doty.

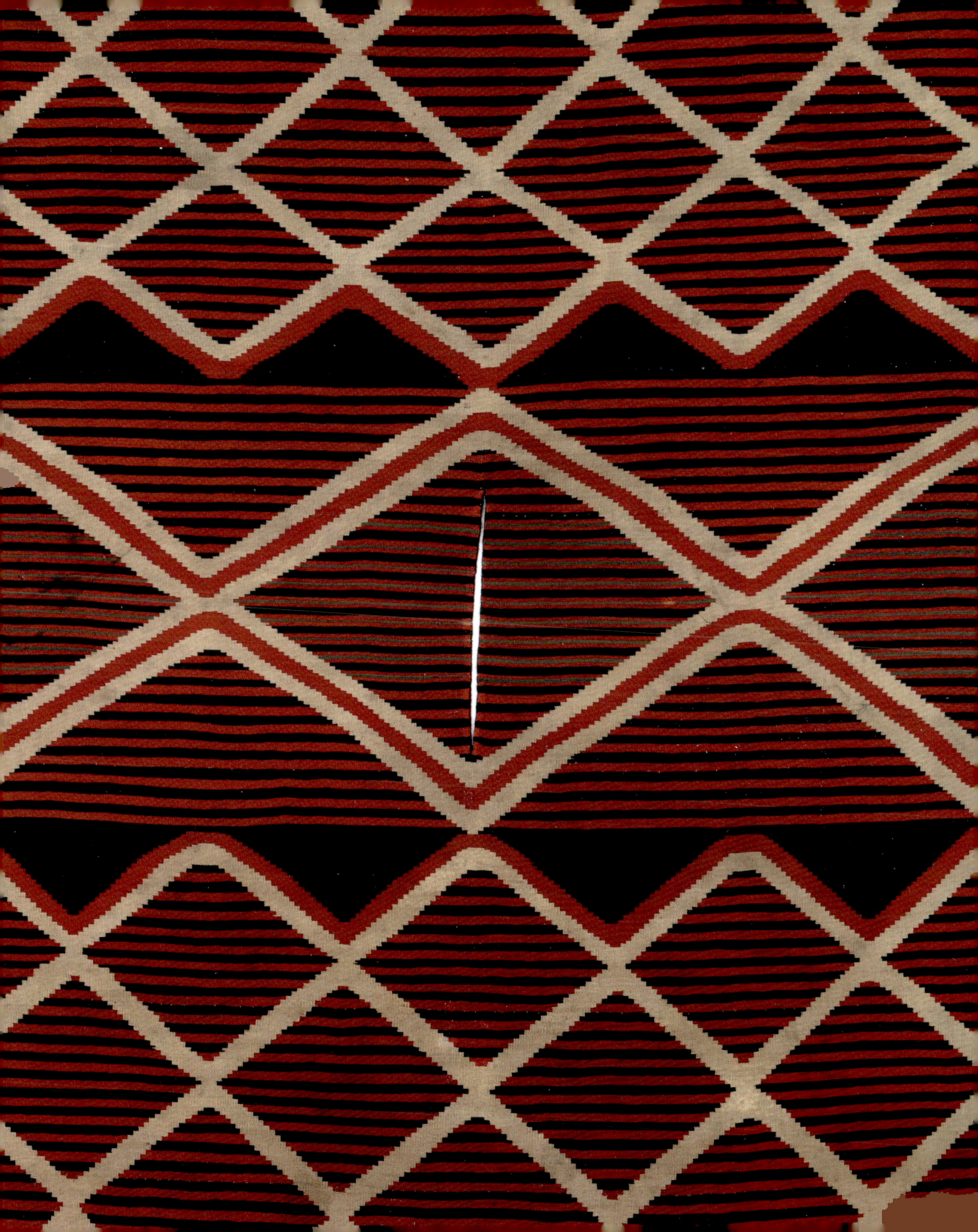

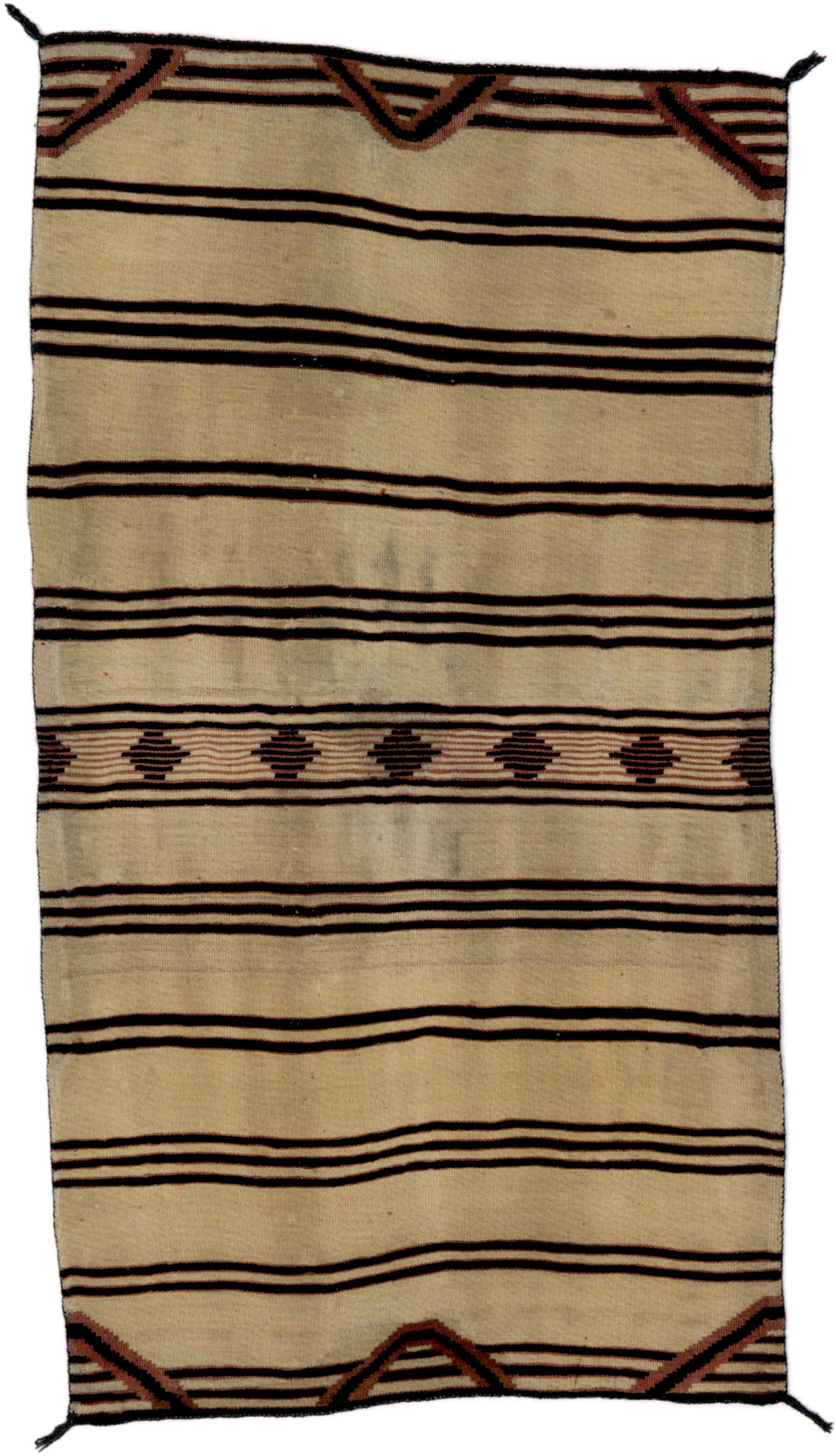

Shoulder blanket or saddle blanket, 1825–1860. Artist once known (Diné). Handspun wool, bayeta, indigo dye, lac dye, cochineal dye. 52 × 30 inches. Museum of Indian Arts and Culture/Laboratory of Anthropology, H. C. Yontz Collection, courtesy of John and Linda Comstock and the Abigail Van Vleck Charitable Trust, 9050/12. Photograph by Addison Doty.

Within the reflective, symmetrical design, the horizontal bands and terraced triangles are created from indigo and outlined with bayeta, composed of a combination of lac and cochineal dyes. The background color comes from handspun wool, which one would imagine being white. Yet it has aged to tan, reminiscent of "Navajo White" paint derived from the Navajo Nation flag.

A visual balance is achieved through the even and odd number of design elements, as well as from the subtle tension between the tones of the weft yarn. Overall, this sense of balance in material and composition offers a feeling of stability and vibrancy.

—RAPHEAL BEGAY

Horizons

WEAVING BETWEEN THE LINES WITH DINÉ TEXTILES

EDITED BY HADLEY WELCH JENSEN

FOREWORD BY
Laura Tohe

PREFACE BY
Tony Chavarria

WITH CONTRIBUTIONS BY
Kevin Aspaas
Rapheal Begay
Wade Campbell
Jennifer Nez Denetdale
Hadley Welch Jensen
Larissa Nez
Lynda Teller Pete
Darby Raymond-Overstreet
Tyrrell Tapaha

MUSEUM OF NEW MEXICO PRESS
SANTA FE

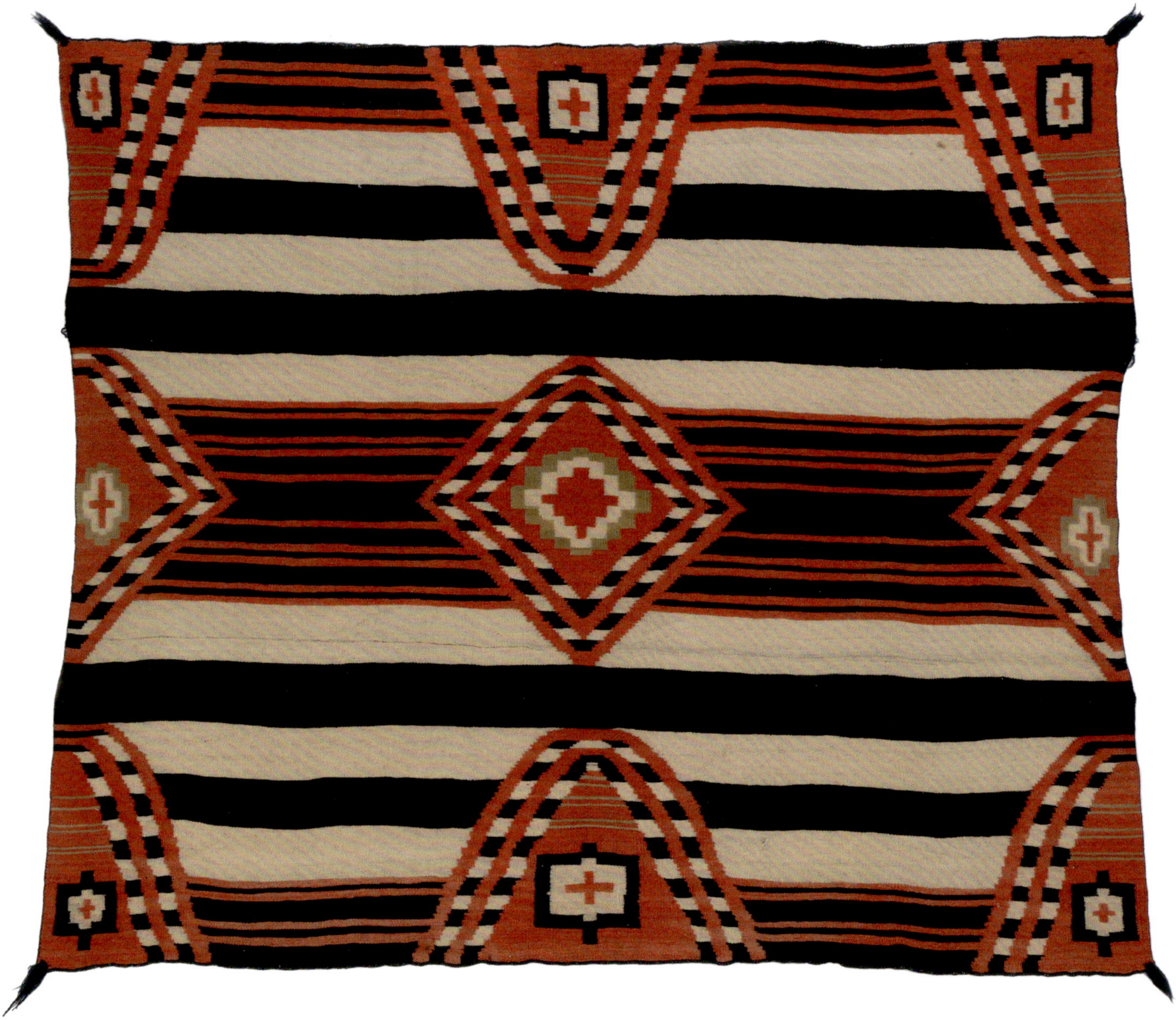

Third Phase Chief blanket, 1875–1880. Artist once known (Diné). Handspun wool, indigo dye, vegetal dye. 55¼ × 65 inches. Museum of Indian Arts and Culture/Laboratory of Anthropology, gift of Mrs. Philip B. Stewart, 9096/12. Photograph by Addison Doty.

Chief blankets have become iconic Diné weavings. They are important not only among the Diné people but across Indian Country, as they were traded widely among the Plains tribes north of Diné Bikéyah. Even to this day, they are sought after because of our ancestors' stylistic design choices and creativity, as we can see in this unusual blanket. Even during times of uncertainty, Diné weavers created Chief blankets. Today, they are a representation of the resiliency of Diné weavers and their families.

—KEVIN ASPAAS

There was once a time that we wove for one another—
pieces of clothing created to protect the wearer from harm.
It is important for our weavers to know their lineage,
to know where they came from.

—KEVIN ASPAAS

Tapestry weave, c. 1960.
Artist once known (Diné). Wool.
Overall: 43 5⁄16 × 24 7⁄16 × 5 7⁄8 inches (as mounted by A. Girard). Museum of International Folk Art, gift of the Girard Foundation Collection, A.1980.1.231. Photograph by Addison Doty.

The psychedelic quality of this weaving is expressed in the shifting black "leaves," or parallelograms, as they move across a white background. This piece centers that movement through the fluidity of the leaves, and the ways they change in size and direction. Although this piece is small, it powerfully and playfully engages with light and shadow, space, and creativity.

—LARISSA NEZ

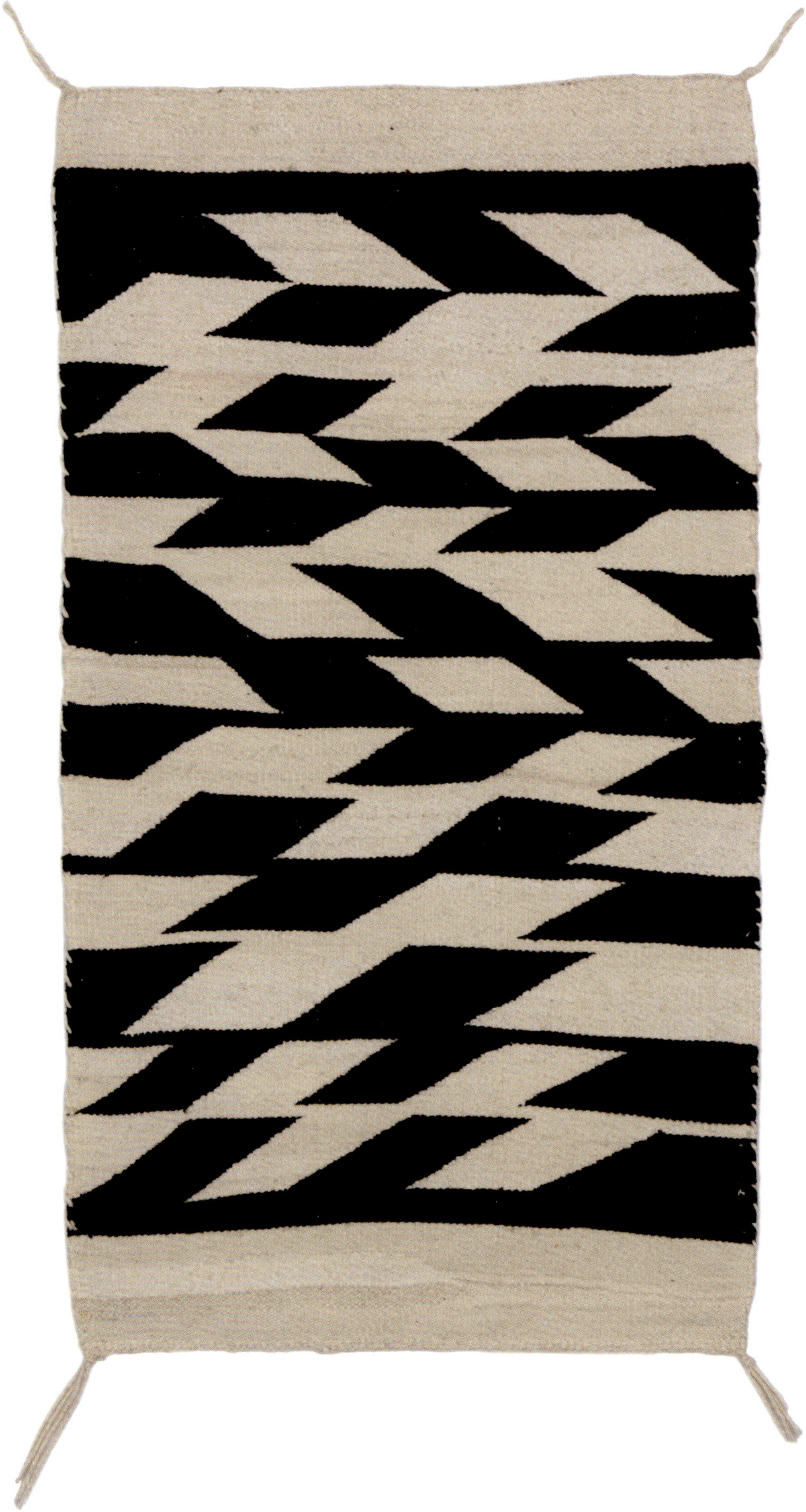

Contents

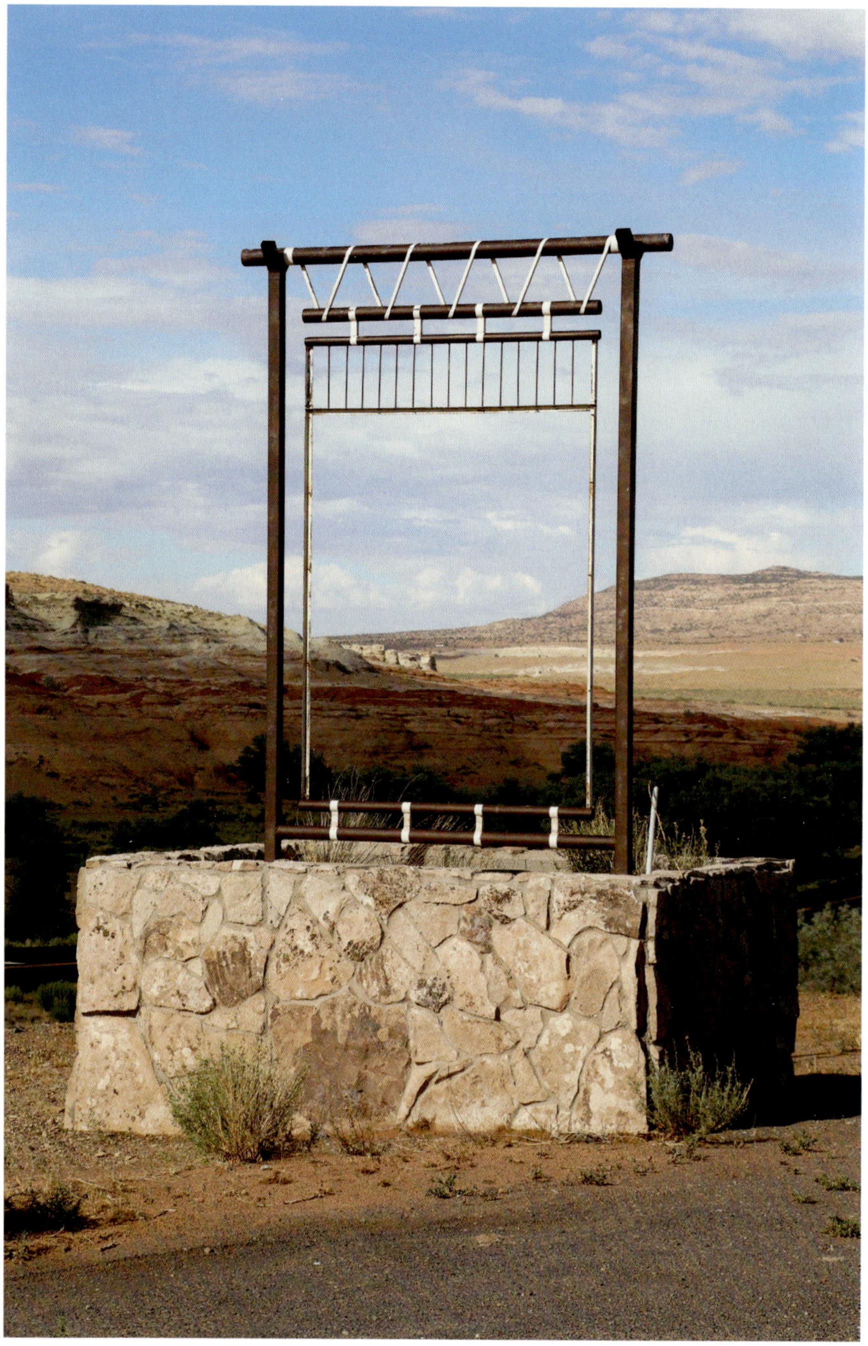

Loom (Tó Nehelíįh—Tonalea, Arizona), 2022. Rapheal Begay (Diné, b. 1991). Courtesy of the artist.

How to Sell a Weaving

LAURA TOHE (DINÉ/LAGUNA PUEBLO)

Trading post day and Masaní
gathers lightning and mountains
she pulled from the sky and

wove onto parallel lines
for she is part geometrician,
part coyote.

She buries her treasure
in the cornfield
damp from desert rains

still fresh from the memory
of the loom before she will walk
to the trading post and get only

half for the weight of mountains and lightning,
half for woolly clouds spun into horizontal lines on her lap,
half for her creation laid down one line at a time.

But in her dwells an old Indian trick:
she shakes off the sand and retains the dampness
for the scale from which the trader will pay her

full for the weight of mountains and lightning,
full for woolly clouds spun into horizontal lines on her lap,
full for her creation laid down one line at a time.

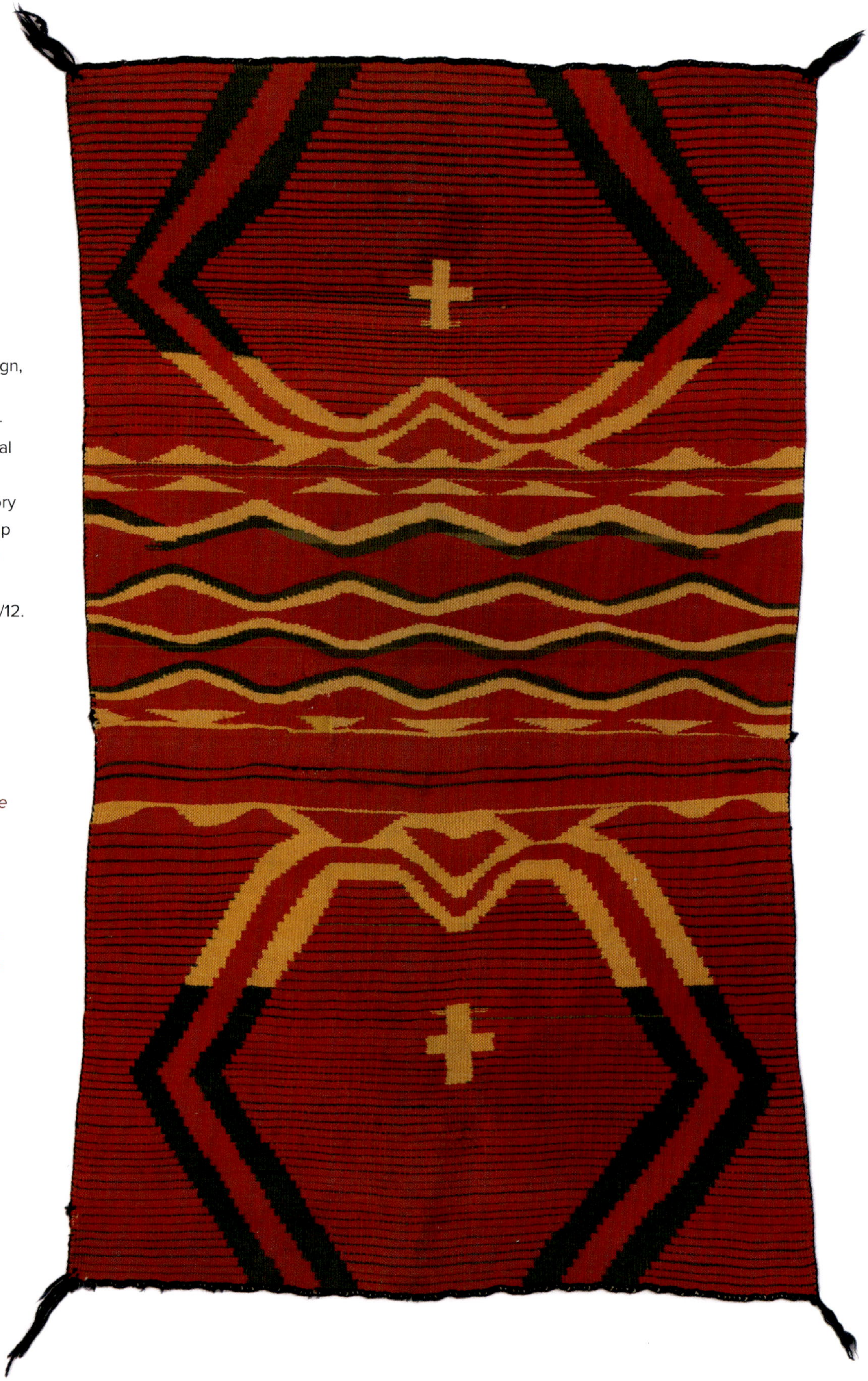

Wearing blanket with spider design, 1860–1880. Artist once known (Diné). Handspun wool, commercial wool yarn, indigo dye, vegetal dye. 51 × 33 inches. Museum of Indian Arts and Culture/Laboratory of Anthropology, gift of Mrs. Philip B. Stewart, courtesy of John and Linda Comstock and the Abigail Van Vleck Charitable Trust, 9124/12. Photograph by Addison Doty.

This weaving is composed of an abstract representation of a spider (na'ashjé'ii). In Diné creation stories, Spider Woman, an important deity, helped create the loom and gave Diné the gift of weaving. The weaver of this blanket honors Spider Woman by exhibiting a distinct practice of creative experimentation and control. The elements reflect the longevity of Diné cosmology and oral history passed down through generations of Diné people and weavers.

—LARISSA NEZ

Foreword
Becoming Mythic

Weaving is a ceremony. Growing up, I was surrounded by family and relatives who created diyogí, woven blankets and rugs considered valuable soft goods, which are part of the cultural wealth of the Navajo Nation in the Glittering World. I observed and heard dah'iistł'ó, the loom, resonate with upward movement sounds as the women in my family wove stories and songs with deft fingers. The loom stood near their bed, in the living area, or under a shade tree in the summer. We were warned not to touch grandma's weaving. If the dogs ventured near the loom, they were chased away with "kwiįį́ʼ" and they would scatter. When finished for the day, they covered their loom with a cloth to protect it. In the morning they removed the cloth, adjusted the loom, and began the daily process of creating an enduring visual and aural work that continues from one generation to the next. With their designs mentally stored and instruments nearby, the weavers in my family became mythic storytellers, composers, musicians, and mathematicians.

On our visits to Shibízhí, my paternal aunt, she would stop weaving to story with us. Her specialties, besides runners, were intricate double-sided weaves and beautiful thick saddle blankets because our family owned horses. Her designs vibrate with movement and musicality and are said to be analogous to sacred ceremonial songs. Indeed, the shapes resemble a musical score. On one of our outings, she said she had forgotten how to weave a particular design. After several unsuccessful tries, she undid the weave and didn't try again until the design came to her in a dream and she was able to recreate it. After she retired from working, she wove full time. "I told my kids when I die, bury me with my loom. If you put me in a rest home, bring my loom," she joked. After our goodbyes, she returned to her weaving and to the sounds that are a large part of growing up among my clan relatives who wove. We buried her years later, but not with her loom.

Shibízhí learned to weave from her mother, Shinálí, my paternal grandmother. Spending part of my summers with Shinálí is among my cherished memories. She was patient, kind, and resilient, and, being Bitter Water clan, told me stories about water after the monsoon rains left their puddles on the thirsty earth. In the summer evenings my cousin and I sat on the floor with a denim cloth on our laps, cleaning the mound of wool of debris and carding it into soft fluffy clouds for her spindle. Lanolin from the wool moisturized our hands. Moths circled the kerosene lamp crazily. It prompted stories from Shinálí with a strong caution to not model our lives after moth behavior.

In the morning, Shinálí settled into weaving for the next few hours. A steady tempo of pulling the even lines of warp, strumming, and tamping filled the room. Alive with her stories, the weaving sang in colors as it grew upward, each line holding the notes of her composition that shaped clouds and mountains she pulled down into her loom. Some notes held momentarily and others sustained continuously in the background; it soothed like medicine. Life was in harmony—the rains had come, the dogs sat under the shade of the hogan flicking their tails, my father read a magazine, life hummed with movement. The earth, slow and deliberate, moved us toward the last warm caresses of summer.

Ałk'idą́ą́'áda, jiní, stories from time immemorial tell that Spider Woman gifted weaving to the Diné women and taught them how to weave. Shimá, my mother, talented with Spider Woman's abilities, could create almost anything made with string—sash belts, biil (the traditional woven dress), winter string games, and many craft arts. She produced tightly woven rugs that could hold water. For her living room floor, she chose the bold colors of the Chief's blanket. Originally a blanket style, after the transitional period and calls from traders and tourists, such weavings were made for the floor and later for display. We watched my mother loosen the weaving from the loom for this special moment, like watching a baby take her first steps. She spread it on the floor, and we admired its striking beauty. "It's okay to walk on it," she said, but none of us wanted to, so we tiptoed on the outer edges.

On one of her hitchhiking trips to the flea market Shimásaní, my maternal great-grandmother Lupton bought sweaters to recycle. The emerald-green, hot pink, and teal colors blended smoothly with the natural and dyed colors in her rug. Narrow strips of eye-catching pink pop and create a minor fusion of traditional and contemporary, as if she wanted to allow only a slight opening to the outside world. It reminds me of how Diné women keep an eye open for found objects, human made and otherwise, to repurpose them.

Navajo weavers hold economic and cultural clout because weaving is essential to the maintenance of Navajo culture and ceremonial life and provides financial support. My Tsénahabiłnii great-great-grandmother developed a shrewdness in her business dealings with the traders who once dictated the sizes and designs of weavings and bought them by their weight. Before she sold them, she buried them in damp sand to absorb the moisture and make them heavier. The trader increased her payment, which enabled her to buy more supplies and food for her family—and perhaps a treat for the young ones at home.

Because I was away at boarding school, I didn't learn to weave. I was an observer and listener until I asked my grandmother to teach me. On my third weaving, the rhythmic sounds and aural tempo drifted back. As if by instinct or by osmosis, it seemed my hands knew what to do. All I had to do was listen to the loom. Though I'm still a beginner, I imagine the computer as my dah'iistł'ó, where I weave my poems and stories just as my ancestors wove theirs.

Weaving is a family collaboration—from herding sheep to constructing the loom, making the weaving tools, and cleaning and preparing the wool. Time consuming and physically demanding, it requires that weavers give themselves fully to their work. I've found strands of hair woven into the rugs given to me as gifts. Spiritual helpers also come to assist the weaver and to remind them that perfection is not sought in creation: to make anything perfect is to take away their aid. In traditional weavings a small line of wool, barely noticeable, is woven into a corner as an intentional mistake called ch'íníť'í, it leads to the outside. This slight imperfection, also called a spirit line, is part of the diyogí that allows it to breathe and not trap negativity. Positive thoughts also enter through this opening, and when the weaver releases the weaving to the world, her hope that it will be cared for like a child accompanies it.

Embedded in diyogí are the numerous collective memories and stories of Diné. Our stories speak of history, sacred ceremonies, mythic journeys, struggles, and triumphs. They honor accomplishments and remember the trauma of the Long Walk—the forced removal from our homeland—and our return from incarceration. They speak of sky and earth beauty replete with plants and animals, contact with the outside world, modern life, and influences from other weaving cultures. This richness of stories and love for weaving has brought international fame to the Diné for their textile art, once in decline until a revival brought Diné youth, including my eldest brother, to the loom. I am always awe struck by the stunning artistry of Navajo weavers whenever I visit museums and trading posts. *Horizons: Weaving Between the Lines with Diné Textiles* displays an astonishing collection of Navajo textile art and photography, demonstrating the ongoing evolution and innovation of Diné arts from traditional to contemporary expressions. Through textile art and the ceremony of weaving, we trace our ancestral identity, cultural sovereignty, and history that ground us culturally and spiritually in the Glittering World within the Four Sacred Mountains of our homeland.

It begins with songs and prayers
she calls the earth and sky
she calls down female mountains
she calls down male mountains
to her loom
to balance the world

LAURA TOHE (DINÉ/LAGUNA PUEBLO)
Navajo Nation Poet Laureate
Arizona State University Professor Emerita

Rug, 1880–1897. Artist once known (Diné). Cotton string, Germantown wool yarn, raveled yarn. 74¼ × 52 inches. Museum of Indian Arts and Culture/Laboratory of Anthropology, gift of Kathleen Lilley, 26091/12. Photograph by Addison Doty.

In 1864, the United States federal government continued the attempted ethnic cleansing and cultural assimilation of the Navajo people through the forced removal from our homelands to Bosque Redondo in Fort Sumner, New Mexico. This campaign is known as "The Navajo Long Walk," or Hweeldi (The Time of Suffering).

Our time at Bosque Redondo exposed us to a plethora of new food, materials, and resources that completely changed our weaving. Vibrantly dyed three-ply Germantown yarn was introduced during this time as a way of continuing textile production, since people couldn't bring their livestock with them. Germantown yarn continued to be steadily supplied after Bosque Redondo through traders and the newly established railway. This piece, with its Bisti stars, now acts as evidence of the adaptation of Navajo weaving post–Long Walk era.

–TYRRELL TAPAHA

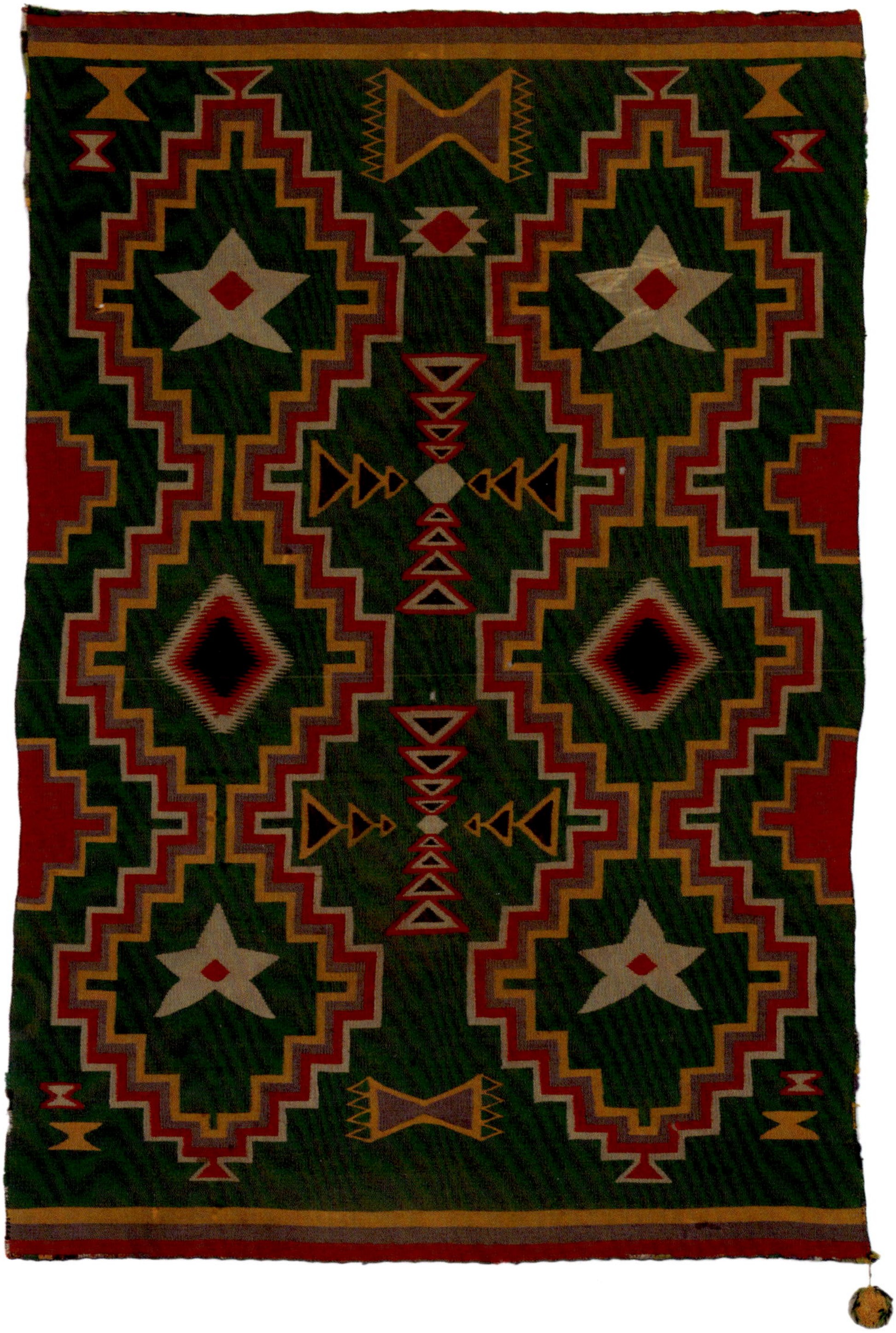

Preface

Museums, with their extensive collections of art, artifact, and history, are often seen as bastions of authority and knowledge. However, as many researchers know, information on museum collections can be scant. Records are often very basic, lacking details about the object itself or the people who created it. In the case of historic Native material, information on makers and the context in which the item was created and later collected is frequently not recorded. It has been the task of museum professionals to delve into the internal and external records and attempt to create a more in-depth understanding. Although this may not seem to be the most exciting venture, it can be a very engaging and rewarding journey. Museums have realized that what information they do have can be greatly enhanced by speaking directly to the communities and cultures from which the objects originated.

Horizons: Weaving Between the Lines with Diné Textiles is a novel examination and presentation of historic and contemporary Navajo textiles. Using the collections at the Museum of Indian Arts and Culture as a starting place, co-curators Hadley Welch Jensen and Rapheal Begay (Diné) assembled an advisory committee of Diné weavers and scholars to review, select, and interpret items that would join works of the past with those of the present. Rather than simply choosing a selection of Classic wearing blankets—often the curatorial default for approaches to Navajo weaving—the *Horizons* team looked toward a larger and more nuanced narrative. Cultural items were chosen to enhance museum knowledge with personal experience of growing up with weavers and keepers of culture. In addition, these woven creations have been augmented with photographs and digital media to reconnect material culture with place. This reactivation lives on in this unique publication.

Horizons positions textiles in the context of culture, history, and art. It is from the perspective of lived experience that woven items can be seen to present everything from the disgraceful internment at Bosque Redondo to the arrival of the railroad and trading posts; from how a dress is worn and shaped to what design and color can tell us about traditions. This is the information that enriches our knowledge of the Diné and lives beyond the temporal span of an exhibition. *Horizons* is at the juncture of developing museum practice in which a new generation of scholars, artists, and practitioners—Native and non-Native—are redefining standard roles of curatorial authority, seeking the expertise of Native communities, and producing a better understanding of art and culture. Jensen and Begay, along with Kevin Aspaas, Larissa Nez, Lynda Teller Pete,

Darby Raymond-Overstreet, and Tyrrell Tapaha, aided by Lillia McEnaney, have enhanced the museum catalogue and created layered meanings that will benefit our future.

As you start your own examination into their efforts, keep at heart the legacy of Diné who have woven stories shaped by the loom, using Spider Woman's gift. The horizon of their past and present creativity remains forever vibrant.

TONY R. CHAVARRIA (SANTA CLARA PUEBLO)
Curator of Ethnology
Museum of Indian Arts and Culture

Acknowledgments

Horizons: Weaving Between the Lines with Diné Textiles offers a new interpretation of the historic textile collection at the Museum of Indian Arts and Culture (MIAC) through the voices, perspectives, and leadership of Diné community members and cultural practitioners. This book grew out of an exhibition of the same name held at MIAC, in Santa Fe, New Mexico, from July 16, 2023, through February 2, 2025. All exhibitions are collaborative enterprises, and co-curator and photographer Rapheal Begay and I are indebted to the many people who contributed to the realization of this project. We were fortunate to work in partnership with an advisory committee whose expertise has grounded the project in Diné knowledges, lifeways, and cultural practices. These efforts were reinforced by MIAC's enduring commitment to integrating intergenerational Native voices into its exhibitions and programs.

We are honored to feature the work and words of contemporary artists, scholars, and writers including Lynda Teller Pete (Diné; advisory committee chair), Kevin Aspaas (Diné), Larissa Nez (Diné), Darby Raymond-Overstreet (Diné), and Tyrrell Tapaha (Diné). For their important contributions to this publication, I also thank Rapheal Begay (Diné), Wade Campbell (Diné), Tony Chavarria (Santa Clara Pueblo), Jennifer Nez Denetdale (Diné), and Laura Tohe (Diné/Laguna Pueblo).

The majority of the works featured in the exhibition and book are drawn from MIAC's permanent collection. We express our appreciation to the individuals and institutions who loaned additional works, including Keeley Aspaas (Diné), Darby Raymond-Overstreet, Tyrrell Tapaha, Peter Goldman and Beverly Werber, DeAnna Goldtooth, the Gochman Family Collection, the Heard Museum, the Museum of International Folk Art, and the Tia Collection.

The exhibition at the Museum of Indian Arts and Culture was beautifully designed and produced by a dedicated team: Natalie Baca, in collaboration with Darby Raymond-Overstreet (graphic design), Tony Chavarria (institutional liaison), Margaret DePond (copy editor), Angela Duckwall (conservator), Lillia McEnaney (project manager), Trilby Nelson (exhibition designer), and the exhibitions staff of the Museum Resources Division. At MIAC, we also thank former executive directors Matthew Martinez (Ohkay Owingeh) and Polly Nordstrand (Hopi) and former deputy director Melissa Powell, as well as Ross Altshuler, Angela Crespin (Santo Domingo Pueblo), Patrick Cruz (Ohkay Owingeh), Marita Hinds (Tesuque Pueblo), and Lisa Mendoza. At the Museum of New Mexico Foundation, we extend our thanks to Jamie Clements,

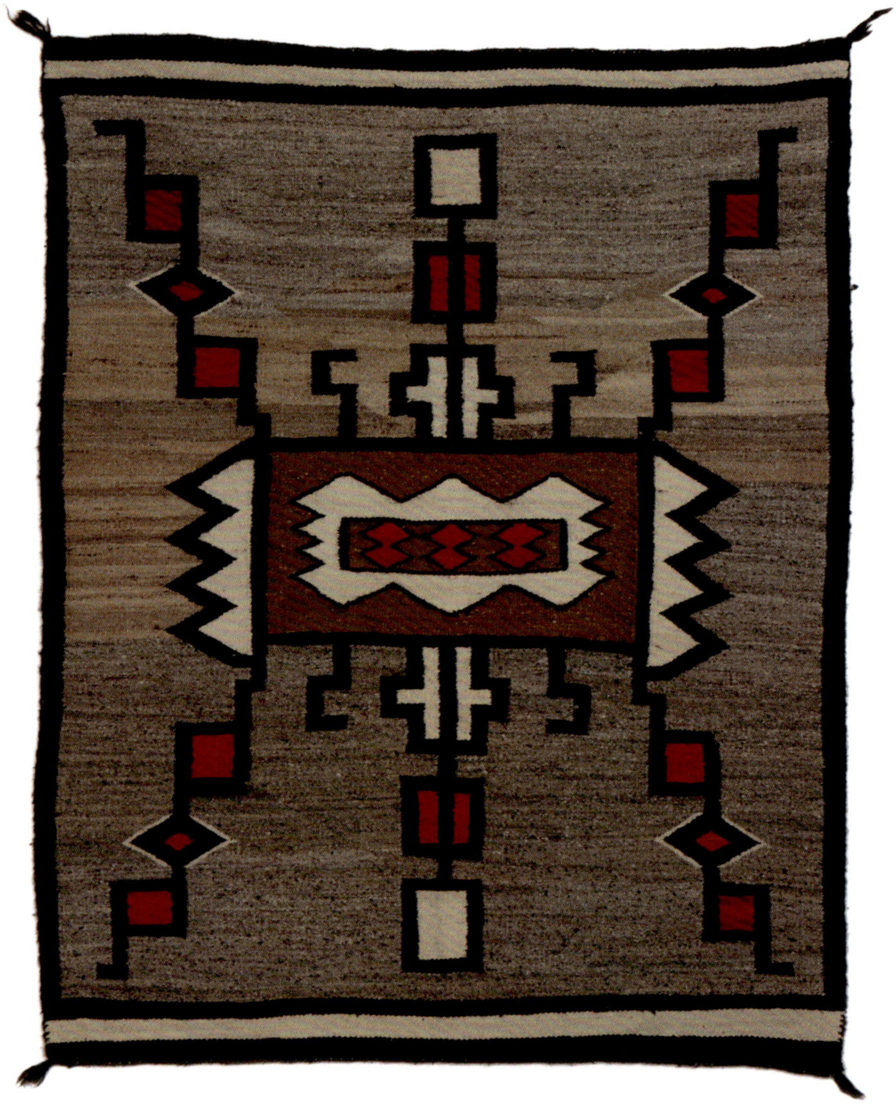

Storm Weaving, 1936. Átł'óhí, "The One Who Weaves" (Diné). Handspun wool, churro wool, aniline dye. 67 × 52 inches. Museum of Indian Arts and Culture/Laboratory of Anthropology, gift of Mrs. Philip B. Stewart, 9532/12. Photograph by Addison Doty.

In 1936, a Diné male weaver, identified as "The One Who Weaves," made this striking Storm Pattern, a rug design from the J. B. Moore catalogue of 1911. The sheer size of this work requires the viewer to engage with the intricacies of its simple design. From the variegation of the handspun yarn to the symbolism of the design layout, this piece is a snapshot of the weaver's life.

Most Navajo weavings were attributed to female weavers, even if males wove the textiles. Not only was this particular rug made by a named weaver, but an identified male weaver! Within our stories and songs, there have always been male, female, and queer weavers. At the turn of the twentieth century, the notion of male weavers didn't fit into the romanticized image of what Navajo weaving was and, as such, was deemed inauthentic to Navajo culture. Now, male weavers are receiving recognition and creating masterpieces like this one.

—TYRRELL TAPAHA

Cara O'Brien, Peggy Hermann, Lauren Paige, and Brittny Wood. Others who contributed to exhibition development included Chloe Accardi, Laura Addison, Jeanne Brako, Connor Chee (Diné), Charine Gonzales (San Ildefonso Pueblo), and Jack Townes.

The multimedia components of the exhibition were created in collaboration with Jesse Merandy, director of Digital Humanities/Exhibitions, Bard Graduate Center; photographer Byron Flesher; Rapheal Begay; and Darby Raymond-Overstreet. Funding for the 360 project was provided by NYU Gallatin WetLab; a film and photography permit was approved by Navajo Nation TV & Film, Division of Human Resources, Window Rock, Arizona. For their time and effort, over several years of project development, I thank each of them.

Invaluable financial support for *Horizons* came from numerous individuals and institutions. In particular, we wish to recognize the exhibition's lead sponsors, France A. Córdova and Christian J. Foster. Additional leadership funding was provided by Tom and Mary James, founders of the James Museum of Western and Wildlife Art; Shiprock Santa Fe; the New Mexico Department of Cultural Affairs; and the Museum of New Mexico Foundation. We thank the Terra Foundation for American Art for their generous support of both the exhibition and its accompanying publication. This collective support has allowed us to advance a model of collaborative curation informed by Indigenous sovereignty and creative cultural expression, providing an opportunity to bring this project to the communities our institutions serve.

Finally, I am especially grateful to Director Anna Gallegos and Art and Production Director David Skolkin of the Museum of New Mexico Press; project editor Kate O'Donnell; and photographer Addison Doty for their contributions to *Horizons: Weaving Between the Lines with Diné Textiles.*

HADLEY WELCH JENSEN

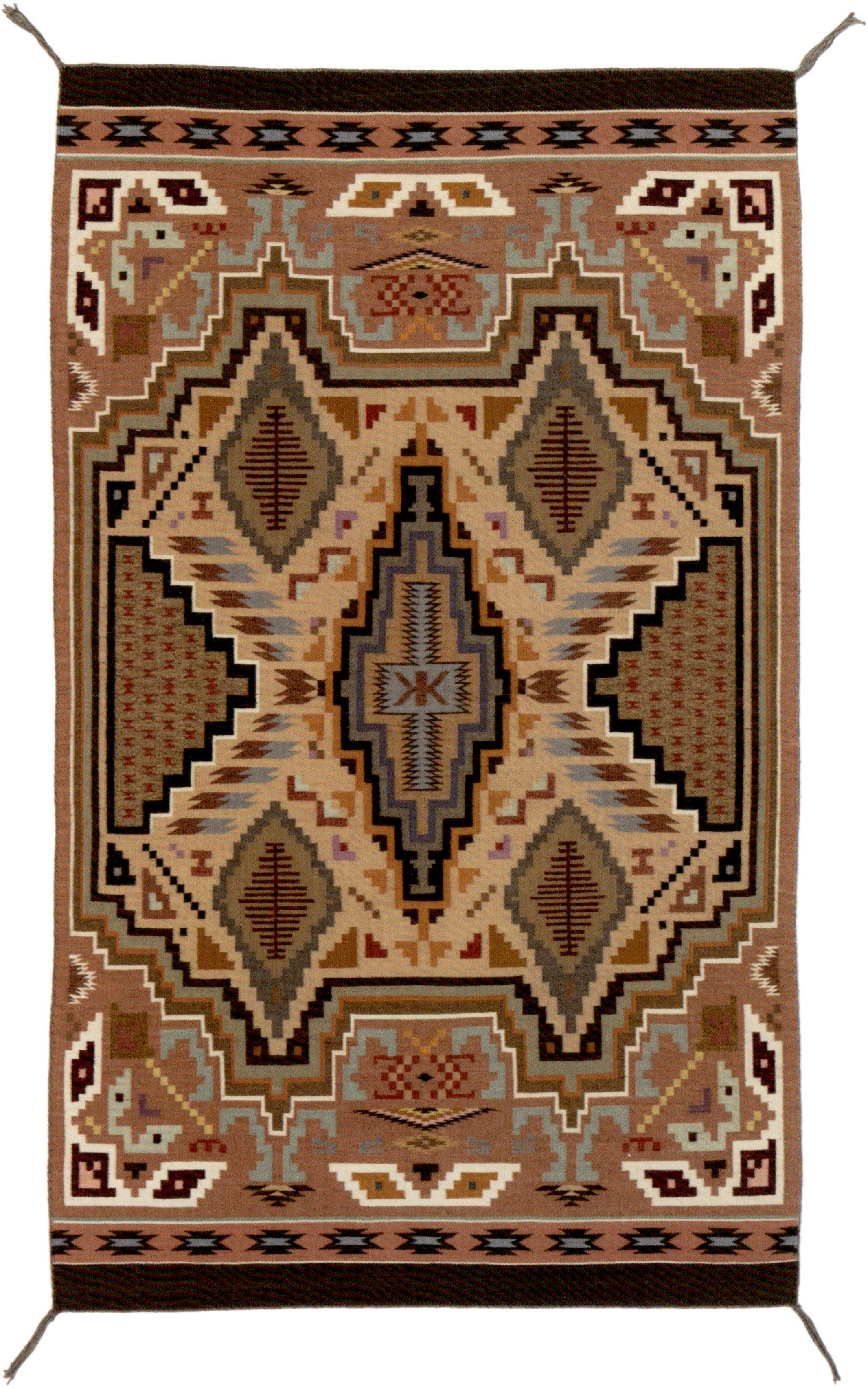

Wall hanging, Burntwater, c. 1980s. Lillie Joe (Diné). Commercial wool yarn. 61 × 38 inches. Museum of Indian Arts and Culture/Laboratory of Anthropology, gift of Jeffery and Carole Katz, 55425/12. Photograph by Addison Doty.

This monumental work is a testimony to a weaver's engagement with the landscape. They imaginatively created a complex web of elements texturized and balanced by the variety of warm and cool colors. The talent, skill, and knowledge of the weaver is expressed in the smallest details. The careful attention to every element of this weaving is evidence of mastering and loving the practice of weaving.

—LARISSA NEZ

Horizons

WEAVING BETWEEN THE LINES WITH DINÉ TEXTILES

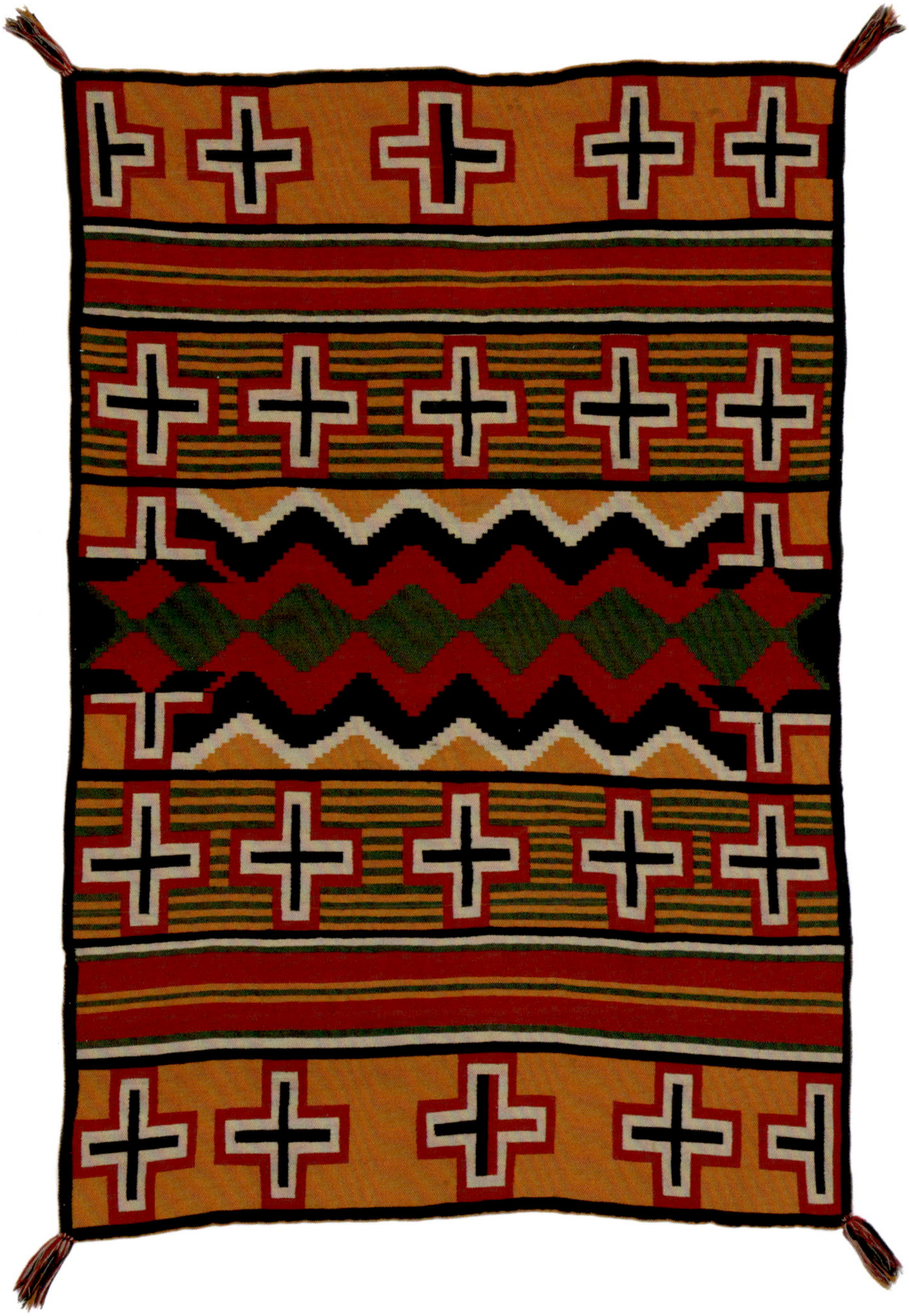

Blanket, 1875–1885. Artist once known (Diné). Germantown wool yarn, aniline dye. 77 × 52 ½ inches. Museum of Indian Arts and Culture/Laboratory of Anthropology, gift of Mr. and Mrs. Ted Otero, 36299/12. Photograph by Addison Doty.

On viewing this piece, I was immediately drawn to the vibrant color palette, which to me implies an energetic artistic vision at the forefront in this textile's creation. I also see this through the blanket's dimensional quality, and the suggestion of movement that is attained through the colorful composition of motifs. As the designs expand from the center, emergence is evoked through the separation of subsequent design elements as though they are layered in space. This compositional feature is another unique quality of this weaving. For me, the vivid colors and dynamic nature portrayed in this piece reflect the continued vibrancy and vitality of our communities, traditions, and artforms.

—DARBY RAYMOND-OVERSTREET

Introduction
Constellations of Thought

HADLEY WELCH JENSEN

Horizons: Weaving Between the Lines with Diné Textiles is not a publication *about* Navajo textiles. It represents instead a curatorial framework for thinking about the culture of creativity that reflects and inspires Diné (Navajo) weaving, both historically and into the present. As this project took shape in 2021, co-curator Rapheal Begay and I began to have conversations about land, space, and light, and specifically the horizon. As both a point of connection between sky and earth and a separation of space, the horizon line emerged as our conceptual touchstone.

We developed the exhibition and its accompanying book to explore the connections between weaving and photography as modes of engagement with place. By situating these media in conversation, we present a way of seeing and knowing Diné Bikéyah, the Navajo homeland, that emphasizes the land-based and relational practices of Diné fiber arts. "As forms of visual storytelling" Begay reflects, "Diné weaving and photography are created in collaboration with one's surroundings. Diné Bikéyah is not only our home but is also a source of inspiration for design, color, and connection

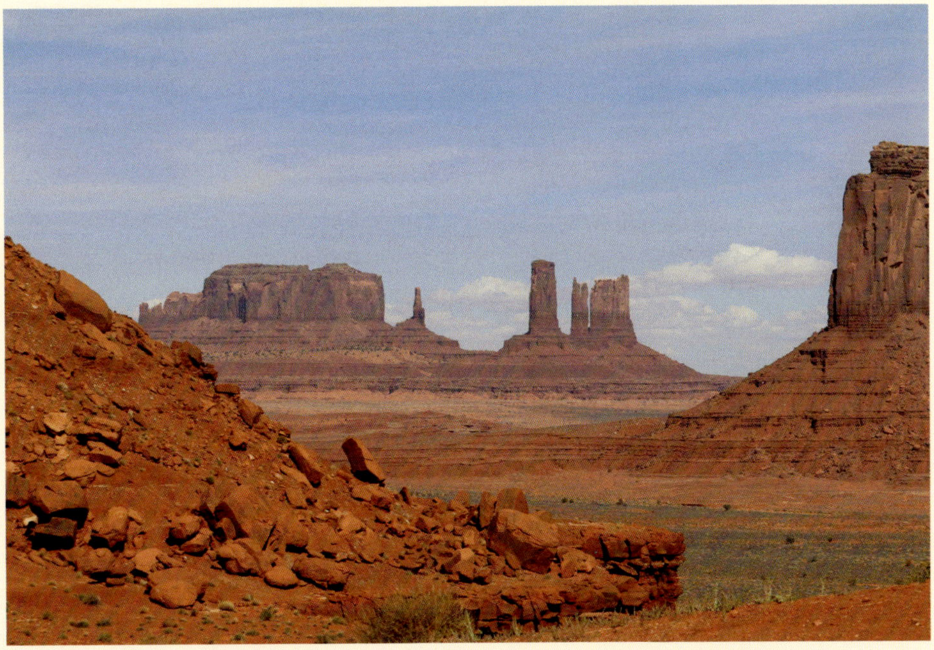

North Window Overlook (Monument Valley, Utah), 2021. Rapheal Begay (Diné, b. 1991). Courtesy of the artist.

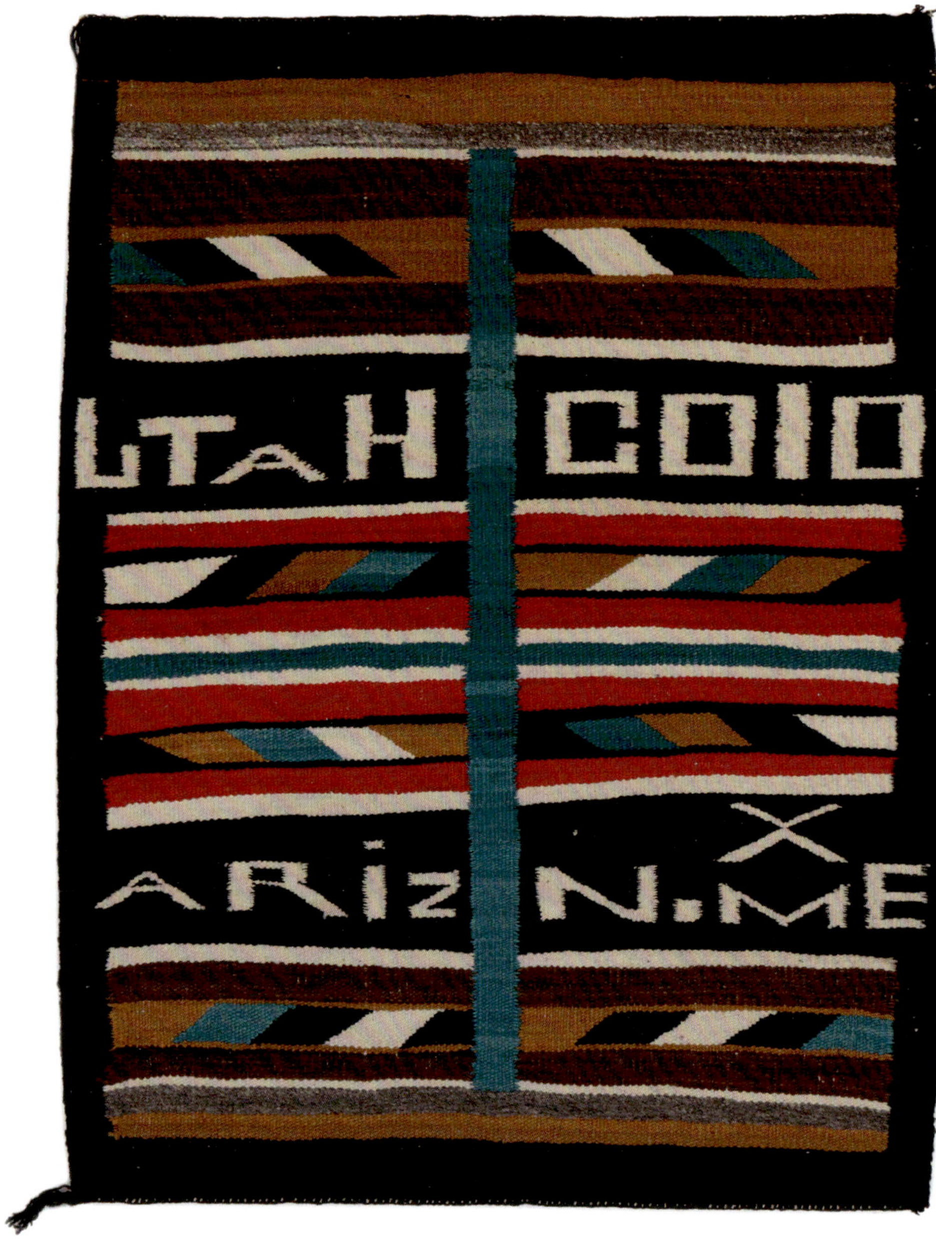

Four Corners weaving, 1950–1967. Artist once known (Diné). Wool. 38 × 30 inches. Museum of International Folk Art, gift of the Girard Foundation Collection, A.1980.1.174. Photograph by Addison Doty.

The Navajo Nation comprises 27,000 square miles of land across Arizona, New Mexico, and Utah. Traditionally, Diné Bikéyah also stretched into Colorado. This particular piece draws attention to state borders, shown as a blue cross at the center of the weaving, and how colonization impacts our conceptualization of traditional territories, homelands, and belonging to these places. The "X" just above the "N.ME" letters may reference the most painful and relevant event of settler-colonial violence—the Long Walk to Bosque Redondo in New Mexico.

—LARISSA NEZ

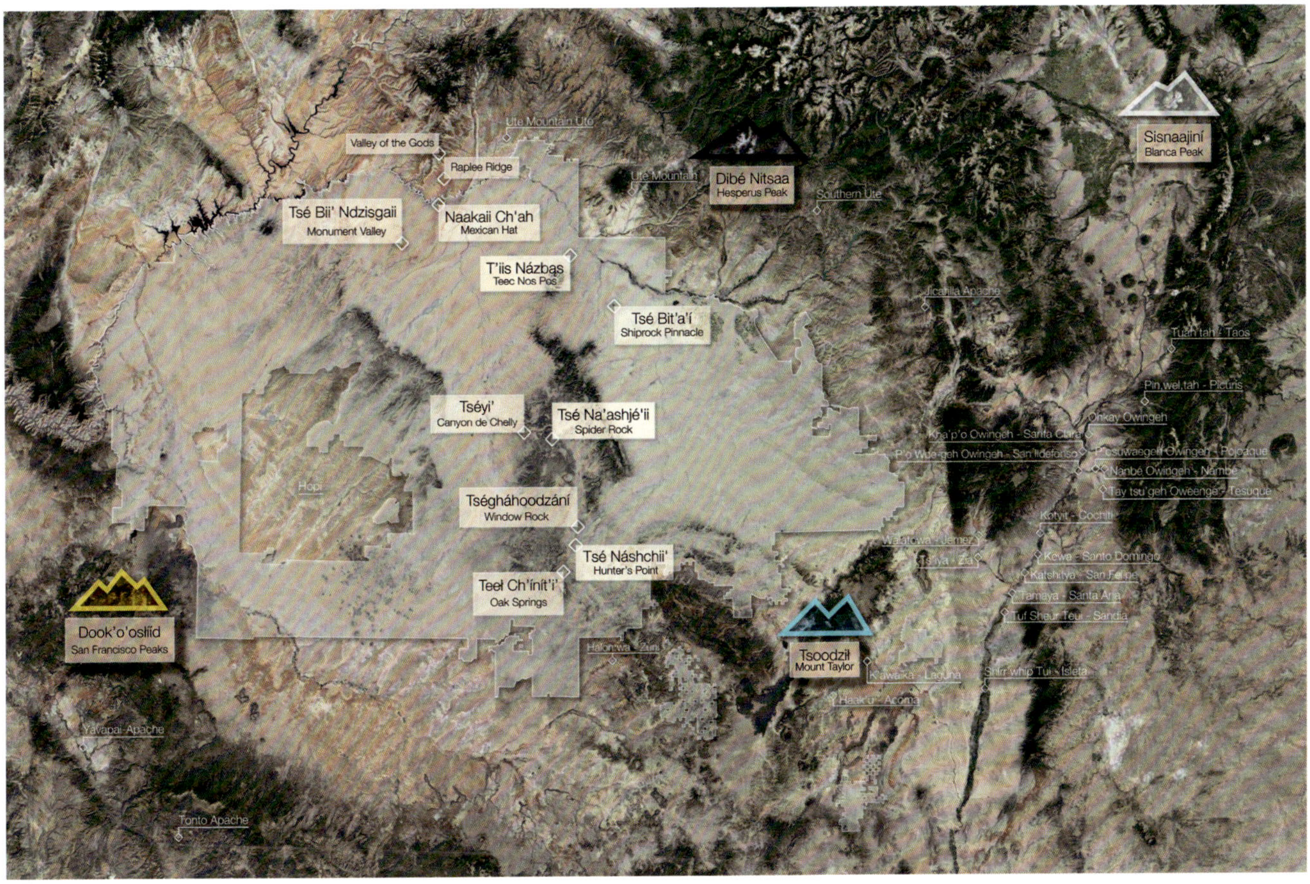

Navajo Nation, 2023. Topographic map by Jacklyn Wang, updated by Darby Raymond-Overstreet (Diné). Courtesy of Bard Graduate Center, New York, and Museum of Indian Arts and Culture, Santa Fe.

to the past, present, and future. Our reciprocal relationship to land, language, and memory reflects our creativity and resilience as five-fingered beings."

Importantly, this project has been the result of an ongoing partnership with Diné artists and scholars through all aspects of exhibition development, programming, and publication. Aiming to both contribute to and expand conversations around accessibility, reciprocity, and stewardship of museum collections, we have prioritized a multiplicity of perspectives centered on Diné thought, language, and practice. *Horizons* strives to bring specificity to the (re)interpretation of the artworks and cultural belongings featured here. Rather than thinking about Navajo textiles as disembodied "objects," our curatorial focus has been on the individual artists who made them.

With this in mind, Rapheal Begay and I assembled an advisory committee of five Diné weavers, fiber artists, scholars, and practitioners: Lynda Teller Pete (committee chair), Kevin Aspaas, Larissa Nez, Darby Raymond-Overstreet, and Tyrrell Tapaha. By incorporating a wide range of interests and expertise, we emphasized intergenerational perspectives, multidisciplinary approaches, and lived experience in the committee's formation. This collaboration unfolded over nearly two years, at least three states, and a variety of spaces—from museum storage areas and regional art markets to many

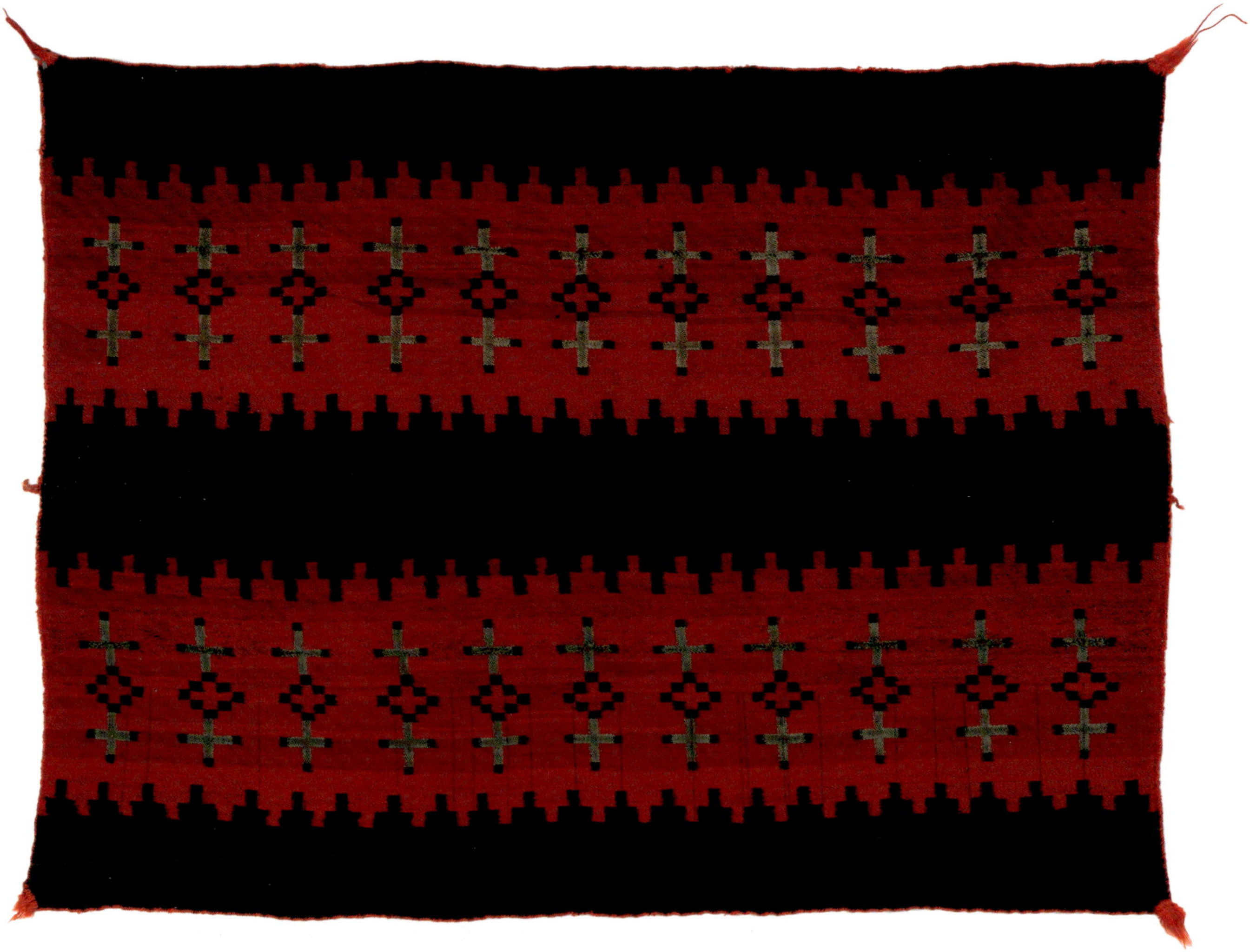

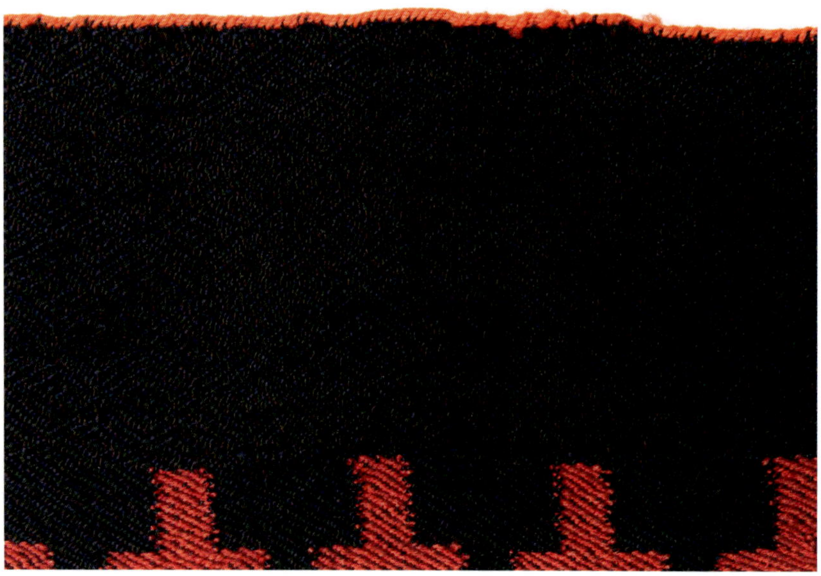

Manta, 1875–1880 (detail, top edge).
Photograph by Addison Doty.
Note the intricate diamond twill edges at top, woven in indigo-dyed yarn.

OPPOSITE

Manta, 1875–1880. Artist once known (Diné). Handspun wool yarn, raveled yarn, cochineal dye, indigo dye, aniline dye, vegetal dye. 42½ × 57½ inches. Museum of Indian Arts and Culture/Laboratory of Anthropology, gift of Mrs. Philip B. Stewart, 9106/12. Photograph by Addison Doty.

A fancy woman's wearing blanket or manta, this inspirational piece was woven for a cherished family member or for the weaver herself. Several different twill weaves that we call I'ímás created a sheen—a polished look that rivals today's manufactured haute couture. The black and indigo-blue wool weft is woven in stair-step designs into the inside field color, a stunning red wool that comes from bayeta. The Spider Woman cross variants are woven with vegetal green. A graceful Diné Asdzą́ą́ should be so lucky to use this for everyday, formal, or ceremonial wear.

Today's collectors particularly value men's blankets, clamoring for the elusive Third Phase Chief blankets. In contrast, women's wear is undervalued. A classic beauty in technique and design, this woman's manta will radiate beauty for ages.

—LYNDA TELLER PETE

shared meals and cups of coffee. Three in-person convenings at the Museum of Indian Arts and Culture (MIAC) in 2022–2023 were supplemented by regular communication over email, text, and Zoom. Together we took on the conceptual elements and practical components of exhibition making: developing a checklist, envisioning a thematic framework, defining the graphic identity, creating a layout and design, and considering each item's presentation. Our work extended to mount making and conservation, as well as writing interpretative text, planning public programming, and leading docent training.

The curatorial team chose items for display that included dresses, wearing blankets, sash belts, rugs, and other woven items across a wide historical scope, as well as tools and dye and fiber samples. We contextualized these selections with interpretation that highlights and restores agency—to individual weavers and to Diné communities—in the history of Navajo textile production. In implementing these aims, advisory committee members authored labels for their own works, for items in MIAC's permanent collection, and for pieces loaned from other institutions and private collections. The resulting exhibition reveals a deep and deliberate investment in this process, manifesting the unique ways in which each person has shaped the project's outcome.

This publication deepens and expands on the exhibition's themes, advancing new interpretive frameworks to situate Diné fiber arts within larger historical, cultural, ecological, and regional contexts. Through the lens of poetry, archaeology, and history, the perspectives of three additional authors—Laura Tohe, Wade Campbell, and Jennifer Nez Denetdale—bring a holistic approach to the study of Diné weaving. Each in their own way, the contributors to this volume emphasize that creative exchange is visible in historical works and continues to resonate through contemporary art. As the interpretive captions, essays, and interviews in this book suggest, these artworks were chosen not for purely aesthetic or historical criteria but rather as reflections of an encultured and enduring process. We center the contributions and innovations of Diné artists, even when the makers remain unidentified. By exploring the ways in which these works can be viewed across time and space, we invite readers to make their own connections—to locate and appreciate the material traces of each weaver's artistic vision, expertise, and experimentation.

Our exhibition and publication rethink assumed boundaries to create connections between media, across generations, and within a continuum of historical and contemporary works. On the printed page as in the gallery, these ideas unfold to emphasize the ecological and holistic process found within Diné art production. Energized by questions of curatorial and artistic practice, *Horizons* offers a dynamic model of collaborative curation. Tracing the intersections of time and place, contributors to this volume reflect on recurring themes of identity and belonging, kinship, storytelling, community, and creation. They focus on intergenerational knowledge and experience to reaffirm key concepts and narratives of Diné survivance, cultural sovereignty, and self-determination while exploring throughlines of memory, transformation, creativity, imagination, resistance, and resilience.

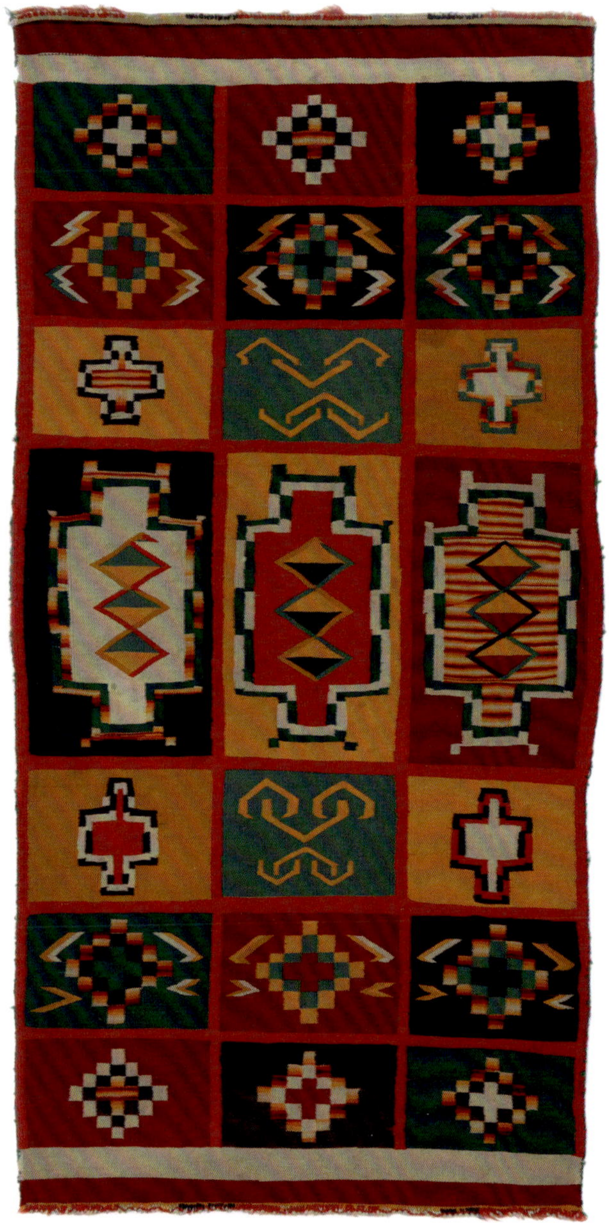

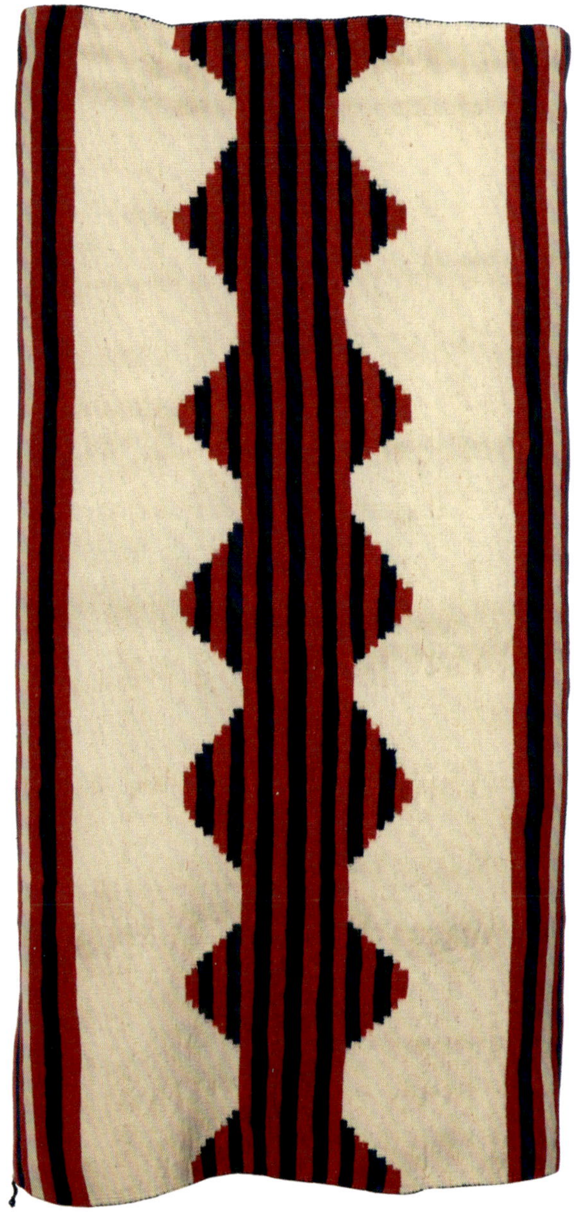

Germantown saddle blanket, c. 1880. Artist once known (Diné). Cotton string, Germantown wool yarn, aniline dye. 60 × 30 ½ inches. Museum of Indian Arts and Culture/Laboratory of Anthropology. Museum purchase, courtesy of John and Linda Comstock and the Abigail Van Vleck Charitable Trust, 9048/12. Photograph by Addison Doty.

This saddle blanket is a snapshot of the transitionary histories of Navajo weaving, showing the influence of other cultures, people, and artisans, as well as accessibility of new materials and resources. What catches my eye with this work is the use of a discontinued Zephyr Saxony Germantown yarn. Produced by an eastern mill, this yarn was a multicolored three-ply yarn introduced via the railway around the late 1870s. It speaks to the weaver's ingenuity in creating an intimate and careful study of color, shape, and experimentation.

—TYRRELL TAPAHA

Shoulder blanket (displayed on form), 1860–1870, possibly owned by Manuelito. Artist once known (Diné). Handspun wool, cochineal dye, indigo dye, bayeta. 70 ½ × 52 inches. Museum of Indian Arts and Culture/Laboratory of Anthropology, gift of the Jennings family, 54593/12. Photograph by Addison Doty.

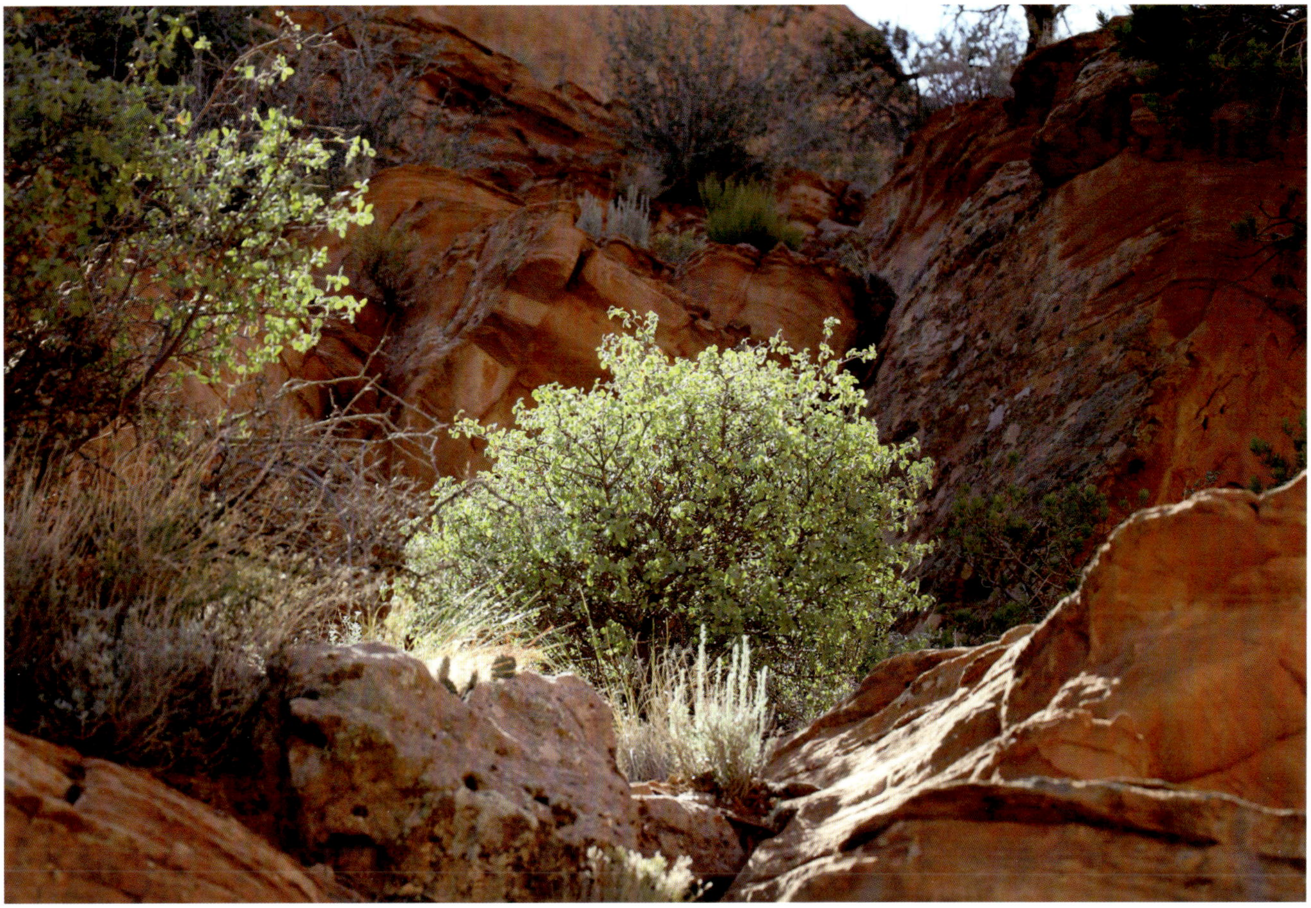

Glow Growth (Tséyi'—Canyon de Chelly, Arizona), 2021. Rapheal Begay (Diné, b. 1991). Courtesy of the artist.

Through a constellation of poetry, essays, interviews, textiles, photographs, and prints, this book aims to establish connections among Diné art forms as ways of seeing, knowing, and relating to place. As this work demonstrates, we conceive of weaving as an expansive, interconnected, and culturally specific practice, situating it as a mode of cultural production, an archive of collective (and inherited) knowledge, and an expression of lived experience.

This book does not present a linear history of Navajo weaving. Similarly, it is not meant to be comprehensive in scope. Rather, it is intended to challenge and reframe conventional categories and perceived chronologies to reflect Diné ways of thinking about weaving. While the project contains elements of a visual narrative of Navajo weaving over time, our aim is to trace the fluid relationships among historic, contemporary, and living artists, inviting a deeper understanding of Diné artistry and ways of knowing—past, present, and future. Just as the horizon line renders a spatial relationship, at once fixed and mutable, so too does it evoke a temporal one, connecting stories, landscapes, and life histories through the visual language of weaving.

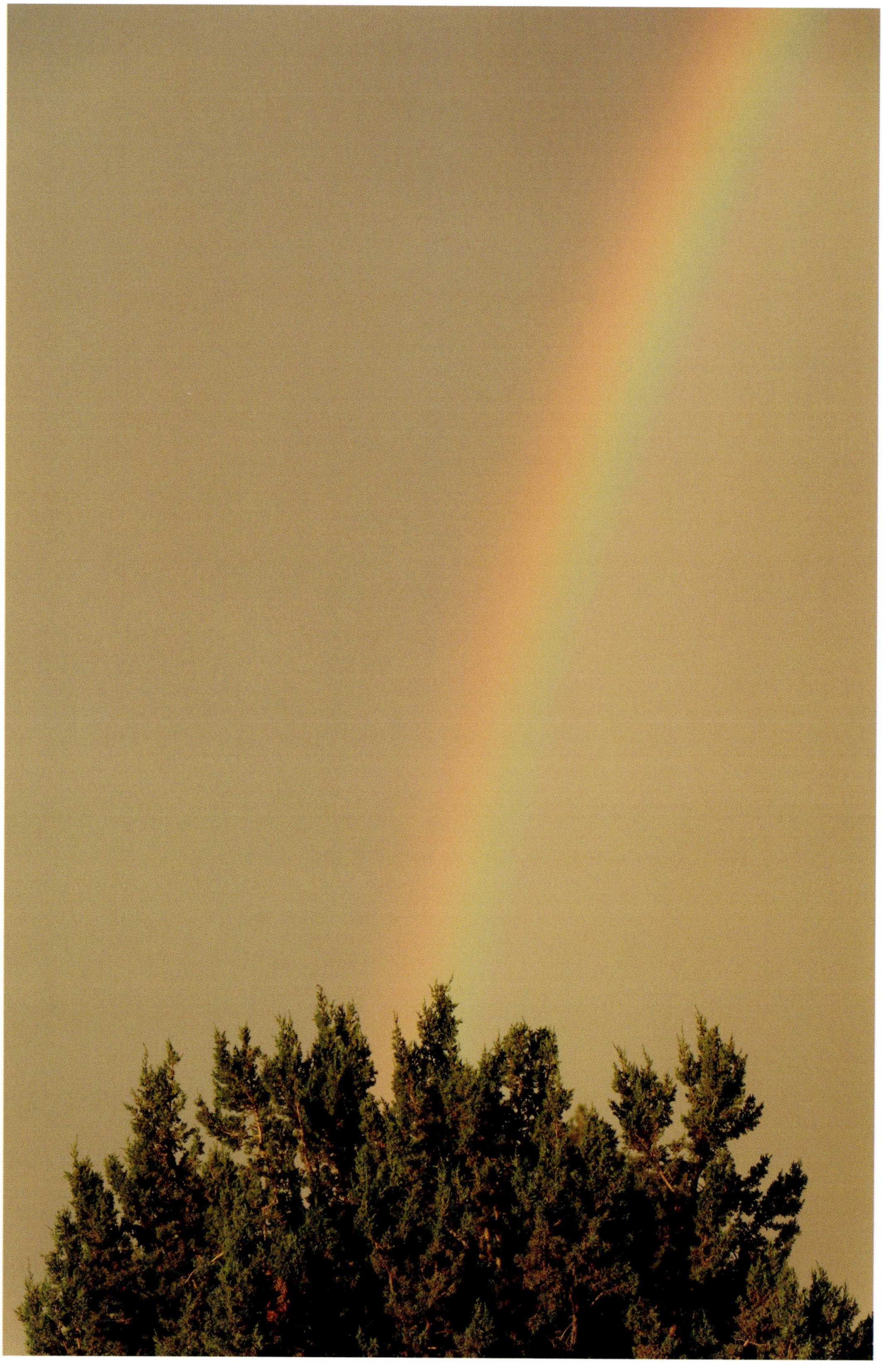

1 Visual Blessings

Seeing and Believing in the Navajo Nation

RAPHEAL BEGAY

OPPOSITE
Juniper Rainbow (Heber, Arizona), 2022. Rapheal Begay (Diné, b. 1991). Courtesy of the artist.

How does one visualize something as elusive and ever-changing as light? As Diné, we are living in the Glittering World where 'adinídíín (light) is divine. It is prayer, projection, and perspective. It is an all-seeing element that permeates every aspect of our being.

Referencing Diné Fundamental Law, our people regard the earth as thinking, water as planning, air as life, and light as wisdom. Within Diné weaving, rainbows serve as tools that act as an extension of the weaver's hand. This image of a rainbow and juniper is inspired by the intangible cultural teachings that inform the creative process of both weaver and photographer.

Honor what you see, for it is a blessing.

—RAPHEAL BEGAY

Yá'át'ééh shík'éí dóó shídine'é. Shí éí Rapheal Begay yinishyé. Hónágháahnii nishłį́. Kinłichii'nii bashishchiin. Tábąąhá dashicheii. 'Áshįįhi dashinalí. Tségháhoodzání kééhast'į́ ndi Tsé Náshchii' naashá. Hello, my name is Rapheal Begay. I am One Who Walks Around. Born for the Red House People. My maternal grandfather's clan is Water's Edge. My paternal grandfather's clan is Salt People. I live in Window Rock, Arizona, but I am from Hunter's Point, Arizona.

As a Diné visual storyteller, my artistic practice is an extension of my holistic being. Using cultural landscape photography and oral storytelling traditions, I document and celebrate the Diné way of life. As Hónágháahnii (One Who Walks Around), I do exactly that—I walk around and create with my camera as I venture across the Navajo Nation to understand and honor everyday rez life. Through a site/sight-specific process, I reflect upon visual blessings offered by my surroundings to culturally express and creatively advocate for land, light, and love.

By identifying and photographing preexisting aesthetic relationships, I explore connections to kéyah (land), hooghan (home), k'é (kinship), and iiná (life). In doing so, the image becomes a record of Diné space and time that stewards collective and individual stories, memories, and teachings. In practice, it is the weaving together of these visual and vernacular elements that allows me to understand and communicate with the world. And so, I aim to inform and inspire my people and remind them of the beauty of our home, our language, and the perseverance of our existence as Diné.

Ahéhee'. Thank you.

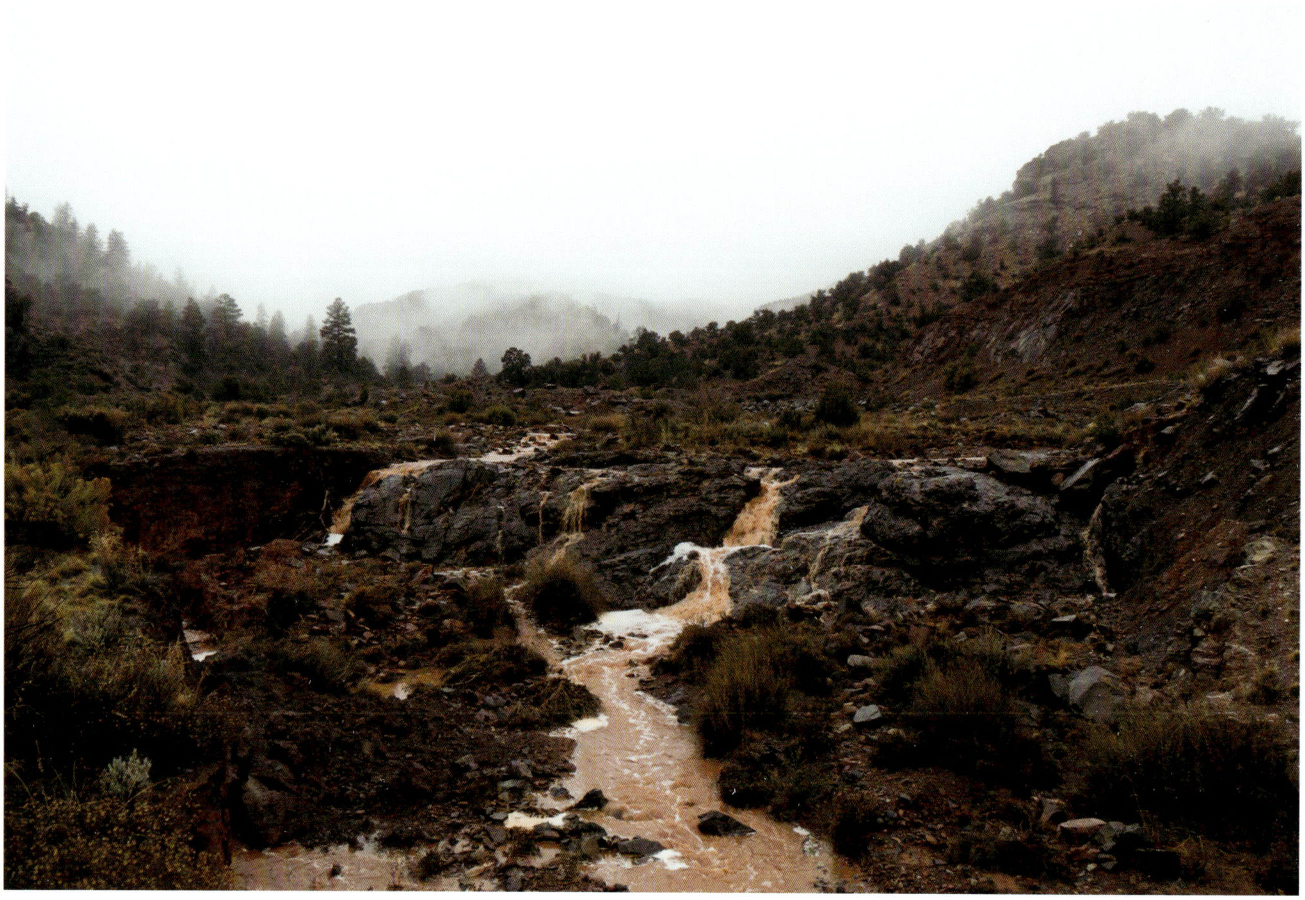

My Backyard (Hunter's Point, Arizona), 2016. Rapheal Begay (Diné, b. 1991). Courtesy of the artist.

With rolling red hills, fields of sage, and open blue skies, my backyard was the ultimate playground. Situated at the mouth of a canyon, it is here that I created my first picture using a Pentax 35mm film camera while working with the Tséhootsooí Middle School newspaper.

I can recall the rushing wash echoing the sounds of my late grandparents' sheep, as well as the joy, laughter, and grief of my relatives. Years later, this image represents the beginning of my journey as a photographer. And like the sheep corral, this place is one of love, light, and life.

The land remembers.

—RB

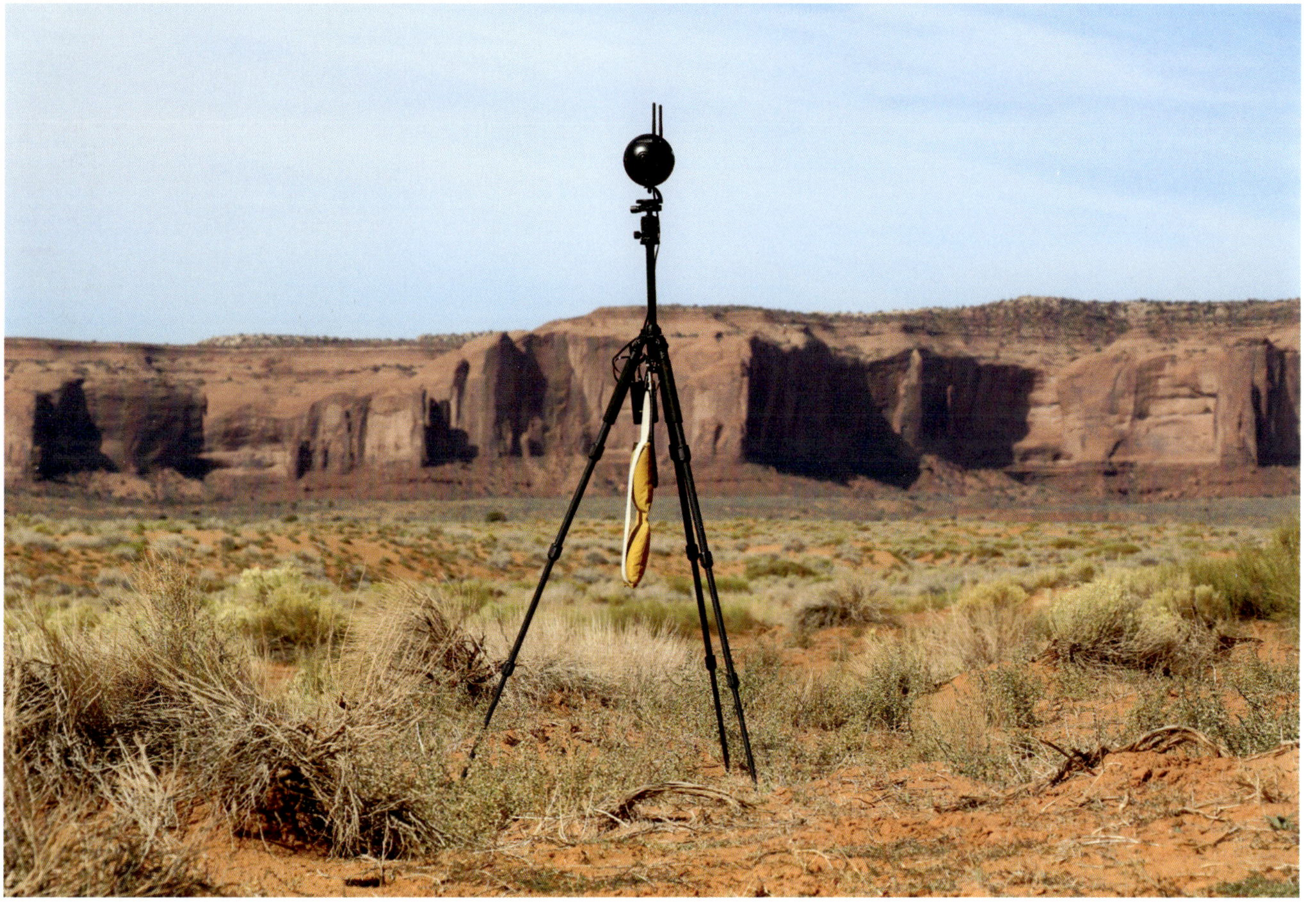

360 (Tsé Bii' Ndzisgaii—Monument Valley, Utah), 2021. Rapheal Begay (Diné, b. 1991). Courtesy of the artist.

The Insta360 Pro II Camera used by our team allows for a new way of seeing and relating to the cultural landscape. Positioned on a tripod and equipped with six lenses, the omnidirectional camera stands above and within the red mesas and buttes, creating a site/sight-specific view.

As visual storytellers, we can reflect and refract the histories of this technology to reimagine, celebrate, and steward our relationships to place. From this stance, photography can be used creatively to activate, inform, and inspire a Diné worldview.

—RB

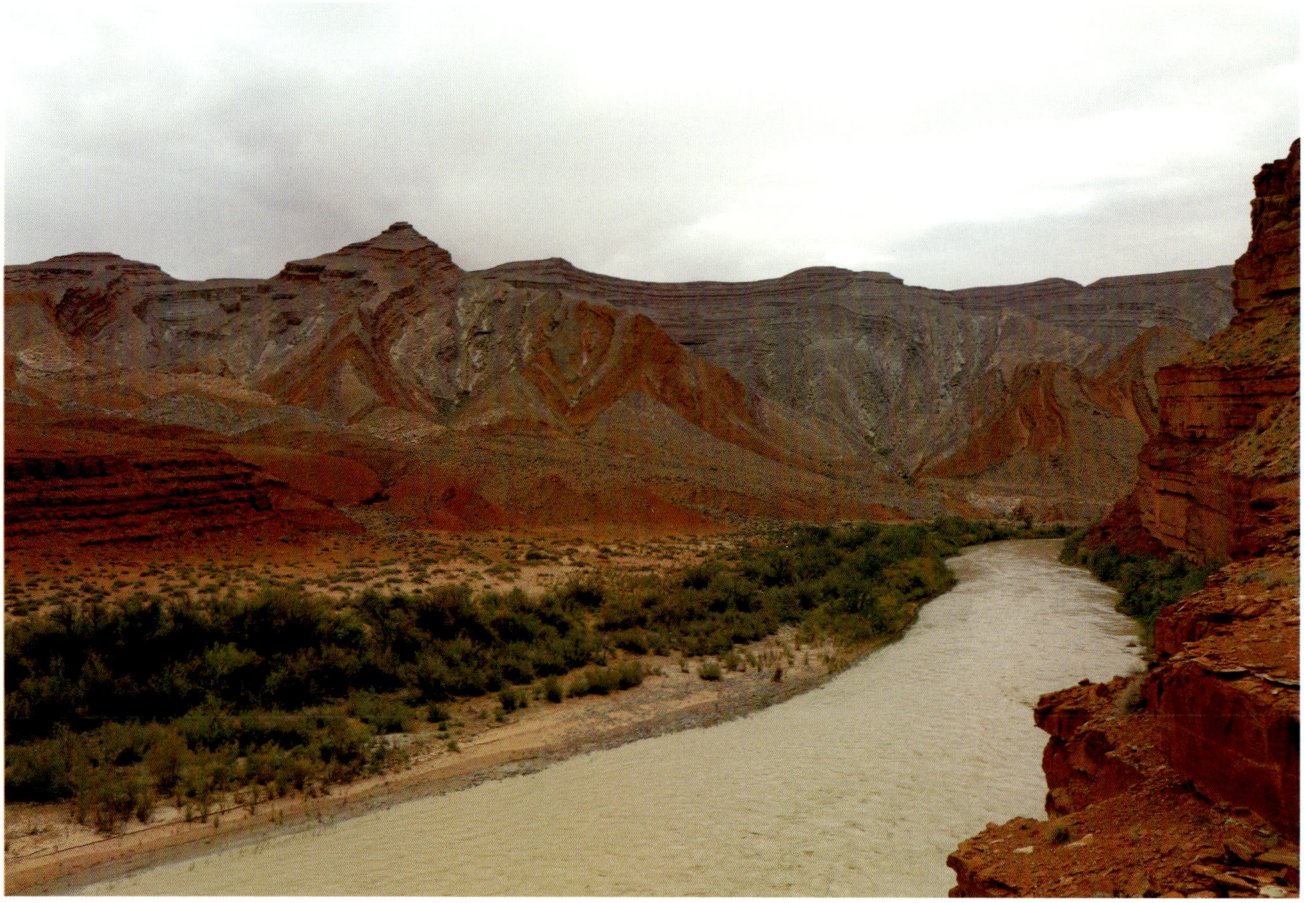

Raplee Monocline (Naakaii Ch'ah—Mexican Hat, Utah), 2021. Rapheal Begay (Diné, b. 1991). Courtesy of the artist.

East of the inverted stone known as Mexican Hat and across the San Juan River, Raplee Monocline rests amid the red lands known as Halchíítah (Among the Red Areas). The monocline has been referred to as inspiration in the development of Diné textile designs. Its multicolored zigzags mirror the visual motion in wedge weave blankets and the geometric lightning motifs found in other weavings. Like the weathered landscape, both weaving and image emulate the natural transformation between space and time.

—RB

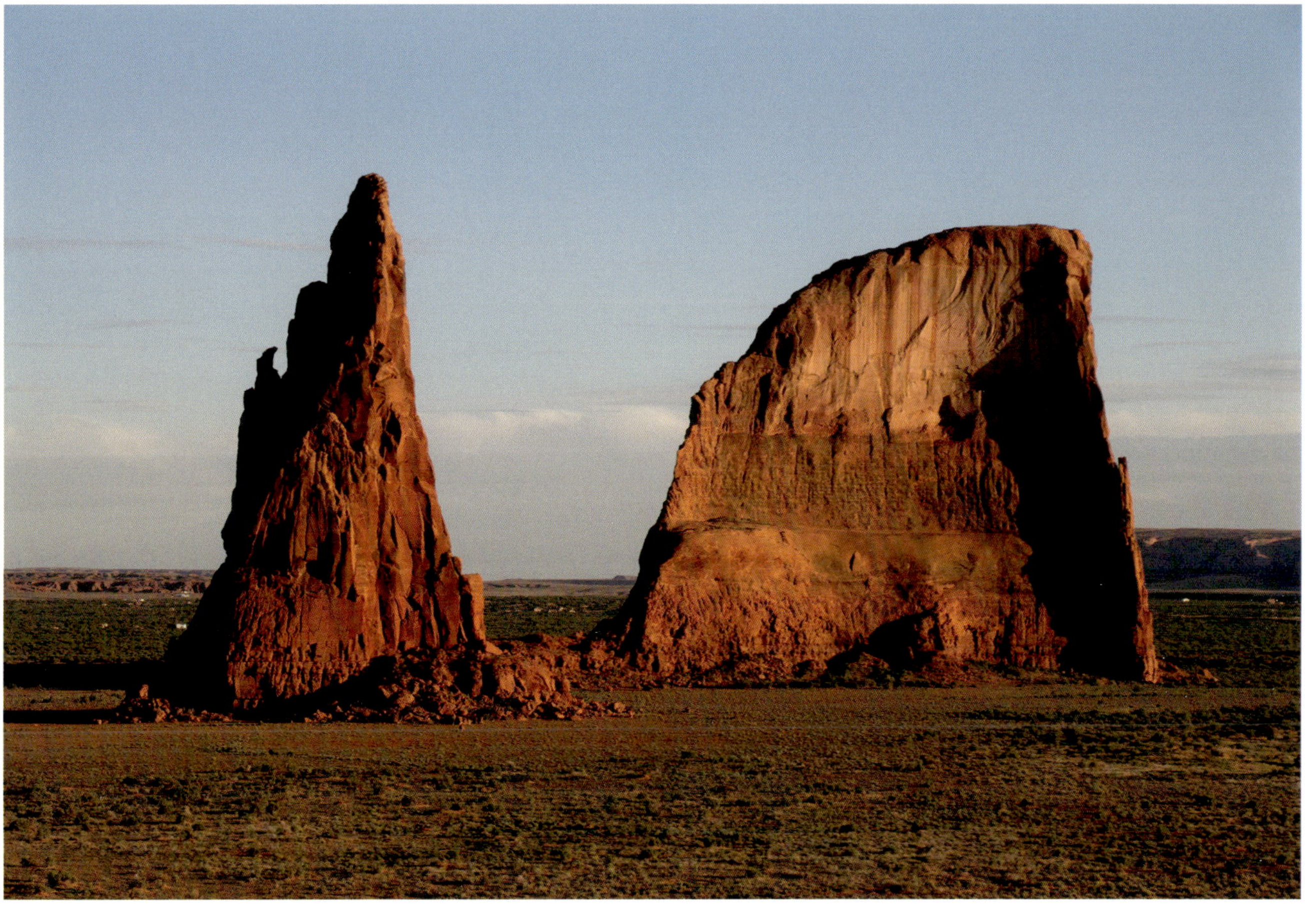

Standing Red Rock (Tsé Łichíí Deez'ahí—Rock Point, Arizona), 2023. Rapheal Begay (Diné, b. 1991). Courtesy of the artist.

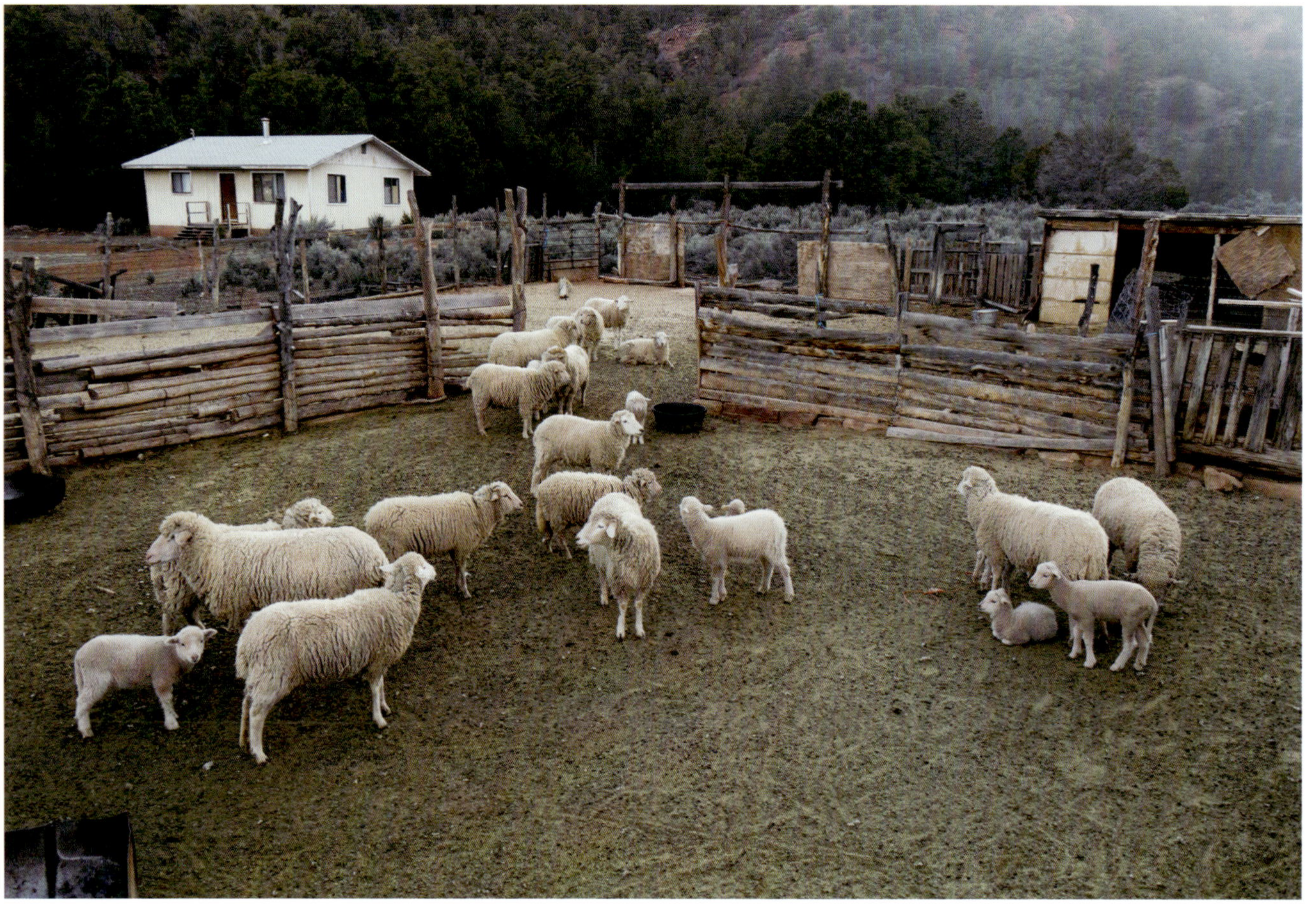

Navel (Hunter's Point, Arizona), 2017. Rapheal Begay (Diné, b. 1991). Courtesy of the artist.

The use and value of Diné textiles have been transformed over time. However, the one thing that remains constant is the Diné relationship with dibé (sheep), kéyah (land), and hooghan (home).

Concerning the Diné lifecycle, this image alludes to where my mother buried my shitséé' (umbilical cord) within the sheep corral. It is the place I return to for direction, inspiration, and strength. Like a flock of sheep, we as people are natural stewards of our surroundings and the stories we hold and tell. As storytellers, weavers, and artists, we embody the teaching of hózhǫ́ (to be in balance and harmony with our surroundings), and just like the land, we will continue to change, adapt, and persevere.

—RB

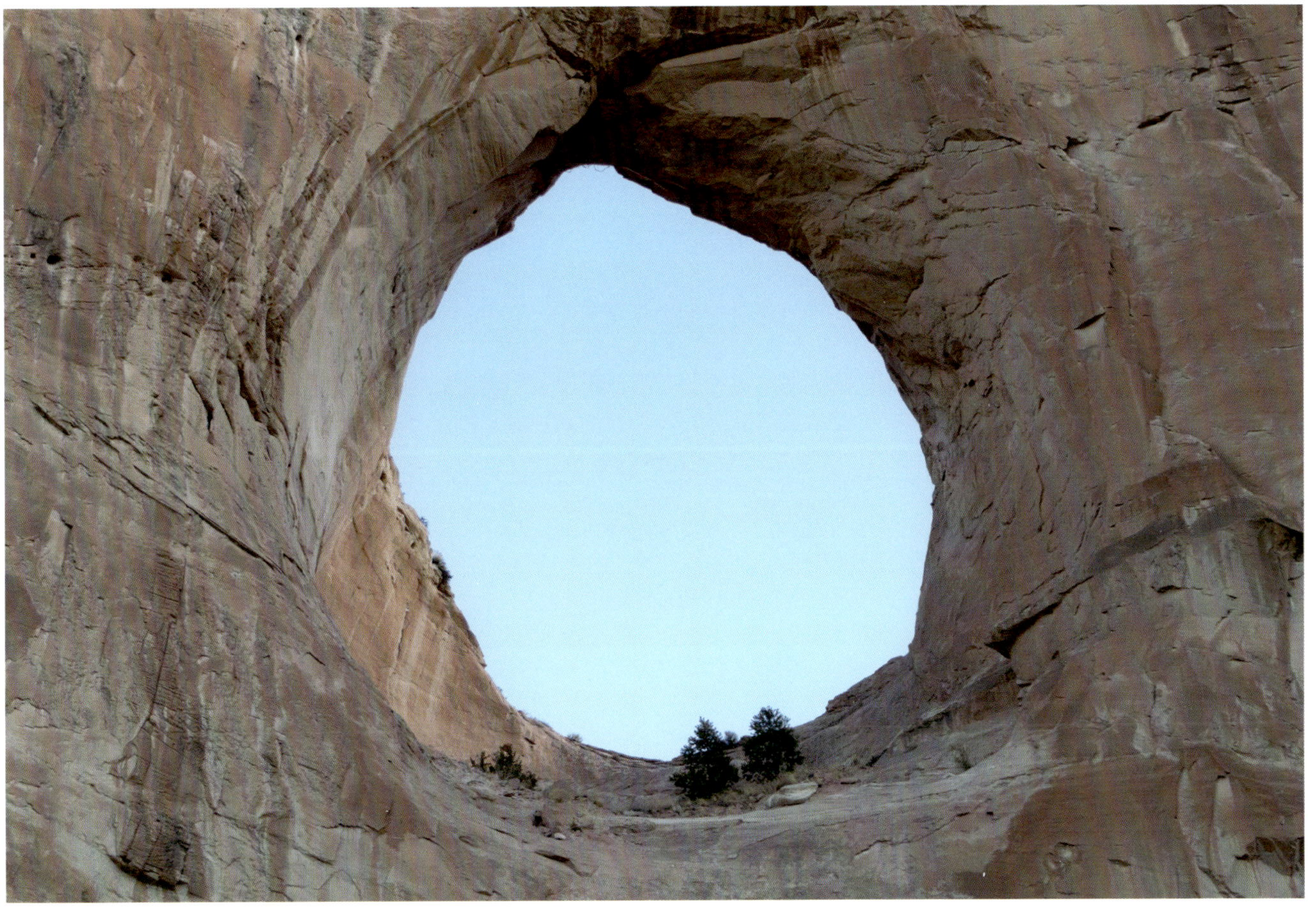

Window Rock (Tséghą́hoodzání—Window Rock, Arizona), 2018. Rapheal Begay (Diné, b. 1991). Courtesy of the artist.

As a tool within Diné weaving, the loom operates as a window to the universe as it reflects the weaver's thoughts and emotions. In Diné Bizaad (the Navajo language), tsésǫ' is translated as "window" in reference to the sedimentary elements and glimmering aspects of glass.

Made of sandstone and sky, the Window Rock, Tséghą́hoodzání (Perforated Rock), is a geological formation that symbolizes strength and pride. Also known as the capital of the Navajo Nation, this sacred monument acts as a portal for Diné songs, prayers, and stories.

—RB

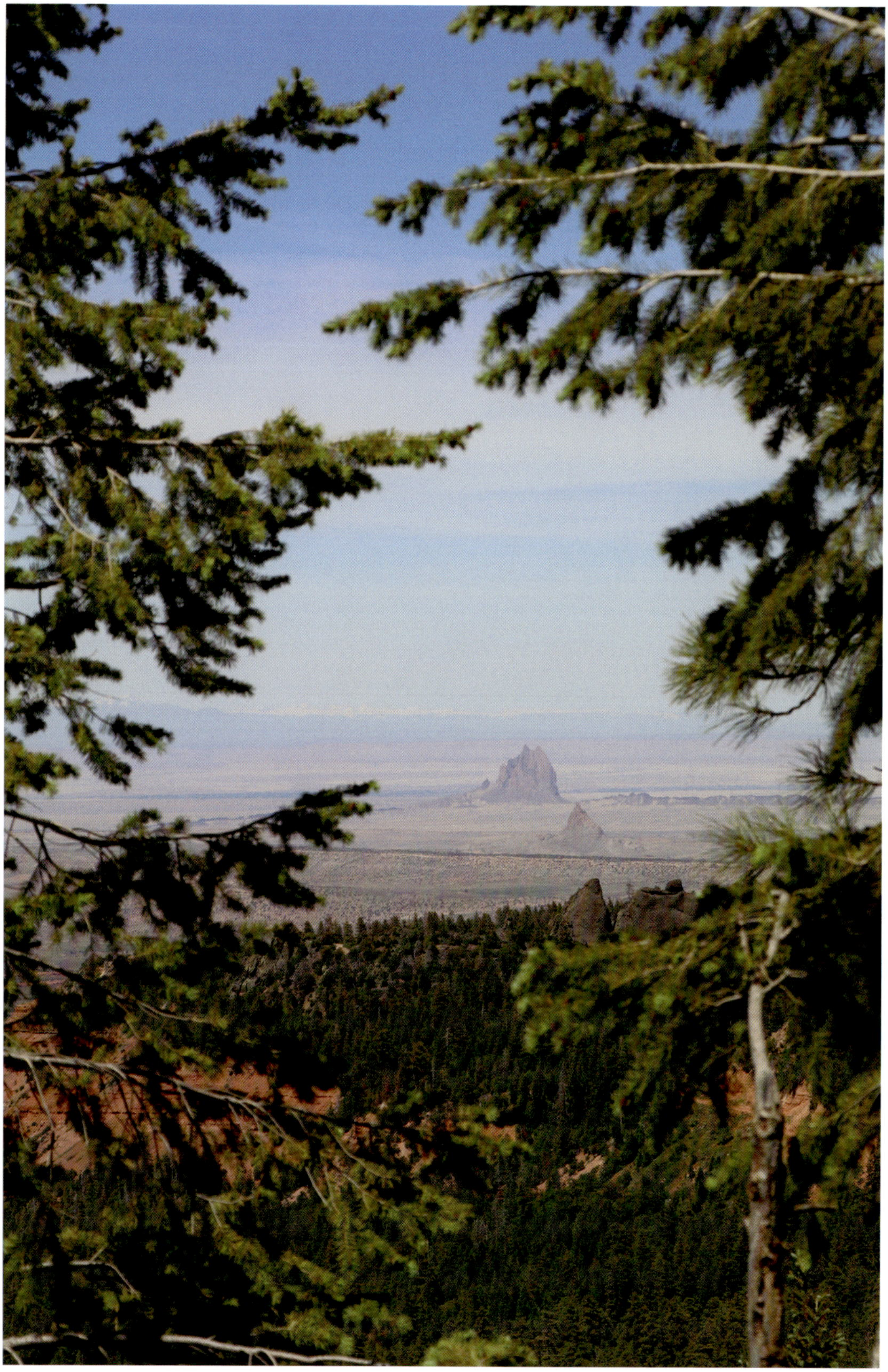

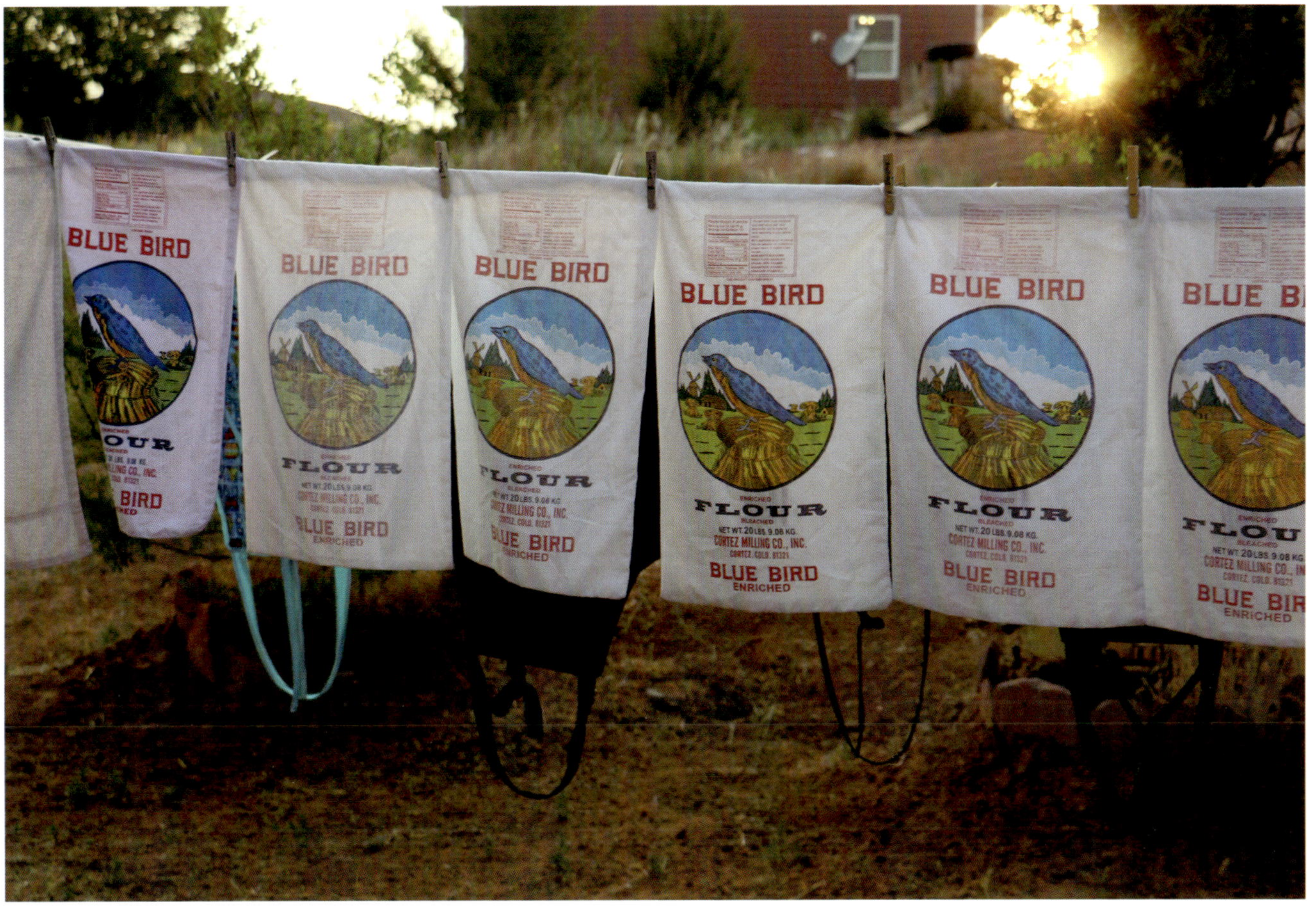

OPPOSITE
Peek (Buffalo Pass, Arizona), 2019. Rapheal Begay (Diné, b. 1991). Courtesy of the artist.

Peering through the ponderosa pines atop Lukachukai Mountain, the viewer gains a glimpse of a small-scale Shiprock in the distance. Entitled "Peek" as opposed to "Peak," the title operates as a humorous acknowledgment of the voyeuristic nature of the photographic process.

Buffalo Pass Overlook enables community members and visitors to form a visual connection between Arizona and New Mexico. Regardless of one's physical stance, "home" exists beneath one's feet and is not bound by border, state, or county line.

—RB

ABOVE
Bluebird Backyard (Window Rock, Arizona), 2020. Rapheal Begay (Diné, b. 1991). Courtesy of the artist.

OPPOSITE

Mesa View (Tsé Bii' Ndzisgaii—Monument Valley, Utah), 2021.
Rapheal Begay (Diné, b. 1991). Courtesy of the artist.

Situated along the Arizona–Utah state line, Monument Valley Navajo Tribal Park is renowned for its iconic Mitten Buttes. Yet this sacred site offers much more than the singular image you may have in mind.

Looking to the north, this valley portrait is framed by the sandstone layers of Rain God Mesa on the left and Spearhead Mesa on the right. Interspersed with juniper trees and yucca shrubs, the receding terrain converges with the blue sky and two red mesas at the vanishing point within the horizon. From this perspective, a visual equilibrium radiates from the center and offers an immersive view that one could describe as hózhó—both beautiful and balanced.

—RB

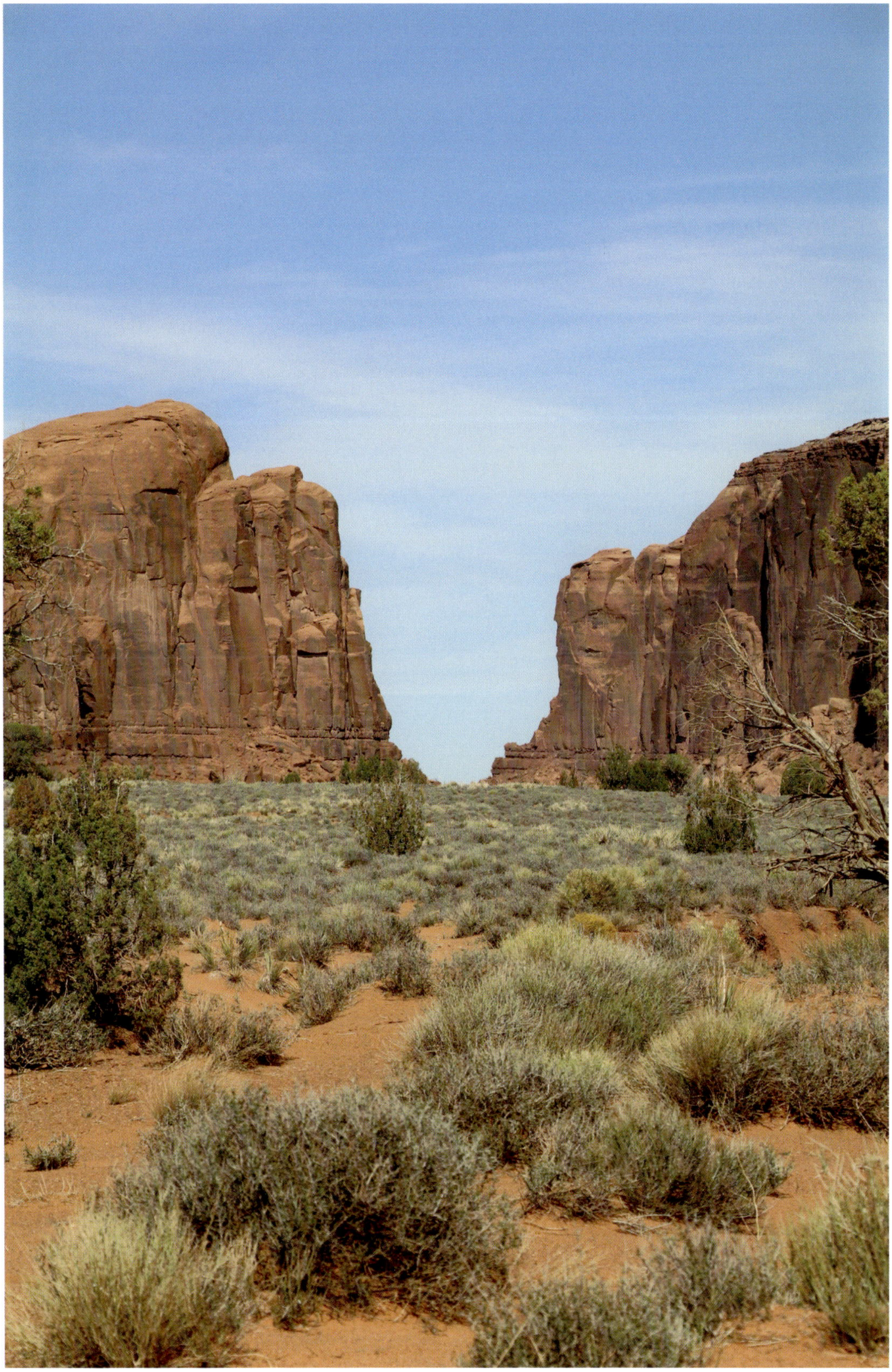

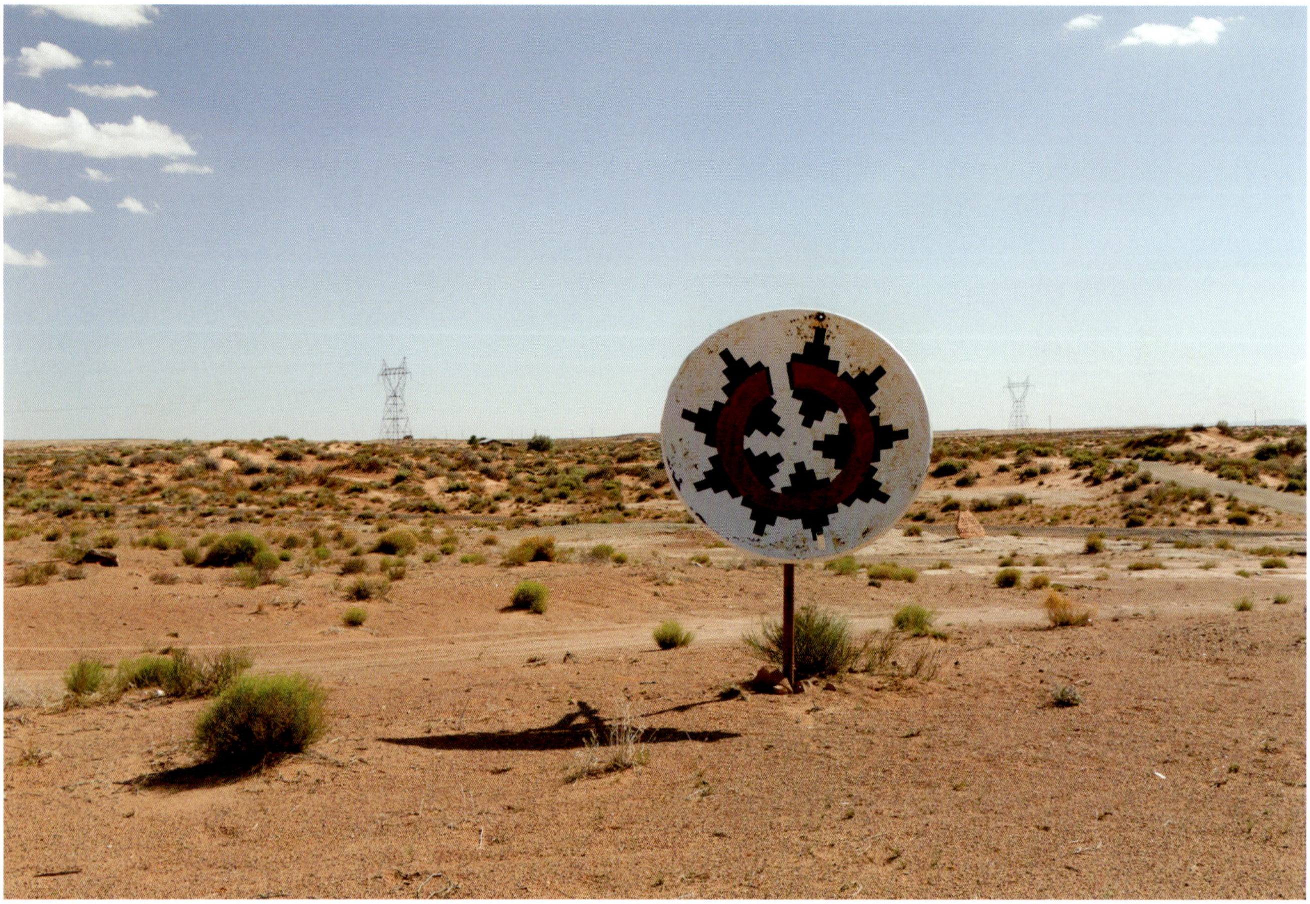

Emergence (Mexican Water, Arizona), 2018. Rapheal Begay (Diné, b. 1991). Courtesy of the artist.

When traveling across the reservation, I am reminded of the endless beauty of the land and the dynamic creativity found within each community. The Diné philosophy of t'áá hwó aji t'éégo (it is up to you) resonates with something as simple as an isolated, reimagined satellite dish along the roadside.

Referencing hajíínéí (coming into being), the center hole of the Navajo basket represents the emergence of life within the Diné universe. Indigenous imagination is both revelation and revolution as it allows us to weave new possibilities of place. There is beauty all around us, and it is up to us to receive and express our understanding of the world.

—RB

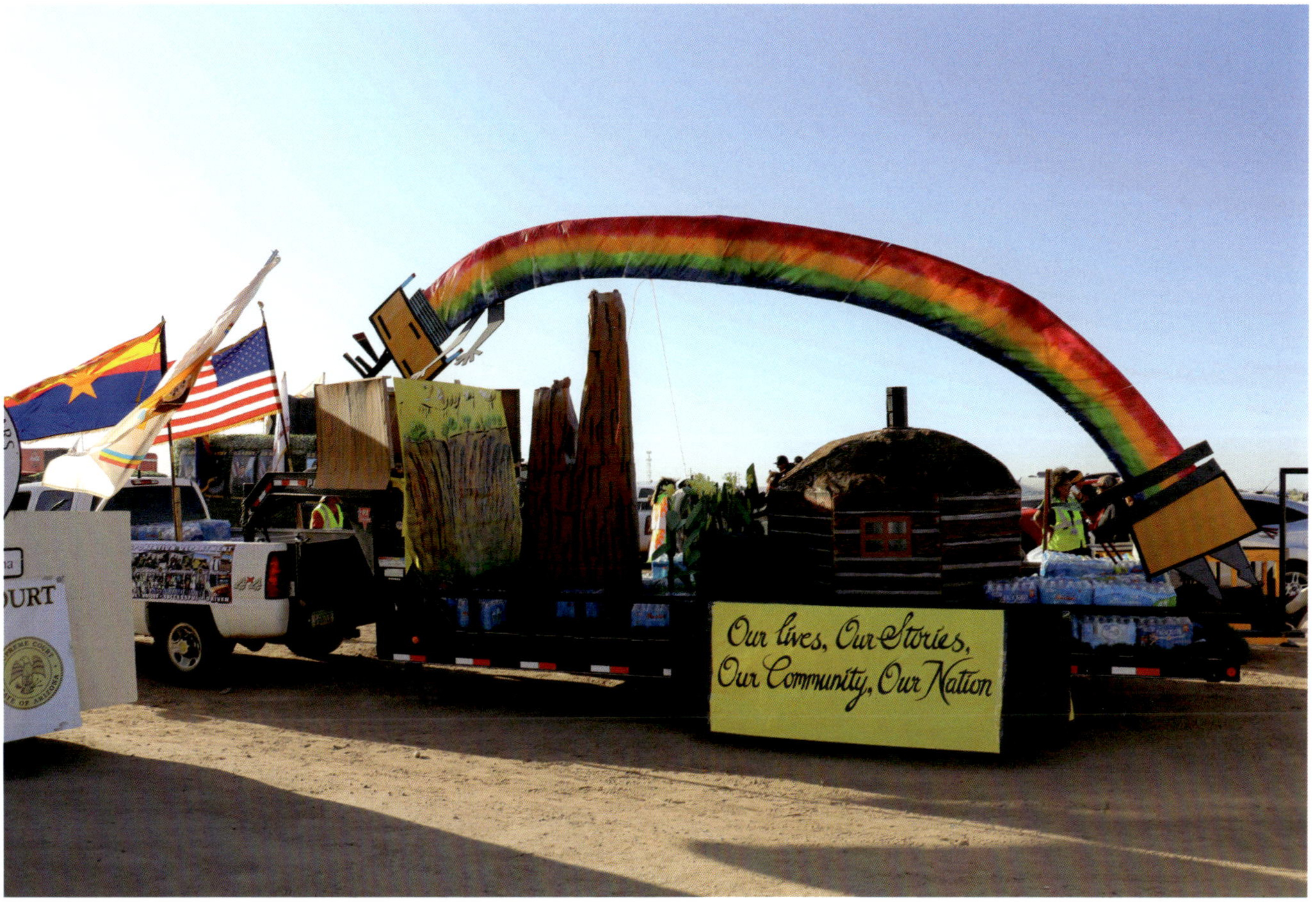

Our Nation (Chinle, Arizona), 2019. Rapheal Begay (Diné, b. 1991). Courtesy of the artist.

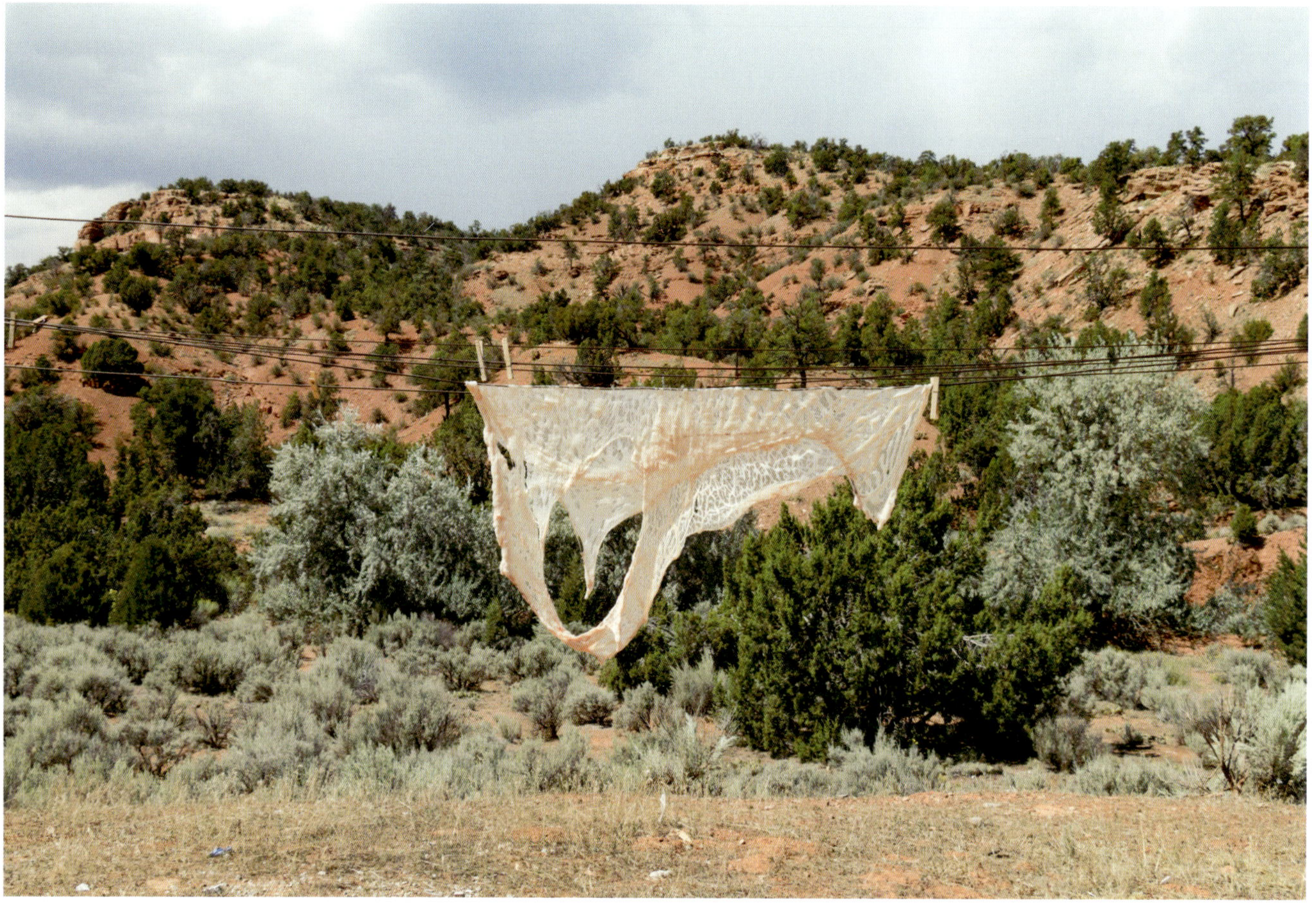

Hung to Dry (Hunter's Point, Arizona), 2017. Rapheal Begay (Diné, b. 1991). Courtesy of the artist.

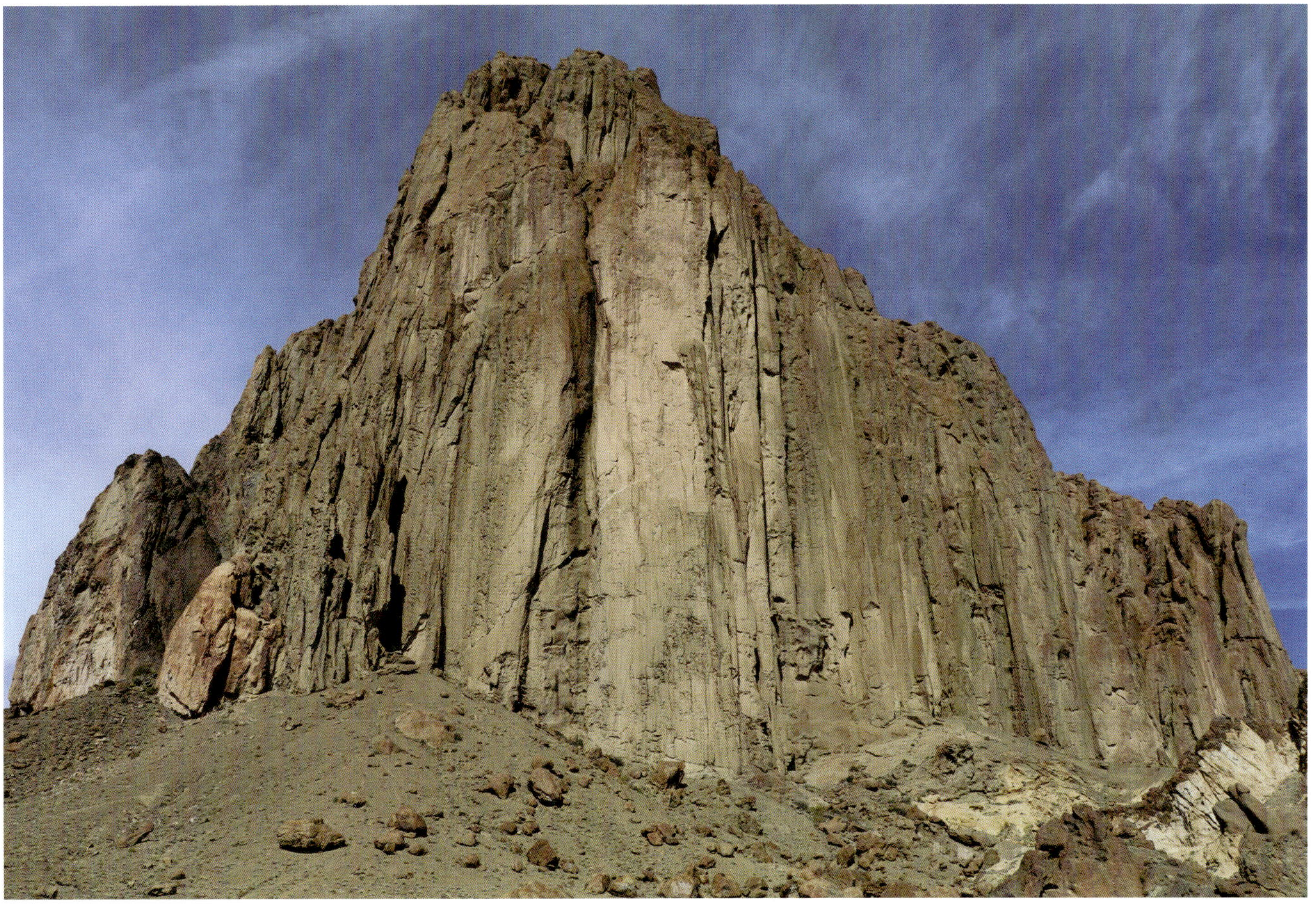

Pinnacle Base (Tsé Bit'a'í—Shiprock, New Mexico), 2021. Rapheal Begay (Diné, b. 1991). Courtesy of the artist.

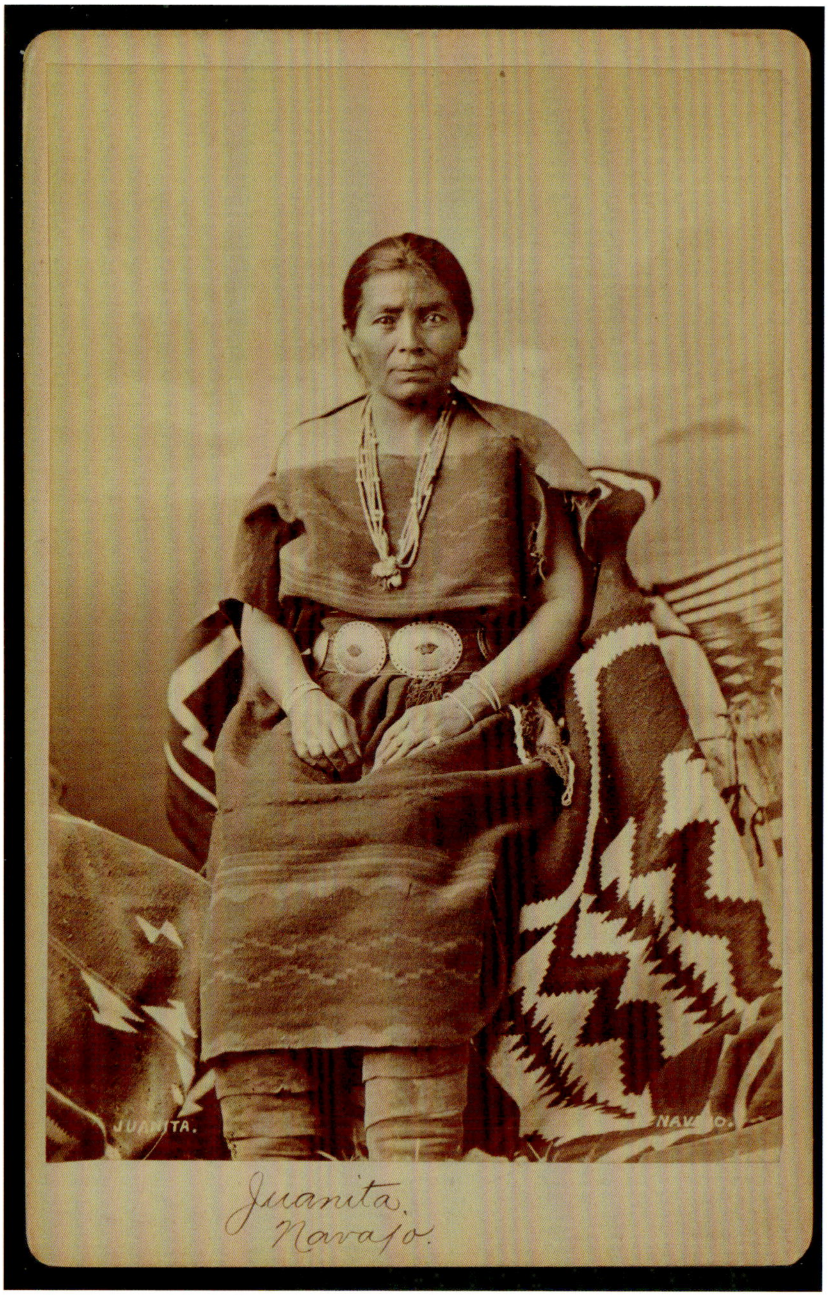
JUANITA.
NAVAJO.
Juanita.
Navajo.

2 Reuniting and Returning

Balancing Our Universe through Weaving

LARISSA NEZ

OPPOSITE
Portrait of Juanita (Asdzáá Tł'ógi), Chief Manuelito's wife, wearing a biil, with silver concho belt, ornaments, and blankets. Washington, DC, 1874. Photograph by Charles Bell. Cabinet card. National Anthropological Archives, Smithsonian Institution, Washington, DC, NAA INV.02274400 NAA MS.4877 OPPS NEG.BAE 2391.

From the original stages of planning *Horizons: Weaving Between the Lines with Diné Textiles*, members of the Diné advisory committee shared their knowledge and explored Diné weaving as an artistic practice connected to Diné cosmology and grounded in Diné creation stories. This interest was exemplified by one weaving that we chose to feature: "Dress, 1890–1895," a Diné biil (woman's rug dress), which was separated into two parts but has been reunited through this project (see pages 32 and 33). This weaving illuminates the ways early twentieth-century capitalist economies in the Southwest violently exploited Diné weavers, especially women, disfigured creative and cultural meanings associated with weavings, and continue to impact present-day understandings of this art form. I am interested not only in examining how historic scholarly engagement with Diné weavings has too often disregarded Diné cultural histories and traditions but also, and more importantly, in exploring how the meaning of weaving in Diné life can be illuminated by viewing it through the lens of our creation stories.

Diné believe that we emerged from four worlds before arriving in the current world, the Glittering World. Since time immemorial, Diné names of celestial bodies and earthly elements, along with their association with the Diyin Dine'é (Holy People), have been passed down. These places, plants, and animals carry powerful names bestowed on them by our ancestors so that we will always recognize them as our relatives and kin and remember how they helped the Diné emerge safely from one world to the next. Moreover, essential meanings and understandings about Diné land, body, and spirit are transmitted generationally through these stories, from which Diné learn the power of songs, prayers, and ceremonies that establish a line of communication between ourselves, the cosmos, and our Holy People. The stories reflect the ways that Diné culture is transmitted, embodied, and enacted. Diné Bizaad (our language) is our lifeline and is essential in furthering our understanding of the deeper epistemological foundations of our origins and futures and how we move between these spaces.

By grounding weaving within Diné cosmology and epistemology, we uphold our ideas about weaving as a multidimensional cultural tradition and artistic practice that is deeply connected to Diné creation stories and to sacred places, plants, animals, and spiritual beings. In Diné creation stories, Spider Woman, an important deity, helped create the loom and gave Diné the gift of weaving. She also helped the People construct the loom and its tools and attributed specific properties to each element that aligned with nature and the universe. We believe that the loom is part of nature, a physical manifestation of the Sky and Earth coming together. Weavers' designs represent their thoughts, life, breath, and spiritual connection to the Holy People and the cosmos. Weaving itself is a practice that connects Diné to the celestial, spiritual, and physical worlds around them. As such, each loom, tool, and weaving has a life and spirit of its own that is activated by the weaver's actions, songs, and prayers. Diné creation stories teach Diné how to care for these weavings through distinctive protocols that are necessary to sustain them. This care nurtures a deep, meaningful connection between past, present, and future; it also subverts colonial ideologies that disconnect our existence from the world around us and create hierarchies of inequality that foster the destruction and exploitation of the natural world.

A critical analysis of literature about Diné weavings shows us that there is a lack of scholarship developed by Diné themselves, and that this absence reproduces and perpetuates colonial violence and capitalism. Some non-Diné scholars have attempted to delineate the historic political economy of weaving throughout the nineteenth and early twentieth century, specifically situating trading posts at the center and placing Diné weavers on the periphery. As Kathy M'Closkey argues in "Weaving and Mothering: Reframing Diné Weavings as Recursive Manifestations of K'e," this type of historiography obscures "the critical role that weaving played in relation to cultural survival."[1]

In *A Critical Theory of Creativity,* Richard Howells investigates the Diné creation story as an entry point to understanding Diné weavings as creative processes grounded in culture, aesthetics, and what Howells calls "Utopia"—or, I would suggest, a future that is decolonized and liberated. Howells argues that Diné weavings are "not simply skillful, abstract designs, but, rather, visual representations of often specific legends, episodes, songs, prayers, stories, and creation myths."[2] Furthermore, he makes the distinction that Diné weavings and culture permeate a space that is not relegated to historical time or mythical time and that Diné are, at once, connected to the vast past, present, and future. I understand this concept to be more fully articulated by Damon Salesa (Sāmoan) as Indigenous time, which "is oriented by ancestors and descendants, not to a 'disembodied calibration of time.'"[3] In situating Diné weavings through the lens of Indigenous time, we can understand a restoration of harmony across time, space, and place that will ultimately heal and repair misreadings of Diné weavings and inaccurate understandings of why our people weave.

Scholarship that centers Diné cultural epistemology must be grounded in traditional Diné culture, language, and spiritual cosmologies. Diné historian Jennifer Nez Denetdale has critically and carefully illuminated the relationship between the materiality of history and the politics of historical interpretation. Denetdale has developed methodologies and strategies that speak to the power of Diné agency in reading and writing our own histories and demonstrates how this in turn empowers future generations. It is impossible to discuss the cultural significance of Diné weavings and weavers without attending to these aspects of Diné lifeways, which are grounded in Diné philosophical thought. This intervention requires us to undo settler-colonial understandings of weaving and restore Diné cultural and visual sovereignty by affirming the significance of Diné epistemologies. Undoing these misunderstandings has come about after lengthy discourse, research, and experiences in the archive and museum collections with the advisory committee members of *Horizons*. Together, we have collectively sought to overturn the ways in which cultural and academic institutions interpret and discuss Diné weavings. This effort to have our voices and knowledge recognized as autonomous and sovereign is among the biggest challenges contemporary Native academics and artists face.

Non-Diné authors have contributed a breadth of scholarship that attempts to interpret Diné history by centering the robust economic market that was structured around the vitality of Diné weaving throughout the nineteenth century. However, not only do Diné culture, language, and epistemologies remain absent from these accounts, Diné authorship of these histories is limited. In her master's thesis, "Woven Kin: Exploring Representation and Collaboration in Navajo Weaving Exhibitions," Teresa Marie Montoya (Diné) writes:

> Based on a survey of literature published on Navajo weaving, there appears to be a dearth of Navajo perspectives and scholarship on the topic. Not surprisingly, an overwhelming amount of literature has been ethnographic in nature and more recently, publications tend to focus on art historical and political economic perspectives while attempting to include a Navajo "voice." Navajo weavers have served as consultants in many publications, but the *authoritative voice* often remains a non-Native interpreter and organizer of the shared cultural knowledge.[4]

This mode of academia has persisted and seeped into scholarship of the twenty-first century. It continues to produce what Stefano Harney and Fred Moten call "the critical academic": scholars who "become unreliable, disloyal to the public sphere, obstructive and shiftless, dumb with insolence in the face of the call to critical thinking."[5] The implications of this mindset can be seen in the ways that weavings are circulated through globalized markets and the ways that Diné and their cultural productions are positioned as curiosities and "objects" of the past. Thus, the dispersal of these capitalistic and settler-colonial projects contributes to the continued exploitation, displacement, and destruction of Diné. As argued by Eve Tuck (Unangax̂) and K. Waye Yang in their groundbreaking article "Decolonization Is Not a Metaphor," these systems of knowledge production are intrinsic to settlers upholding "problematic relationships to land and to Indigenous sovereignty."[6] By turning to Diné philosophies and creation stories in this essay, I seek to no longer reproduce violence in researching Diné weavings. Instead, I aim to move toward a practice of research that is rooted in decolonization—a practice in which "decolonization is accountable to Indigenous sovereignty and futurity."[7]

I center these arguments by focusing on a particular weaving selected by the *Horizons* advisory committee for exhibition and discussion. This weaving, catalogued as "Dress," consists of a front and back panel of a Diné woman's rug dress (see pages 32–33). The front panel (designated "side A") and the back panel ("side B") are catalogued separately within the collection of the Museum of Indian Arts and Culture in Santa Fe. On side A, the design is a traditional stepped-diamond pattern with narrow stripes in indigo blue on a red background. The panel is very worn, with abrasions that result in exposed and broken white warps. On close examination, we see that the ends of the dress are also worn, while the dress itself retains stains from its wearer. Both panels are dated to the period of 1890 to 1895, about thirty years after the Treaty of 1868 was signed by Diné headmen and the US government at Bosque Redondo in Fort Sumner, New Mexico. This treaty recognized the Diné as a sovereign nation after five years of imprisonment at Bosque Redondo and allowed the People to return to their homelands, which were then politically designated as an Indian reservation.

Weaving—prior to, during, and after Diné imprisonment—has been subject to different interpretations: as craft, art, fashion, and decor. For Diné, however, weaving has always embodied cultural, spiritual, and creative resistance, expressing the many forms of life and the resilience of Diné. How is it, then, that a rug dress was separated into two pieces? How does this separation illuminate the ways in which early twentieth-century capitalist economies in the Southwest violently exploited Diné women and simultaneously disfigured creative and cultural meanings associated with weavings? Grappling with these questions allows us to formulate counter-histories that vocalize Diné and present-day understandings of weavings. This rug dress is presumed to have been produced during the Transitional Period (c. 1860–1890), which alludes not only to the Diné people's physical transition back to their homelands following their imprisonment at Fort Sumner but also to a transitional period in styles, materials, and purposes available to weavers and their communities. During Diné incarceration, weavers obtained cloth that they unraveled, reworked, and integrated into their textiles. They also acquired mass-produced yarn from Pennsylvania and synthetic dyes from as far away as England.[8]

Diné traditionally created weavings to wear as blankets or dresses for their own personal or familial use, but during this period of transition, the influence of reservation-based traders ushered in a new era in which weavings became commodities that entered non-Diné markets.[9] By 1890, there were forty trading posts on or adjacent to the Diné reservation.[10] These trading posts, and the traders who operated them, reaped enormous wealth and benefits by engaging in a "two-way commodity trade," which meant that weavers were never paid cash but were granted "book credit" or "seco" (tokens), redeemable only at that particular post.[11] Data from archival sources, particularly the Hubbell Trading Post in Ganado, Arizona, show that the Hubbell family "shipped 208 tons of weaving from Ganado between 1892 and 1909 and that textile production increased 800 percent over the same period." During this time, it is also known that 85 percent of the Diné population was "destitute, moderately poor or average."[12] By 1930, Diné weavers' production was valued at one million dollars annually.[13] Adjusted for inflation, one million dollars in 1930 is equivalent to nearly eighteen million dollars today. In the case of this dress, Lynda Teller Pete, in conversation with the other Diné advisory committee members in October 2022, stated that in order to ensure they would receive the most profit possible, traders would sometimes cut a dress in half to be sold as two separate items. Pete's deep knowledge about trading post economies is supplemented by oral histories that were passed down through her family and by other weavers whose experience with traders goes back five generations.

I believe the separation of "Dress" into two pieces is of great significance. Typically, a rug dress would be woven for one specific individual. The weaver would take careful consideration of the woman for whom it was being made, tailoring the size, thickness, and design for that individual. Historically, anthropological scholarship around the associated history and emergence of the Diné rug dress has focused on borrowed designs and motifs.[14] However, rug dresses are intimately tied to Diné female identity and culture. Diné believe that Changing Woman, one of the most revered female deities, was gifted a rug dress by the Holy People when she transitioned into womanhood upon having her first menstrual cycle. Changing Woman had a special four-day ceremony called kinaaldá to honor this transition—a ritual that remains one of the most widely practiced ceremonies by Diné women and their families today. During kinaaldá, the young woman having the ceremony is said to embody the spirit of Changing Woman and is dressed in her image. On the first day of the ceremony, she is adorned with moccasins, belts, necklaces, earrings, rings, and material hard goods, collectively known as nitł'iz. These symbolize the family's prayers and hopes that the young girl will attain material wealth and prosperity throughout her life.[15] Each component of the young girl's attire has special significance and is "predicated on the dressing of Changing Woman at her kinaaldá."[16] When the young girl wears a rug dress like Changing Woman, she is "emulating Changing Woman here on earth at this time."[17]

Similarly, Pete has said that for Diné women, the rug dress is not viewed as secular.[18] A Diné rug dress is our protection; as we step out into the world, it represents our sacred womanhood. Diné rug dresses are meant to be worn for many years, protecting us not only from the elements but also protecting us spiritually. In traditional Diné families, weavers do not weave their own dresses. Instead, they are made by Diné weavers who have mastered the special designs and techniques. Overall, the dress represents the universe. The lines that are woven vary by family but are commonly understood to represent the rainbow, sun beams, or the sacred mountains that surround our homelands. The edge cords or tassels that hang on each corner are representations of female rain; for others, they can be referred to as umbilical cords. The woven sash belt, wrapped around the woman's waist, is also used during childbirth.

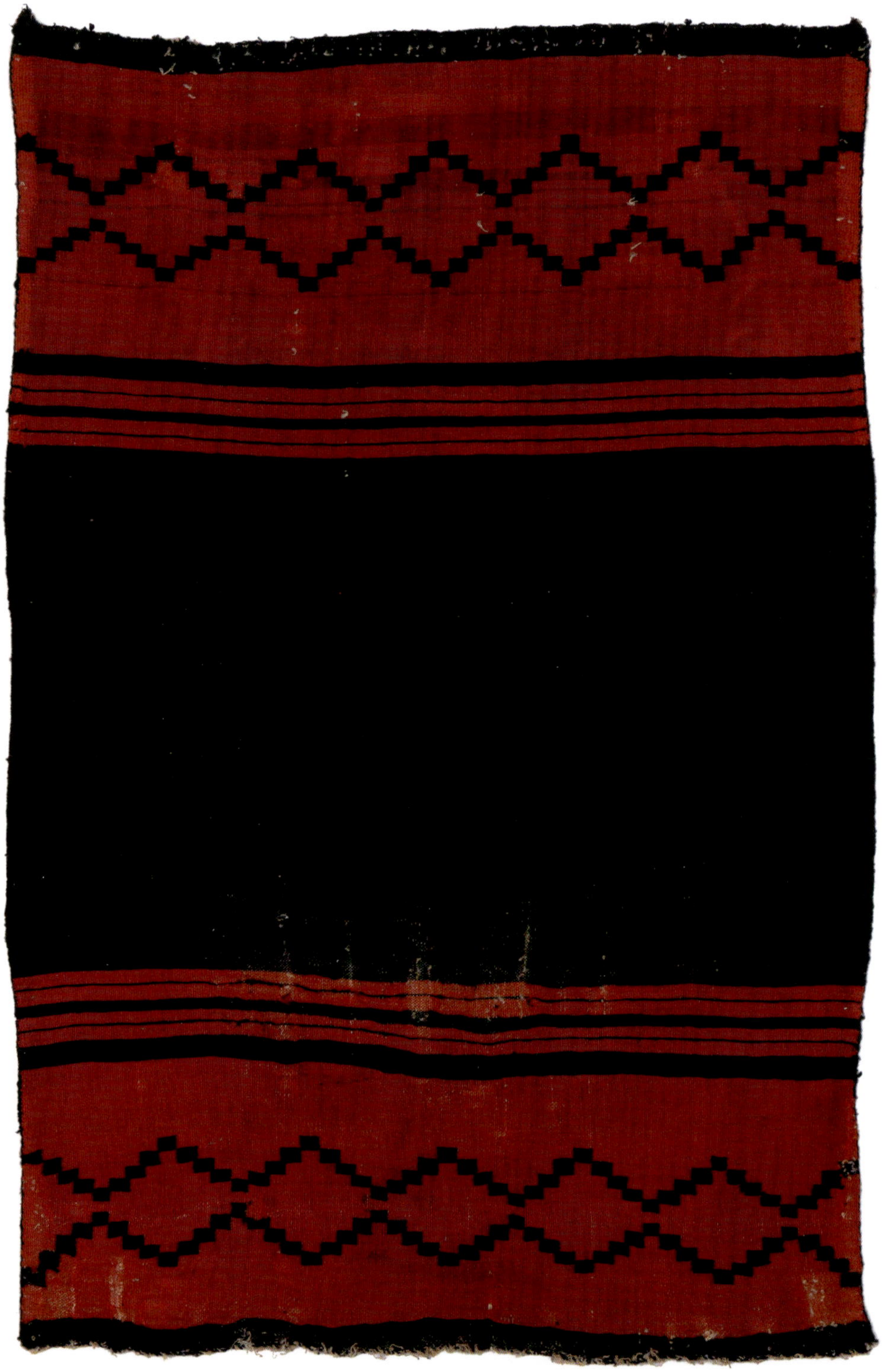

Dress, 1890–1895, side A. Artist once known (Diné). Black handspun wool, indigo blue handspun wool, red raveled wool yarn. 49 × 32 inches. Museum of Indian Arts and Culture/Laboratory of Anthropology, 23236a/12. Photograph by Addison Doty.

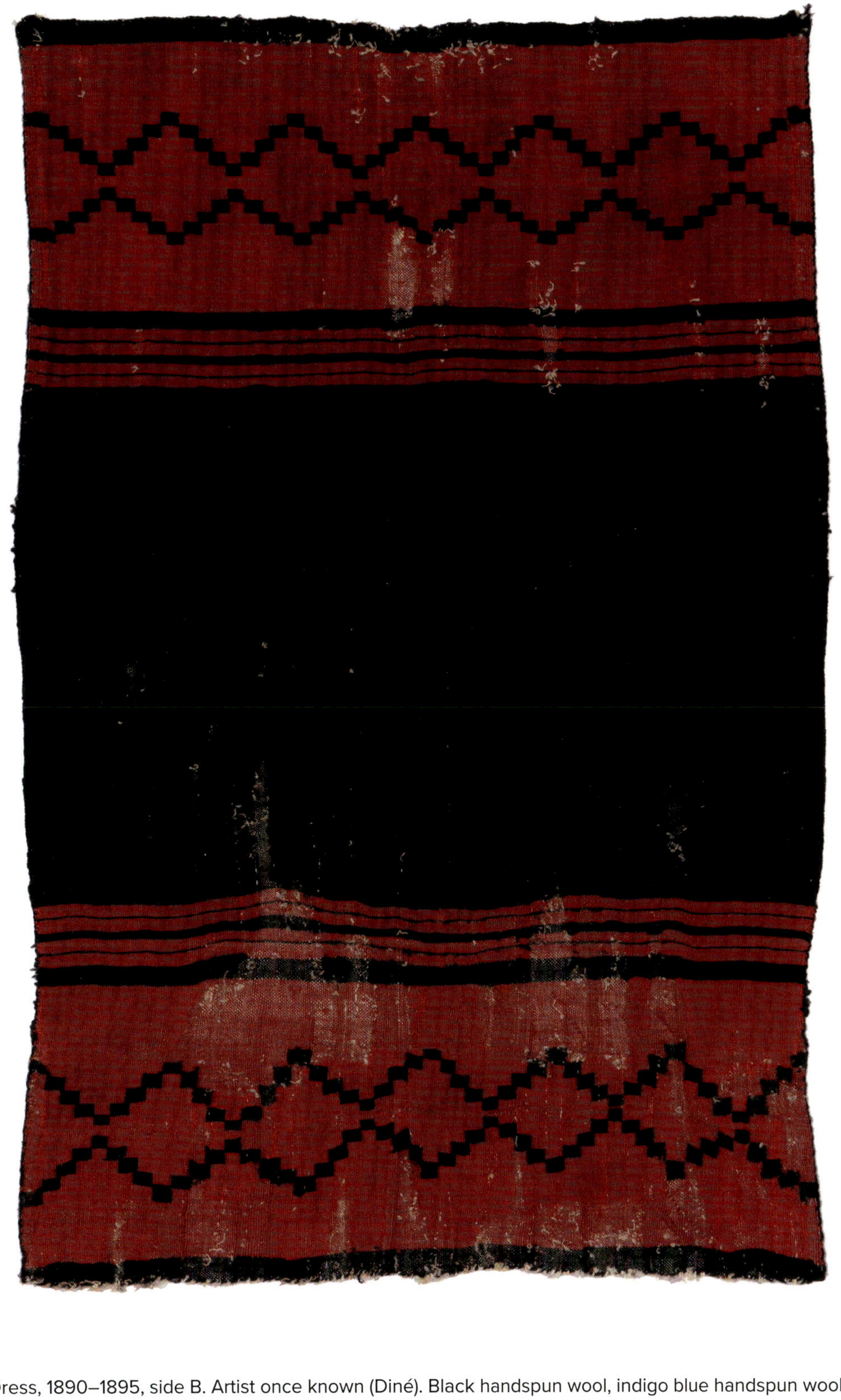

Dress, 1890–1895, side B. Artist once known (Diné). Black handspun wool, indigo blue handspun wool, red raveled wool yarn. 49 × 32 inches. Museum of Indian Arts and Culture/Laboratory of Anthropology, 23236b/12. Photograph by Addison Doty.

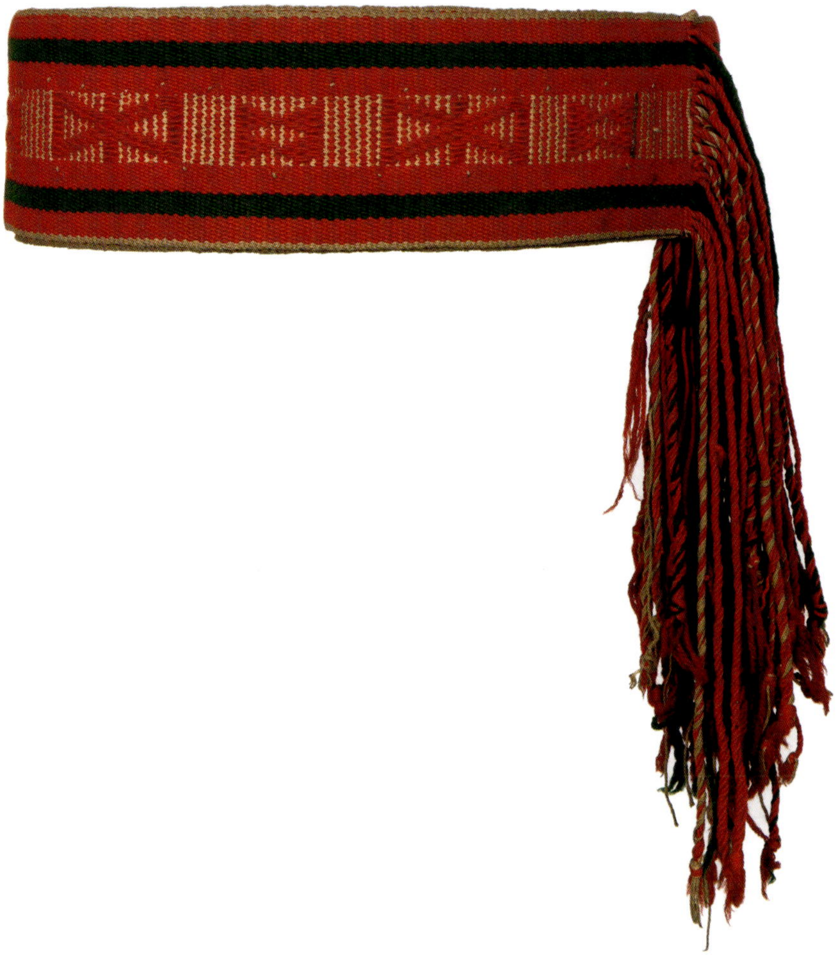

Sash belt, c. 1880–1937. Artist once known (Diné). Commercial cotton string, Germantown wool yarn. 74 × 4 inches. Museum of Indian Arts and Culture/Laboratory of Anthropology, gift of the Chicago Art Institute, 36428/12. Photograph by Addison Doty.

There is continual change in Diné clothing, but one item will always remain constant: the sash belt. I hold these items in very high regard. I learned how to weave them from my mother at a young age, and she was very strict in how they should be made. I see those same teachings visible in the belts woven by my ancestors.

All aspects of the sash belt are representative of womanhood—they are used in the puberty ceremony and even in the birthing of Diné children.

—KEVIN ASPAAS

The fringes of the sash represent the female rain, and the green lines again represent the rainbow and the rays of the sun.

The jewelry commonly worn by Diné women also bears cultural meaning. The necklace represents aging: the left side represents being newborn, and as you move clockwise, the top of the necklace represents the completion of life, or old age. The attachment to the necklace, a pendant that hangs down the center, represents our mothers, as it leads down to our belly buttons where our umbilical cords were cut. The pin signifies White Shell Woman and represents our heart and soul. Women's bracelets are our bowguards, our protection. Our rings lead us toward good decisions, while our earrings prevent us from listening to negativity.

I believe there are three types of destruction occurring with "Dress, 1890–1895" that should be articulated in order to understand the drastic harm that its separation has inflicted on the object itself, on the wearer, on the weaver, and ultimately, on Diné as a whole. First, this separation is a destructive act of capitalist exploitation, most likely done at the hands of traders with the sole intent of accumulating more profit.

For the reasons explained below, Diné would never intentionally separate a rug dress into two pieces, either for alteration or for sale. If adjustments were necessary—say, if the wearer was pregnant—the weaver would take these life and body changes into account prior to weaving the dress. As Lynda Teller Pete wrote in an exhibition label regarding this dress, "In my many years of assisting with curatorial work, I have been angered and saddened to see dress panels separated. I believe that the weaver prayed and sang for the dress as it was given to the wearer. The universe answered with the panels' reunion."[19]

Second, the forced separation of a rug dress into two pieces is an act of violence to both the weaver and the wearer. The weaver has the intention to create two pieces that would ultimately be joined together to create the dress. Despite the two identical panels being woven separately and subsequently taken off the loom, a rug dress is not considered complete until the two panels are sewn together to create the garment. The weaver takes into consideration the wearer's height, weight, and preferences for the dress itself. Upon completion, and when it is given to the woman for whom it was made, the rug dress is a blessing and a gift. The story of Changing Woman receiving and wearing her first rug dress is part of the gifting process of this item. Within the context of the kinaaldá ceremony, both the wearer of the dress and the dress itself take on new significance: the woman and the dress become connected. When a woman is pregnant and has children of her own, she can pass down her biil to her children. This long-standing practice of weavers gifting their productions, and those gifts being subsequently passed on to future generations, is an act that honors our creation stories, livelihoods, and the Holy People. To separate the panels of a rug dress into two pieces damages not only the woven garment but the weaver and the wearer of the biil.

Finally, if a weaving is destroyed or taken apart, it is as if the person undoing it is taking apart the weaver's spirit and unraveling the spirit of the weaving itself. If a weaver decides to start a piece, it must be completed—a belief that honors traditional Diné teachings and creation stories. Each weaving is brought into existence by the maker, whose careful actions activate its life and whose breath becomes part of the textile. According to Diné worldview, if a textile is left incomplete, it is as if the weaver's life remains incomplete. If for some reason it cannot be completed, the unfinished piece will be laid to rest in a special place with offerings, and a special ceremony must take place to restore balance in the weaver's life. The weaver, the weaving, and the loom are manifestations of the celestial, spiritual, and physical worlds coming together. To destroy or damage a weaving once created is to tear those worlds apart.

Diné weaving practices are tied to our creation stories in profound ways, and contemporary scholarship about weaving must focus on Diné culture as the foundation for reassessing what weavings have meant to our people and how we orient ourselves within the world. In the instance of "Dress, 1890–1895," it was a blessing to see both panels reunited under our care, prayer, and presence. I hope that my analysis of the dress will help to restore healing and life to this weaving—and that the *Horizons* project will initiate a new kind of conversation and understanding of Diné weaving from a uniquely Diné perspective.

BIBLIOGRAPHY

Harney, Stefano, and Fred Moten. *The Undercommons: Fugitive Planning & Black Study*. Wivenhoe, UK: Minor Compositions, 2013.

Howells, Richard. "The Aesthetics of Utopia: Creation, Creativity and a Critical Theory of Design." *Thesis Eleven 123,* no. 1 (August 2014): 41–61. https://doi.org/10.1177/0725513614543414.

M'Closkey, Kathy. "Weaving and Mothering: Reframing Navajo Weaving as Recursive Manifestations of K'é." In *Transgressing Borders: Critical Perspectives on Gender, Household, and Culture,* edited by Suzan Ilcan and Lynne Phillips, 115–27. Westport, CT: Bergin & Garvey, 1998.

Montoya, Teresa. "Woven Kin: Exploring Representation and Collaboration in Navajo Weaving Exhibitions." *Electronic Theses and Dissertations*, January 1, 2011. https://digitalcommons.du.edu/etd/443.

Reichard, Gladys A. *Spider Woman: A Story of Navajo Weavers and Chanters.* New York: Macmillan, 1934; Albuquerque: University of New Mexico Press, 1997.

Salesa, Damon. "The Pacific in Indigenous Time." In *Pacific Histories: Ocean, Land, People,* edited by David Armitage and Alison Basford, 41. New York: Palgrave Macmillan, 2014.

Schwarz, Maureen Trudelle. *Molded in the Image of Changing Woman: Navajo Views on the Human Body and Personhood*. Tucson: University of Arizona Press, 1997.

Tuck, Eve, and K. Waye Yang. "Decolonization Is Not a Metaphor." *Decolonization: Indigeneity, Education & Society* 1, no. 1 (2012): 28, 35. https://jps.library.utoronto.ca/index.php/des/issue/view/1234.

NOTES

1. M'Closkey, "Weaving and Mothering," 116.
2. Howells, "The Aesthetics of Utopia," 51.
3. Salesa, "The Pacific in Indigenous Time," 41.
4. Montoya, "Woven Kin," 42.
5. Harney and Moten, *The Undercommons*, 34.
6. Tuck and Yang, "Decolonization Is Not a Metaphor," 28.
7. Tuck and Yang, 35.
8. Howells, 46.
9. Howells, 47.

10. M'Closkey, 118.

11. Ibid.

12. M'Closkey, 119.

13. M'Closkey, 120.

14. See Reichard, *Spider Woman*.

15. Schwarz, *Molded in the Image of Changing Woman*, 181.

16. Schwarz, 183–84.

17. Schwarz, 184.

18. Lynda Teller Pete, personal communication, 2023.

19. Lynda Teller Pete, exhibition interpretation, *Horizons: Weaving Between the Lines with Diné Textiles*, Museum of Indian Arts and Culture, Santa Fe, New Mexico, July 16, 2023–February 2, 2025.

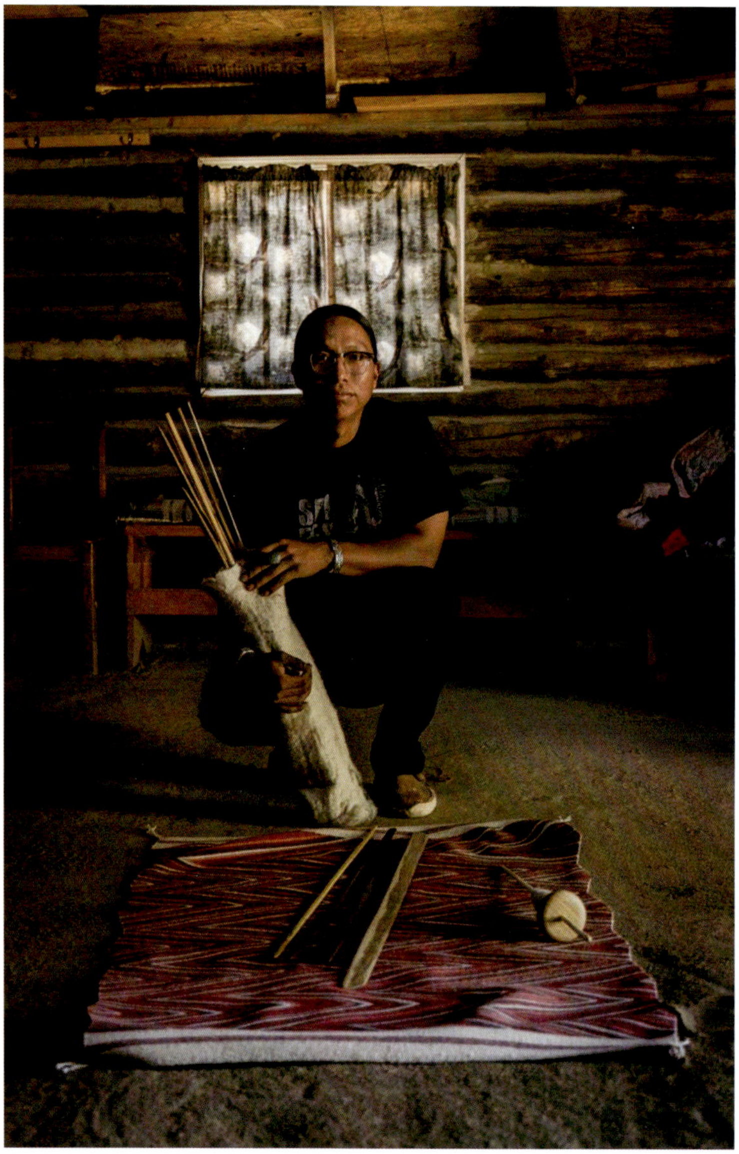

Kevin Aspaas, August 2021.
Photograph by Minesh Bacrania. Courtesy of Kevin Aspaas.

3 To Weave for One Another

Wedge Weaving, Sheepherding, and Memory

KEVIN ASPAAS with Lillia McEnaney

The following conversation between Diné weaver and fiber artist Kevin Aspaas and museum anthropologist Lillia McEnaney was recorded on April 14, 2023. It has been lightly edited for length and clarity. –HWJ

Kevin Aspaas (KA): Yá'át'ééh shí éí Kevin Aspaas yinishyé. Kinyaa'áanii nishłį́, Tódích'iinii báshishchiin, Tł'izíłaní dashicheii, Háshtł'iishnii dashinalí. Tóóhdi shighan. Hello, my name is Kevin Aspaas. I am of the Towering House People Clan, born for the Bitterwater People Clan, my maternal grandfathers are of the Many Goats People Clan and my paternal grandfather is of the Mud People Clan. I live in Shiprock, New Mexico.

Lillia McEnaney (LM): What is your earliest memory of art?

KA: My earliest memory of art is of my mom. Looking back at it now, I didn't consider her an artist then because she was always home with us. Now that I'm older, I think about these things differently and know that she is an artist—she is a weaver. She was always spinning yarn, creating sash belts, and sewing baby blankets in a way that was special to me. It was a significant privilege to grow up in that environment. Being a stay-at-home mom is hard enough in itself, and she was constantly moving between these two roles.

I can still hear her spindle dancing on the floor, the squeak of wood on linoleum, the pounding when she was weaving her belts. Those were the sounds we went to sleep to.

LM: How did you learn to weave? Who taught you?

KA: I began weaving because of my mom. My dad worked at a power plant in the Four Corners area, so he stayed up in Shiprock or Farmington during the week. We lived in

Santa Fe because my sister attended the New Mexico School for the Deaf. While we were in Santa Fe, my mom would sew and make sash belts, and on the weekends, we would go out to the Plaza and sell. I always felt like she was the best at what she was doing, and I still think that way. Her teachings are reflected in the work that I do. At home, I have old belts that she wove and frequently look at them. We are completely different people, but I still try to emulate her—her style, her texture, and her structure.

The first thing she taught me was how to re-spin yarn. At the beginning, she was very strict with how many times I had to roll the spindle on my lap, which determines the tightness of the spin. It wasn't until I mastered spinning that I started weaving—my mom did that intentionally as part of the learning process. Because of this, I have learned that the process is just as important as the final product. You need to have fun with the process!

Eventually, I moved onto learning how to weave. She would let me sit at her loom and practice on pieces she was working on. Once I was done practicing, she would take out everything that I had done and continue with her project, but after she finished each weaving, she would set up another one for me to practice on.

Eventually, we got to the point where I wanted to weave my own belt. My dad made me a loom for it. I spun the yarns and picked the colors. I still have these first two belts—they don't have any designs. I was nine or ten years old at the time and was very proud of them.

After my sister graduated, we moved back home to Shiprock, and we've been there ever since. Once we went back home, I wanted to learn how to weave rugs. It was really helpful to be living near people who knew how to weave in that way. In the summer of 2005, I started learning from Rose Blueeyes [Diné], who is from the Two Grey Hills area. Around this same time, there was a summer weaving class at the local school, Tohaali Boarding School. The classes provided looms, tools, and yarn—everything that you needed. All you had to do was attend. Most of the students were in their fifties, but I was about ten years old. I finished my first rug in that class—my mom has it in a frame on the wall of her house. After that, I continued to learn from my neighbor Elsie Whitehorse [Diné], and then just kept going.

LM: Coming out of those learning experiences, what brought you to wedge weaving?

KA: When I was in high school in Shiprock, weaving fell a bit to the wayside, but after graduation, I taught myself to weave again. Soon I was going to community weaving events, where I met Roy Kady [Diné], a master weaver from Teec Nos Pos. He taught me and a group of us all different types of techniques—Navajo and non-Navajo, European tapestry, everything. For me, a lot of it was muscle memory at that point—it was very fluid and natural. I was picking up different techniques very quickly. My goal was to master all of the different regional styles.

A huge part of the learning experience was going to sheep camp. Every June, we take the flock up to the top of the Carrizo Mountains in Arizona for summer grazing.

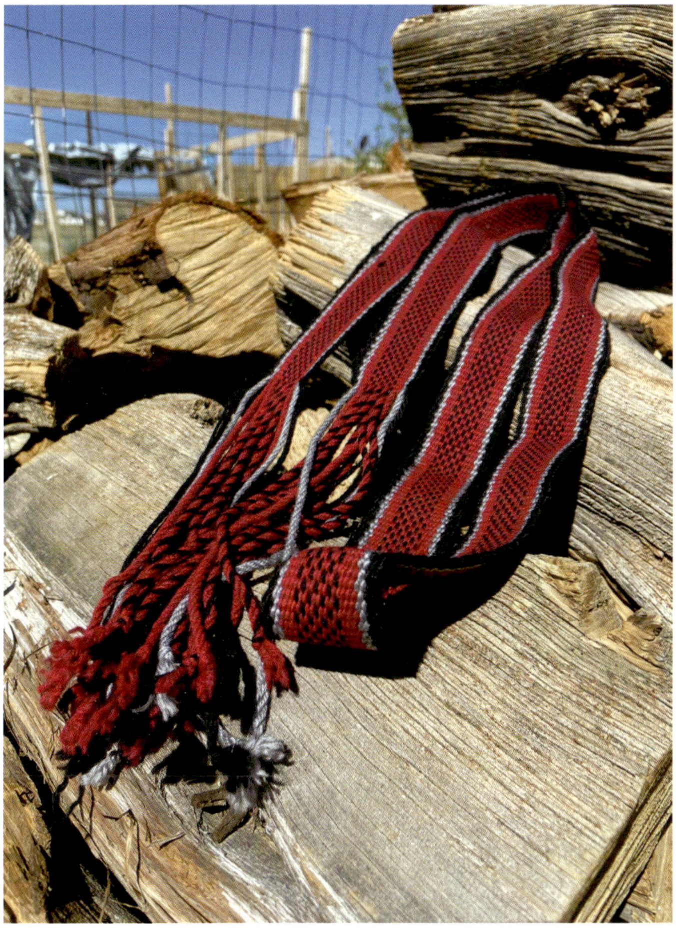

First weaving, July 2004. Kevin Aspaas (Diné, b. 1995).
Sash belt. Acrylic red, grey, and black yarn. 28 × 3 inches.
Photograph by Kevin Aspaas. Courtesy of the artist.

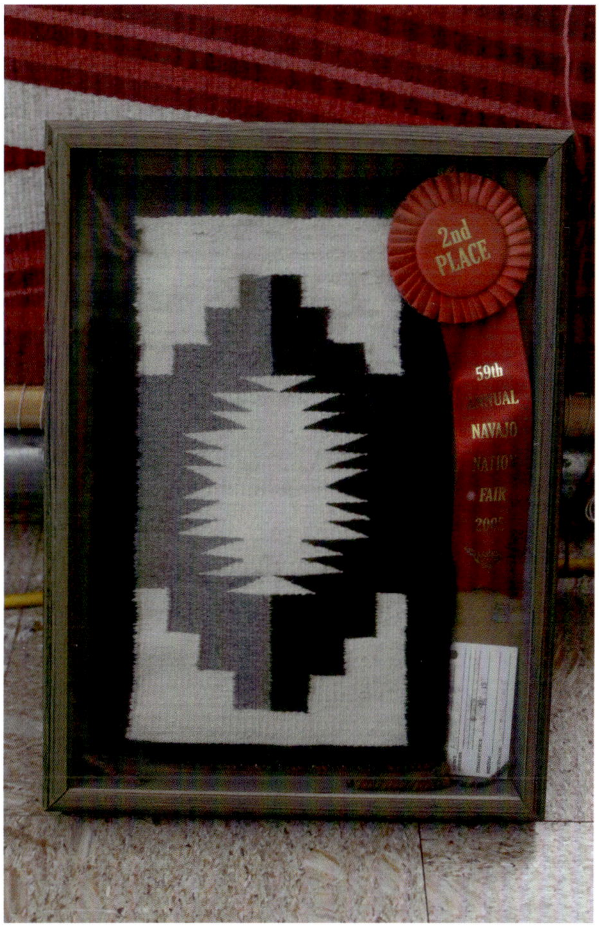

First woven rug, August 2005. Kevin Aspaas (Diné, b. 1995).
Framed; wool with natural (undyed) colors. 18 × 12 inches.
Photograph by Kevin Aspaas. Courtesy of the artist.

The mountainous high country typically has more vegetation and cooler temperatures, and this is where we keep the sheep for the summer, from June to October. The Kady family has a cabin and camp on the northwest part of the mountain, in a very remote area of the reservation. A lot of Diné families have a portion of their homelands that they call sheep camp.

In 2014, while we were there, Roy asked each of us what we wanted to weave. He told us that nothing is holding us back, that we—the younger generation—don't have the restrictions of the trading posts. At this point he introduced me to wedge weaving, and he taught it to me in one afternoon. I was sitting on the ground on the mountain, and I knew that I had to do this. I felt almost immediately motivated to do large-scale wedge weaves, and so I went home and finished a four-foot by five-foot piece in one month.

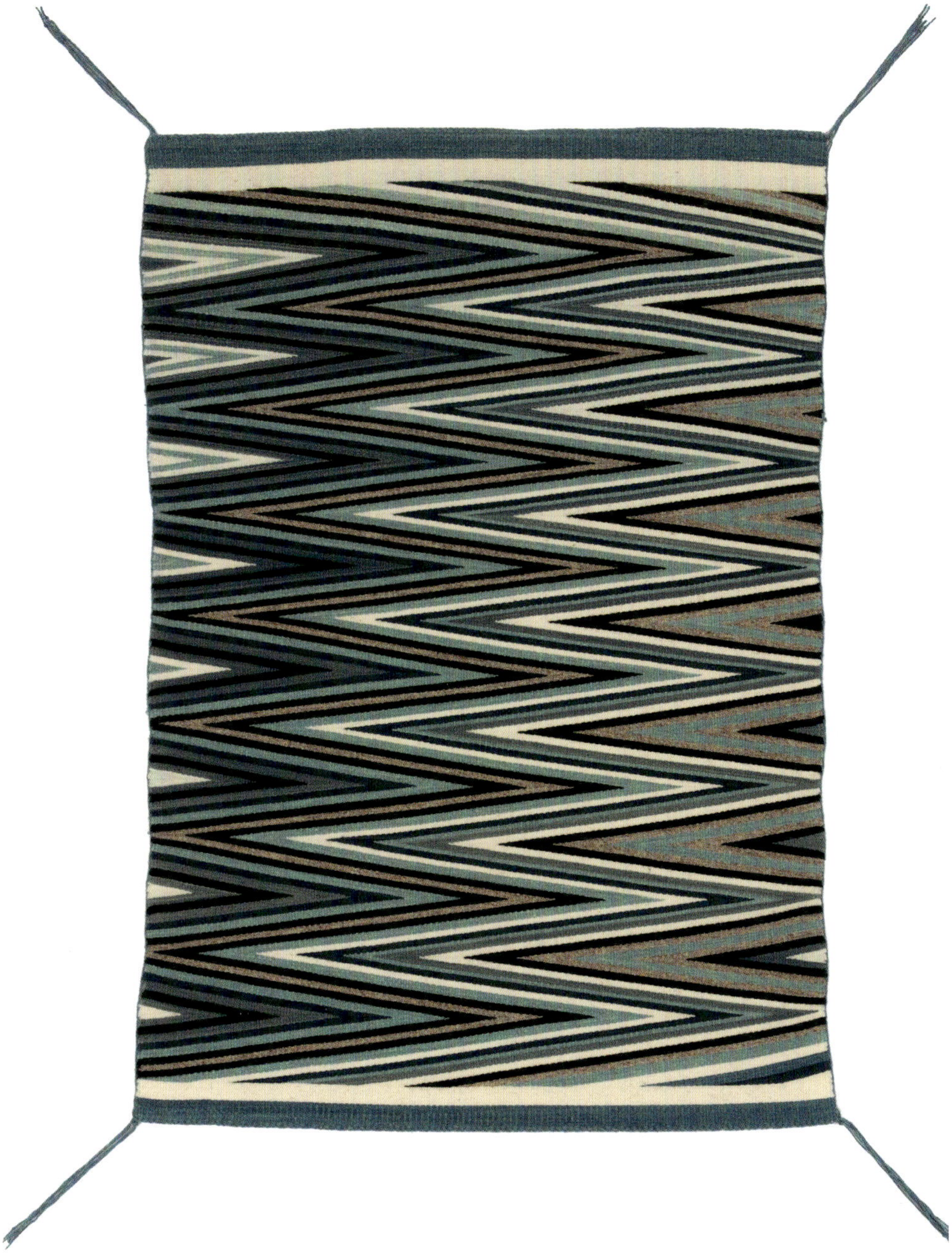

Untitled, 2022. Kevin Aspaas (Diné, b. 1995). Wedge weave, wool yarn (including wool warp), indigo dye, natural (undyed) white and grey wool. 42 × 32 inches. Gochman Family Collection. Photograph by Addison Doty.

One of the first things I was taught about weavings is that they are an extension of your very own being. The act of weaving and the interactions with the tools can provide healing. Thoughts and emotions play an important part of any artistic expression. I wove this piece during a very difficult time in my life, and I think my grief made itself evident through the choice of the varying shades of blue.

Although it was a tough piece to complete, it brought me healing and comfort. Looking back now, I realize this is what my ancestors went through with their own grief and in times of trouble. There is beauty in that sadness, but only if we sit with it and have that conversation.

—KEVIN ASPAAS

By 2018, I had finally developed my own niche—I am now known for wedge weaving. A truly Diné weaving innovation, wedge weaving was first done between 1850 and 1880. The weft is woven on a diagonal angle throughout the entirety of the piece. I start to build an angle on one side of the warp. To clarify, I always start the wedge on the furthest/last warp string on the right. I weave the weft to the left, turn around and take it back to the right. Each time I work the weft to the left, I turn around on the next warp string over. Because of the angle, the weft creates tension and pulls the warp in each row, creating a scalloped edge. This gave wedge weave another name: it's also known as a pulled-warp weave or pulled-warp technique. The weavings hardly lie flat—there are always ripples here and there.

Wedge weaving does not fit your idea of what a "normal" Diné weaving is, as that ideal was constructed and encouraged by trading posts. The traders had very particular ideas of "perfection" and wanted weavers to fit into their Euro-American boxes. This is part of the reason that the wedge weave technique was lost. That's part of why I

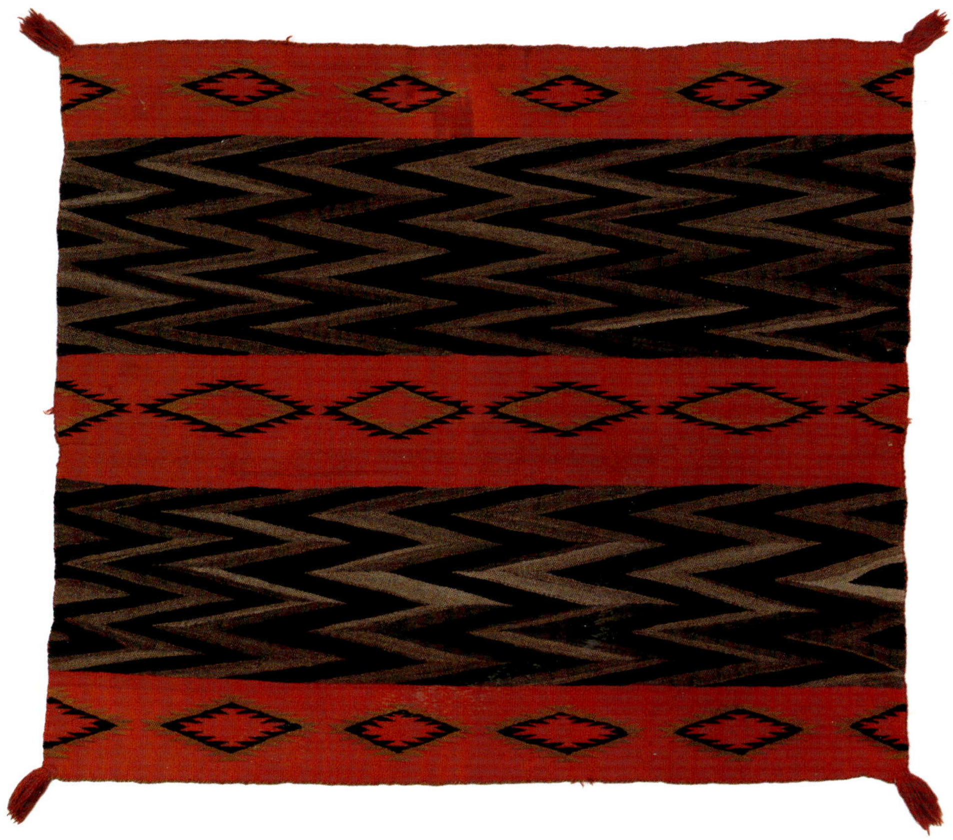

Woman's shoulder blanket, c. 1860–1890. Artist once known (Diné). Handspun wool, vegetal dye, indigo dye, aniline dye, sinew, plant matter. 43 × 52 inches. Museum of Indian Arts and Culture/Laboratory of Anthropology, gift of Mrs. Philip B. Stewart, 9100/12. Photograph by Addison Doty.

In Diné weaving, there is a history of evolution and experimentation. Here, the creator of this piece made a one-of-a-kind blanket. What could have been a standard woman's blanket with horizontal stripes was altered with the addition of the wedge weave technique. This transformed the weaving into a piece that makes a powerful and striking statement. Due to its structure, the wedge weave also creates a type of movement, offering protection and camouflage for the wearer. While it is not widely practiced among Diné weavers, wedge weaving is making a comeback with a younger generation of textile and fiber artists.

—KA

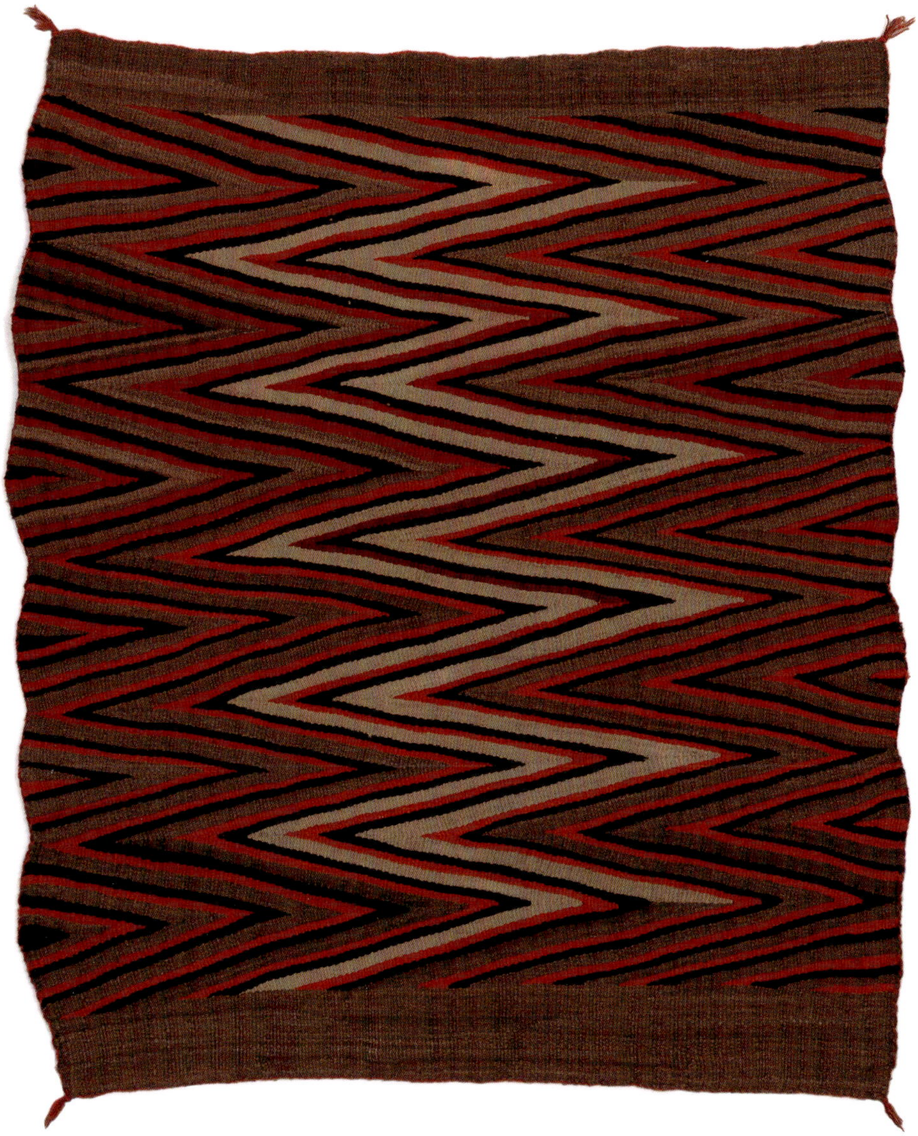

Wedge weave blanket, c. 1895. Artist once known (Diné). Commercial cotton string, Germantown wool yarn. 52 × 45 inches. Museum of International Folk Art, gift of Lloyd E. Cotsen and the Neutrogena Cooperation, A.1995.93.1038. Photograph by Addison Doty.

I see wedge weave blankets as both a rare treasure and an "orphaned child" of Diné weaving. The technique itself had a short lifespan in the late nineteenth century that was specific to one area of Diné Bikéyah.

Wedge weave textiles have a lot of movement, visible in the way the warp pulls at an angle in each section and in the scalloped edges on the sides of the textile. They raise the questions of "how?" and "why?" We may never know the answers, but as an artist who specializes in wedge weaves, I'm always excited to see historical examples of this technique. It reaffirms my own work and inspires me to keep moving forward.

—KA

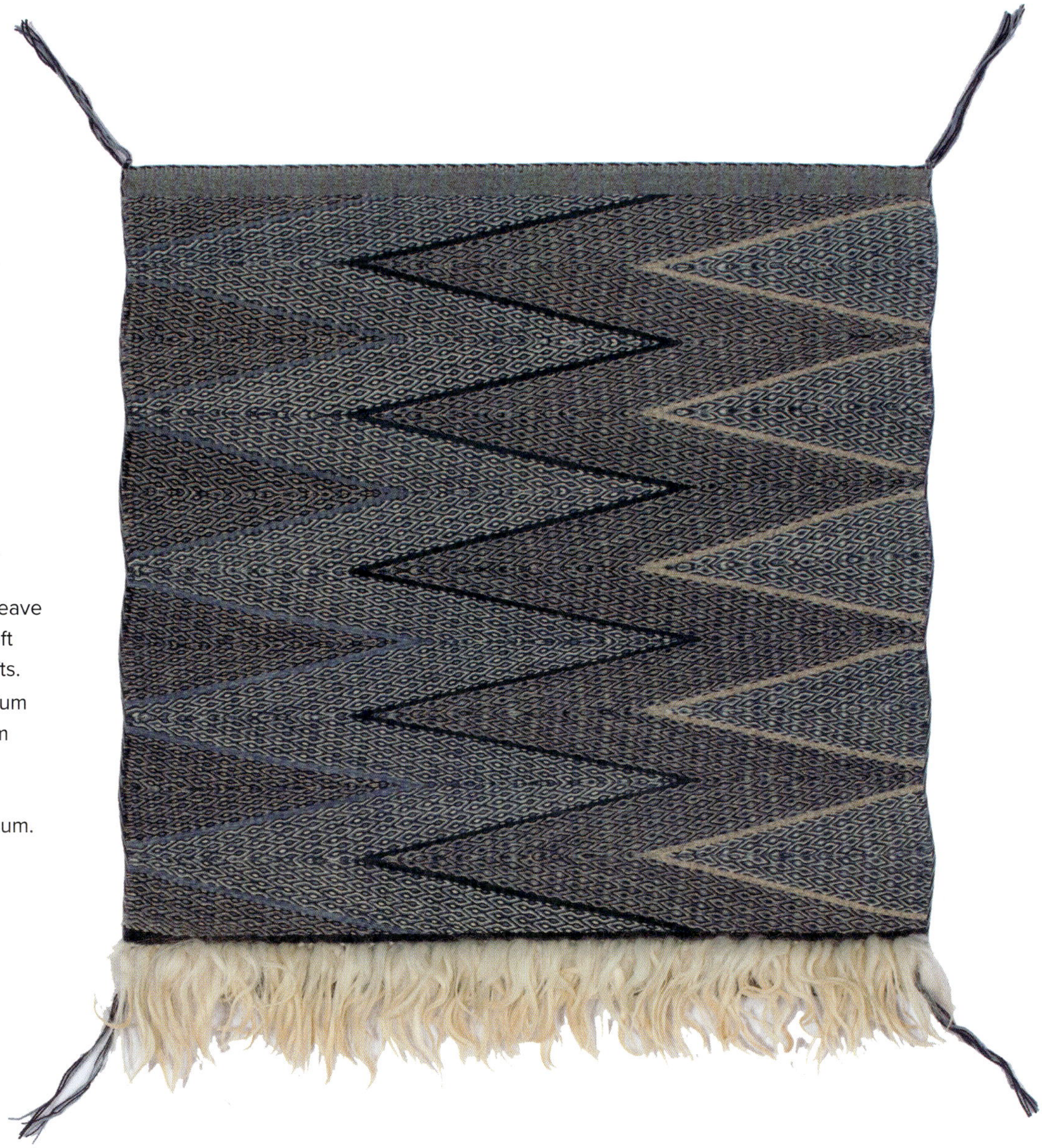

Horned Toad and Lightning, 2022. Kevin Aspaas (Diné, b. 1995). Indigo dyes, twill weave with wedge weave, wool weft and warp, Navajo-Churro tufts. 32 × 32 inches. Heard Museum Collection, gift of Drs. William G. and Kathleen L. Howard. Photograph by Craig Smith. Courtesy of the Heard Museum.

love it so much—I'm a sucker for the things that are thrown off to the side, the underdogs. Wedge weaves have nothing to prove and give me the freedom to experiment. Last year, I combined a twill weave with a wedge weave, and it was the first of its kind. That piece was purchased by the Heard Museum.

LM: How has managing your own flock changed the way you think about weaving? What does that relationship look like?

KA: Sheep are really connected with us—they have a long history with Diné people. When I started learning from Roy Kady, I quickly realized how much work having a flock is, but I still wanted to learn. Both of my parents were raised with sheep, but the flocks were sold as my grandparents aged and couldn't care for them. Once we moved back home to Shiprock, I had a goal of eventually starting my own flock.

Before the onset of the pandemic, I finally decided to start. I was saving up to build a corral. My family kept warning me of how much work it is and how difficult it is to travel once you have sheep, but my mentality was, "Someone's got to do it, and I'm going to do it." I'm a homebody, I like being home, so that was my way to justify getting sheep. I started off with five sheep, but then soon had eight. Somewhere along the way I had as many as thirty, but since then I've reduced. It's been three years now—it's crazy to think that I've had them for three years. That seems like a pretty short amount of time to have them. I don't see it as work because I truly enjoy them. My flock brings me happiness.

Shearing my own sheep has changed the way I think about weaving. This was also part of the reason I wanted to raise them: I wanted them to be shorn in a very particular way. When I shear, I put tarps out, put the sheep somewhere that's clean, and stay outside all day with them. The most rewarding part is actually getting to see the work that was done over the fall and winter. Seeing the fleeces in the spring and summer is really exciting—you check the cleanliness of it and how long the fibers are.

I've learned that you're going to make a lot of mistakes. Learning how to shear was a whole different challenge in itself, and that brought me an even deeper appreciation for weaving.

After you shear, you clean the wool, card it, and spin it. People think that weaving is the hard part, but really for me, weaving is the fun, easy part. It's everything else that comes before that is difficult—the dirty work. The journey from sheep to loom is a very intimate process. Each animal has its own personality. You're dealing with a living, breathing being. They are part of your process and part of your family. Even when I'm away from them, I'm thinking about them all the time. The sheepdog is part of all of this, too. My sheepdog Bailey takes very good care of them.

Now that we've gone through several lambing seasons, lambing feels like Christmas! Seeing the ewes' stomachs getting big, slowing down, waddling around, you're constantly checking on them to see if new additions show up. It is exciting to see the young ones grow—it's like having children grow up in front of you and develop their own personalities.

LM: This seems like a good time to talk about process. Where does your process start? How do you think about your process?

KA: I think my process really starts when I see the colors that I'm working with. When I'm doing a dye session, I start to feel that creativity once I see the end product. I'm able to envision what's going happen next, what I'm going to put on the loom—matching colors, doing swatches, seeing it come together. My designs aren't planned ahead. I see and envision the colors coming together in my mind, but it is not until I have the warp set up that I have a tangible sense of what's going to happen. When I'm working, I don't actually "see" it until I get three rows in.

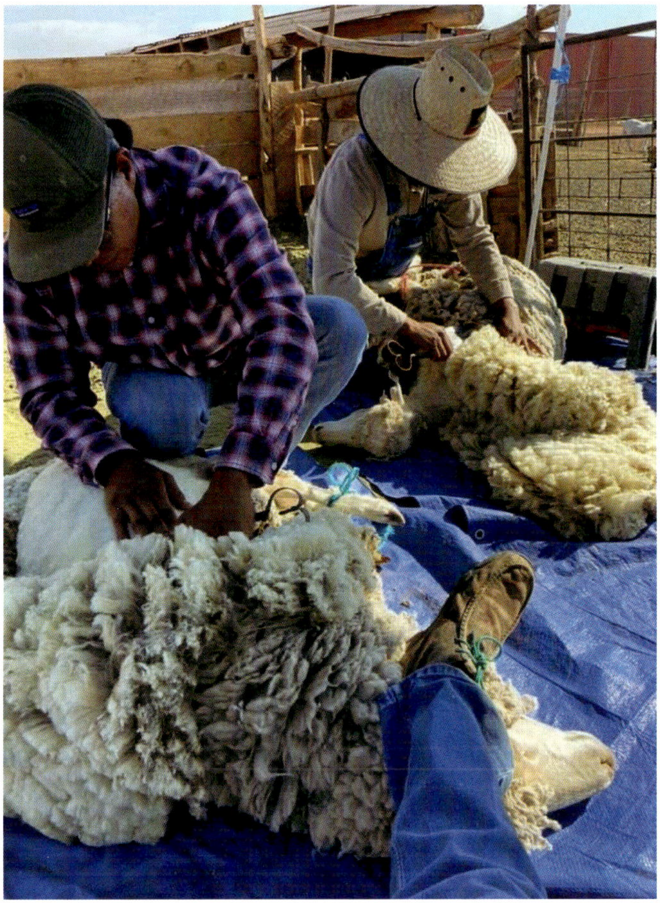

Shearing for relatives, June 2021. Chinle, Arizona. Photograph by Kevin Aspaas. Courtesy of the artist.

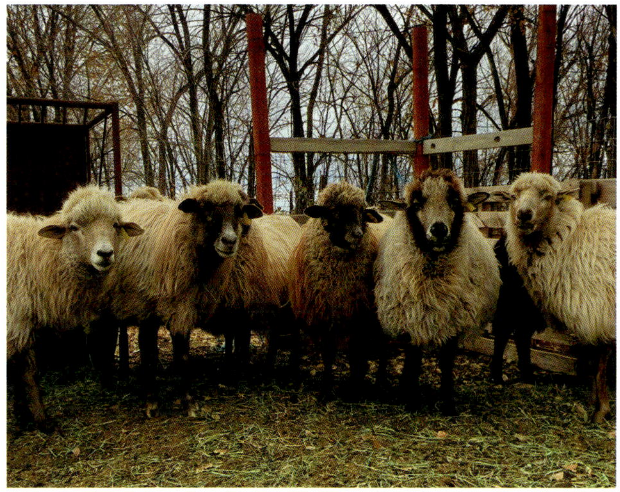

Kevin Aspaas's flock of Navajo-Churro sheep, November 2023. Shiprock, New Mexico. Photograph by Kevin Aspaas. Courtesy of the artist.

Shearing is an integral element of flock management. Many Diné families recall memories of their spring and summer seasons gathering to assist with shearing their family's flock. The act of shearing provides relief for the sheep during hot weather and allows shepherds to assess the health of their flock.

Over the course of the fall and winter seasons, weavers look forward to shearing, as it provides new material for their work. During this time, weavers are able to make their choice of wool fleeces, often selecting the best wool available.

—KA

Sometimes when I'm working I don't like it and then have to ask myself if I'm going to start over or leave it. Most of the time I do leave it, and just grin and bear it. My sisters will give me encouragement. Even some of my better-known pieces, I didn't like them when they came off the loom. It sometimes takes me a few days to warm up to them—I need to spend time with it. For example, the twill and wedge combination—when I took it off the loom, I said that I didn't like it and I was almost on the verge of tears because it was my only piece for the Heard Market. My sisters don't let me complain—they were all telling me to get it together!

My process starts in seeing the colors. For a good amount of time I was fixated on cochineal and indigo—that was my bread and butter. And for a time, I was only using two shades of cochineal and indigo—I was using a cardinal red and a dark navy blue, and then white as a buffer color. Then there was one Saturday night where I was experimenting with shades of indigo, shades of cochineal, learning about the chemistry of these two dyes. Learning that process is really frustrating but fun.

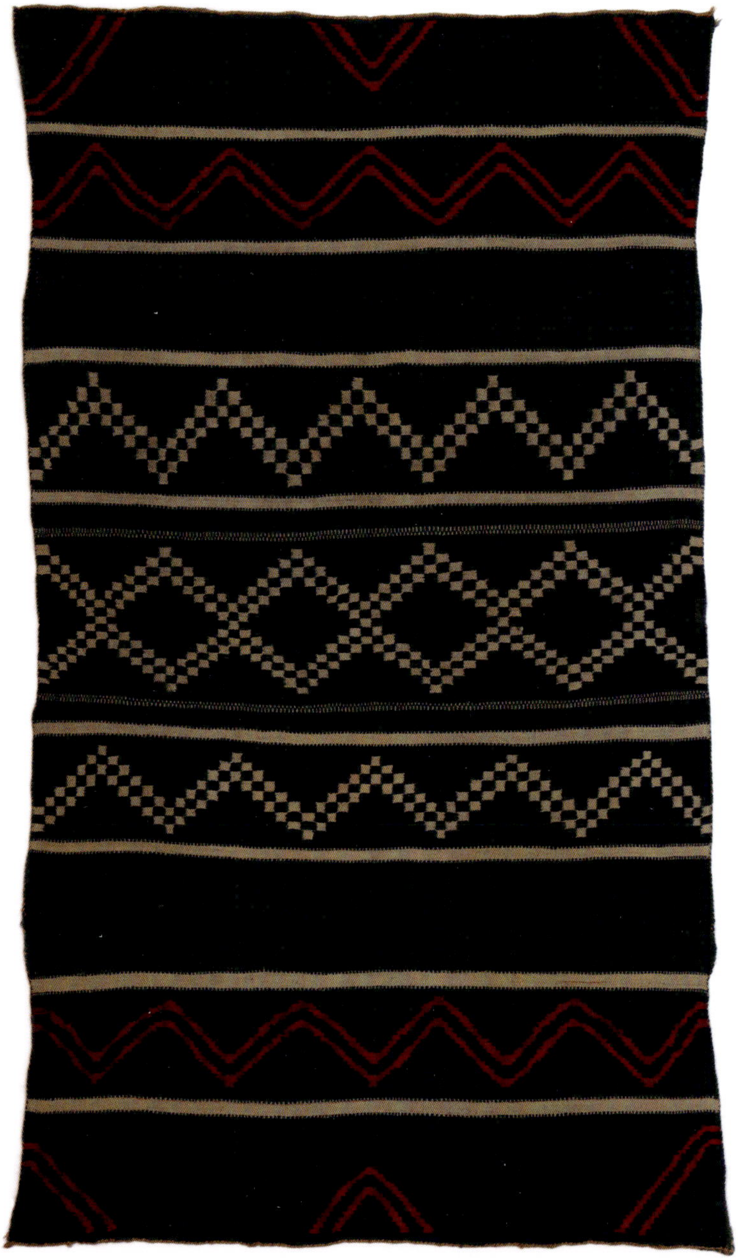

Blanket, c. 1850. Artist once known (Diné). Handspun wool yarn, raveled yarn, cochineal dye, indigo dye, vegetal dye, handspun churro yarn. 82 ¼ × 49 ½ inches. Museum of Indian Arts and Culture/Laboratory of Anthropology, gift of Mrs. Philip B. Stewart, 9319/12. Photograph by Addison Doty.

From the perspective of a weaver and dyer, the amount of blue wool dyed with indigo is an incredible feat, especially given the size of the blanket. The knowledge and work that goes into reaching this deep blue with natural dyes does not go unnoticed and should be appreciated.

—KA

LM: What are your relationships to these materials and tools?

KA: Everything branches out of sheep. Weaving embodies community—everything is connected in one way or another, and we are always developing these relationships. When I say we are interconnected, I mean it—we are all woven together in a very real way. Weaving is so community oriented, especially now. It is important to learn from within your community—you learn from different people, you learn different stories, different techniques.

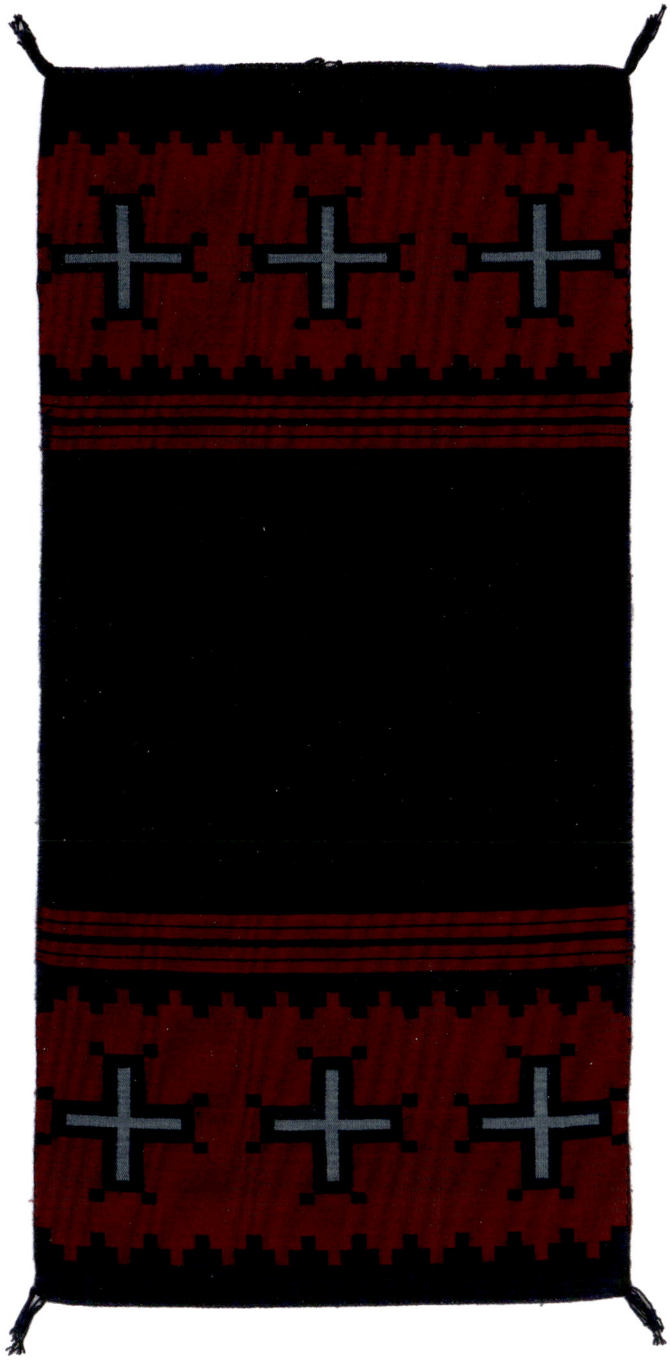

Dress, 2021. Kevin Aspaas (Diné, b. 1995). Two-panel dress, side B. Wool yarn, indigo and commercial acid dyes. Each panel: 47 × 27 inches. Collection of DeAnna Goldtooth. Photograph by Addison Doty.

There was once a time that we wove for one another, pieces of clothing created to protect the wearer from harm. Woven dresses are a prime example of that. I wove this dress with the intention of honoring the ancestors. I wanted to create a dress that emulated those of the past, down to the colors and the layout of the design. The life we give to these pieces—how they are worn and displayed—is amplified by the individual that wears them. It's not often one sees a woven dress that looks as if it would have been worn by the ancestors. As a weaver, it's important to create at least one woven dress in your lifetime.

—KA

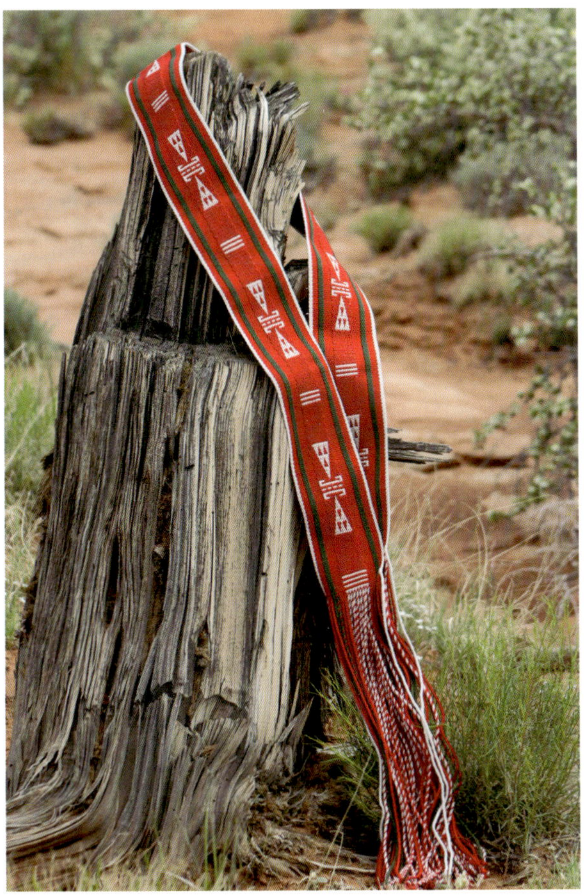

Diné-style sash belt, May 2023. Kevin Aspaas (Diné, b. 1995). Wool warp and cotton weft, float-warp technique. 85 × 4 inches. Collection of Megan Johnson. Photograph by Kevin Aspaas. Courtesy of the artist.

LM: Speaking of sheep, can you tell us about Diné Bé'liná?

KA: Diné Bé'liná is a Navajo-led organization; more than 90 percent of our board is Diné. We support weavers and shepherds, and also specifically highlight Navajo-Churro sheep. Navajos valued churro sheep from the beginning, even when outsiders told us they weren't as "good" as other breeds.

Diné Bé'liná supports the preservation and the continuation of fiber arts through community outreach, mentorship programs, and the annual Sheep is Life celebration each June. We get visitors from all over the west for Sheep is Life—folks bring their sheep to Window Rock and set up mini sheep camps in the parking lot of the Navajo Nation Museum.

LM: How does weaving relate to your understanding of home, landscape, and community?

KA: When we participate in the act of weaving, we are participating in a universal, worldly theme. The loom isn't just a loom, the weaving isn't just the weaving, the tools aren't just tools—they are all representative of something in our world. The loom itself is the home of the weaving—the bottom of the loom is the ground, the pillars represent the beams that hold up the sky, the cords create tension and represent lightning. Many of the elements of weaving are representative of Earth itself. Growth, plant life, moisture.

In a sense, what I've been taught is that weaving is a prayer for rain, for moisture. We take care of the land. We use natural dyes, we don't overharvest one area, and we are conscious of the movements and needs of plants. Just like we move our sheep to different camps based on what they need, the plants also do the same.

Weaving is at the core of the universal themes of Diné philosophy and identity. It is amazing to think about the ways a little animal like the sheep transformed our society. We have songs for them, prayers for them, we protect them. Sheep are also representative of clouds, growth, and the renewal of life. We are very blessed to have our sheep.

LM: From your perspective, what role does weaving have in Diné communities? What role does it have in your own life?

KA: Weaving evokes memories for a lot of people—memories of mothers, aunts, grandmothers. Many of us still have our grandmothers' tools in our home. Fundamentally, weaving is about community—you cannot do it alone, it is a community process. Families come together to help each other with their flocks, to card wool together, to dye yarn.

There's a common saying, "When you take care of sheep, they take care of you." During the pandemic, it was a very scary and lonely time. I felt lucky not to be stuck inside, but for anyone, if you're not out there, out in your community, interacting with people, your mental health and emotional well-being become strained. The sheep really helped me get through the pandemic, and that's when I fully came to understand that saying. Emotional support sheep!

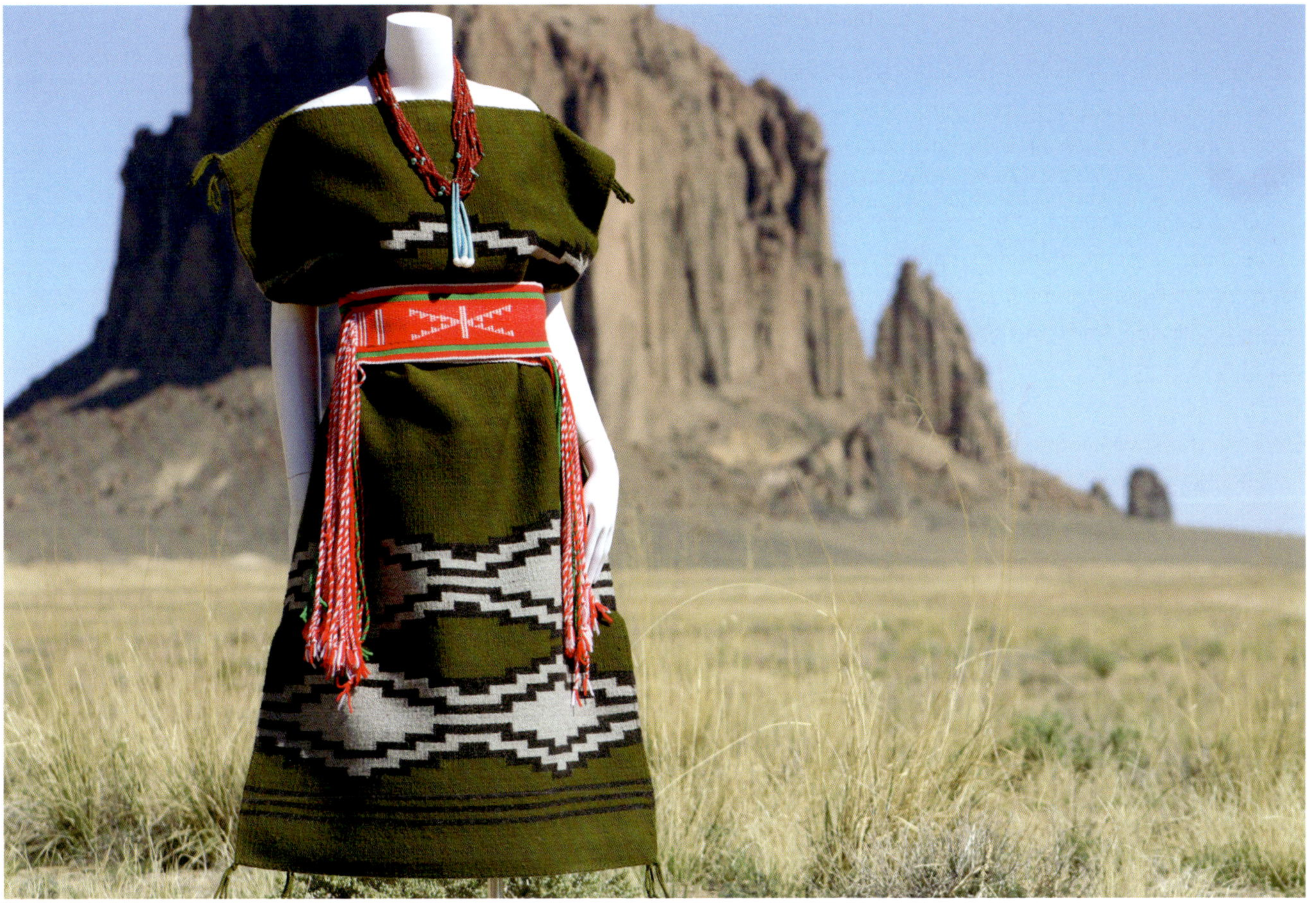

Woven wool dress with sash belt, May 2023. Kevin Aspaas (Diné, b. 1995). 48 × 28 inches. Collection of Rachel Tom. Photograph by Kevin Aspaas. Courtesy of the artist.

LM: What role does weaving have in your life?

KA: When I first started learning how to weave it was mainly to continue a legacy that my grandma left. I realized at the age of nine or ten that I didn't see any of my relatives and peers weaving. But when I picked the weaving back up, in 2013, my main reason was financial. These reasons overlap; they don't contradict each other.

Now, I always think about what else I can do to continue this practice within my community. What am I going to contribute to our history? My goal is to make an impact on the wedge weaving—to bring back a technique, expand upon it, and move it forward. I have the opportunity to practice what our ancestors did—*to weave for one another*. I get a chance to do that, to be a part of our community in that way. I also weave functional, utilitarian pieces for my sisters and for other members of my family. There is a constant outside tension between artistic and utilitarian, but I don't see it that way.

I view weaving as a responsibility. Navajo people need access to traditional garments. Families now give me two-years' notice when they ask me to weave something for them. Weaving in that way is very satisfying for me. We also bring things down to the Pueblos for feast days—there's one family who has all my family's belts in a glass case, and when we visit, we are able to identity who wove which ones. I like weaving belts for their intended purpose, to be worn—that gives me a little fire to keep me going. That's where our belts belong.

LM: What roles do museum collections and curatorial projects have in your own artistic practice or your life?

KA: When I first started doing art shows, it was my dream to be in a museum! It is important for the public to see contemporary, diverse pieces of weaving. I am lucky to see museum items that many members of my community are not able to see, but I want my community to have access to collections—to be able to see these things that I have the privilege to work with.

The textiles selected for *Horizons* work against a lot of misconceptions about what constitutes a "good" weaving. We were not restricted to regional or trading post styles, and we are not looking at grand masterpieces. We've selected pieces that attract weavers. This is a special group of people—this project is *by* weavers *for* weavers. We chose pieces that were woven by our ancestors to remind us that we don't have to be a certain way. A lot of people have difficult memories of their grandmothers going to trading posts and being told that their work isn't "perfect," not symmetrical enough. It was really harmful. I've had gallery people say this to me, too—they have made me feel like I'm not good enough.

Some people may think that the pieces in this book go against everything that we know about Diné weaving. But really, at their core, they represent Navajo weaving at its finest: the creativity of the weavers themselves—their individual choices. Our ancestral weavers wove what they saw around them, touching on different parts of their lived experience, of their history. *Horizons* represents the history of weaving through the weavers' eyes, and that is what I want people to see.

Diné people are surrounded by beauty every day, and we take it for granted. Photographs of the Diné landscape remind me of pictorial weavings—how can we hold these two things hand in hand? For Evelyn Yazzie's piece, I can imagine someone taking a photograph of that same scene.

LM: Given all of this, where do you see Diné weaving moving into the future?

KA: Even though I'm part of the younger generation, I still see Diné folks who are even younger than me doing fantastic work. Some of us are raising sheep. We are all very supportive of one another. The internet and social media offer so much potential for the future of weaving—we can really support each other and lift each other up in new ways. When I speak with my nieces and nephews, I explain that it's important to start early so that you have your whole lifetime to work on your craft. They comment on my work sometimes, telling me what they like and don't like. Kids are like sponges, so I hope they are learning a lot by watching me.

The future for weaving is very bright.

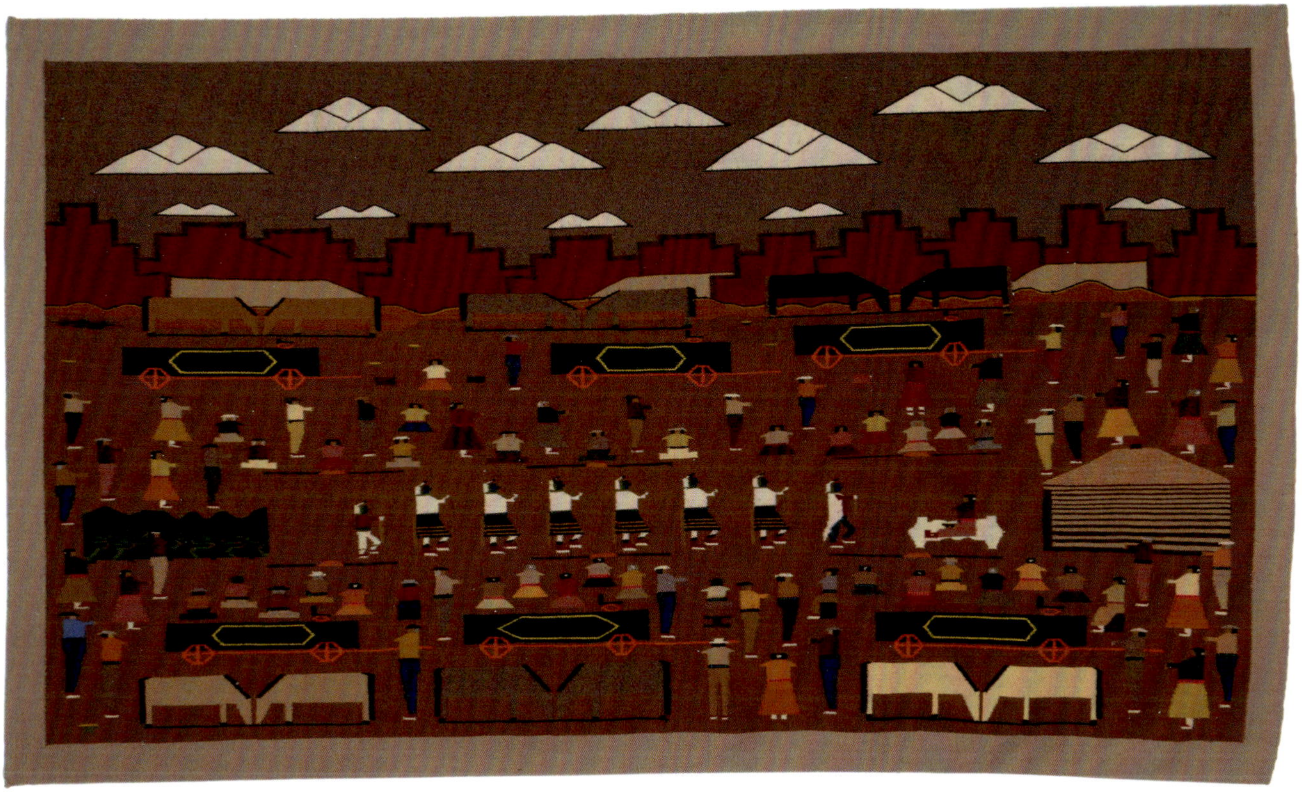

Pictorial Weaving, c. 1989. Evelyn Yazzie (Diné). Wool, cotton, natural dyes. 54 × 92 ½ inches. Museum of International Folk Art, gift of Lloyd E. Cotsen and the Neutrogena Cooperation, A.1995.93.990. Photograph by Addison Doty.

Representative of our relationship to land and what it provides for our community, pictorial weavings are visual documentations of the daily life of a Diné community. Through depictions of livestock, herbs, and food, we get to see what modes of transportation were used, what fashion looked like, what kinds of animals roamed the pastures, and even the season based on the type of community event or ceremony shown.

—KA

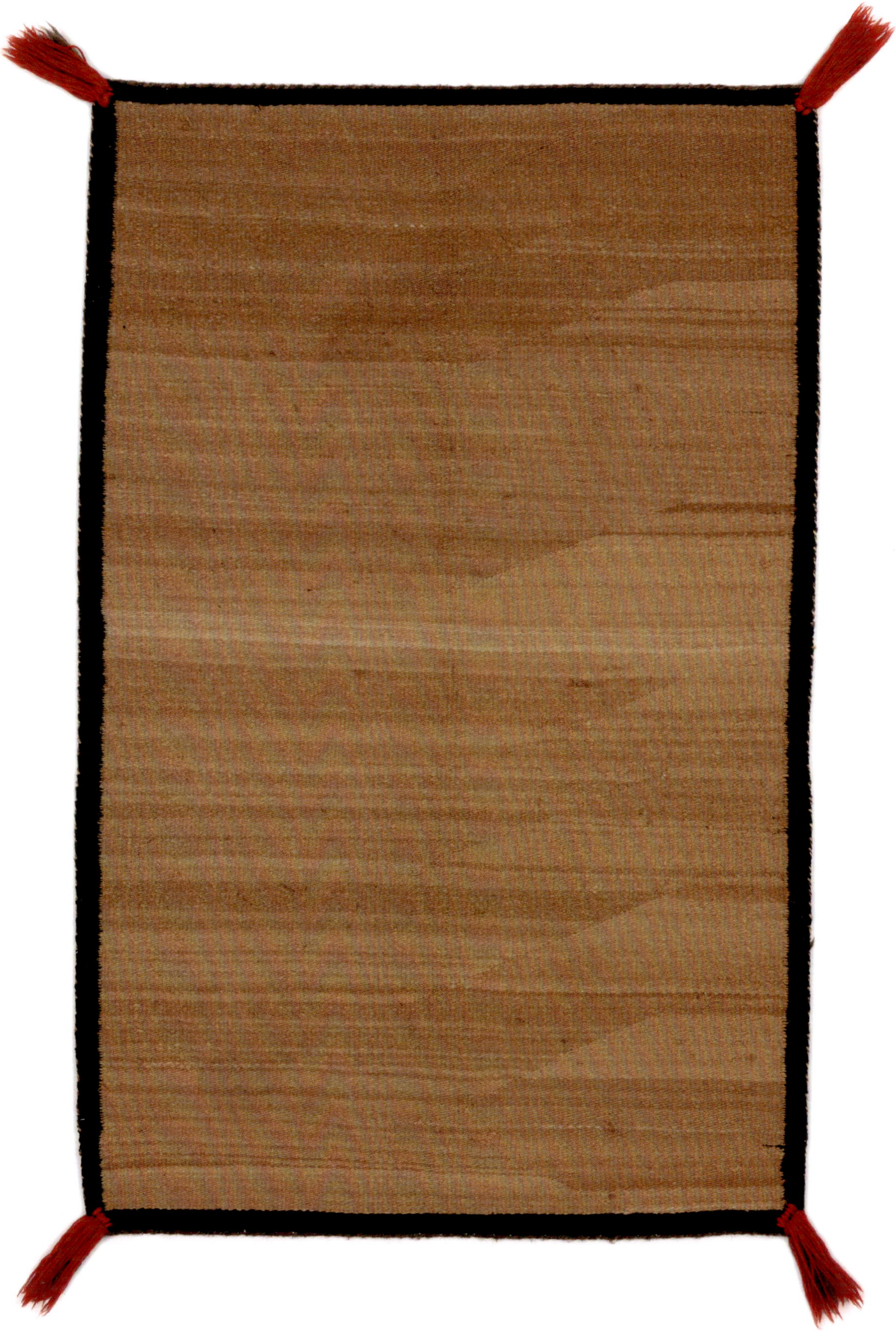

4 Rethinking Early Diné Weaving in the Four Corners

History through an Archaeological Lens

WADE CAMPBELL

OPPOSITE
Textile, c. 1960.
Artist once known (Diné). Wool.
Overall: 48 ¼ × 31 ⅛ × 5 ⅞ inches (mounted by A. Girard).
Museum of International Folk Art, gift of the Girard Foundation Collection, A.1980.1.223.
Photograph by Addison Doty.

Through color choice and design, this weaving engages with the viewer in a direct and personal way. The weaver opens up a space to connect with this piece's meditative, emotional, and spiritual qualities. By choosing not to engage in representational elements such as traditional or regional designs, the artist invites viewers to think about weaving as a distinct art form that offers room to explore the almost indiscernible design along with its soothing character.

—LARISSA NEZ

Over the past century, most discussions about the history of Diné weaving in the American Southwest have approached the topic through the analysis of textiles themselves. Such a focus makes sense, as readily appreciated shifts in Diné blanket designs chart a "Classic–Transitional–Modern" typological progression that mirrors key economic and political developments in nineteenth- and twentieth-century Diné life.[1] Furthermore, close examinations of these objects can shed light on a variety of sociocultural considerations that are literally woven into the very fabric of Diné society past and present, including traditional teaching/learning systems and conceptions of value and hozho ("beauty").[2]

Textile-centric interpretations, however, lead to challenges when considering the Diné weaving tradition during earlier time periods. Prior to European colonization, the Southwest was home to a well-established cotton textile tradition that was in turn supplanted by a wool textile tradition following the introduction of sheep, goats, and other Eurasian animal domesticates by the Spanish settlers of New Mexico in 1598.[3] Colonial texts clearly attest to the adoption of a pastoral lifeway by early Diné communities and a well-established trade in both wool and cotton textiles between Diné, Pueblo, and Hispanic communities in northwest New Mexico circa 1700,[4] yet only five sets of pre-1800 Diné textile fragments—all wool—have been identified. The materials span a period from roughly AD 1710 to the early 1800s and come from Chaco Canyon, Canyon de Chelly, and Dinétah—the traditional Diné homeland centered on the Largo, Gobernador, and San Juan drainages in northwest New Mexico.[5] The poor archaeological preservation of organic materials and a history of early Anglo-American looting thus make pre-1800 textiles exceedingly rare. The few examples we do have also present contemporary researchers with unique ethical concerns, as they were all removed from burial contexts at the turn of the twentieth century.

This tantalizing glimpse into the wider world of Diné weaving prior to the nineteenth century raises a host of questions. What roles did weavers play within early Diné society? What kinds of textiles were produced for trade with Spanish colonists? How did new exchange networks impact existing intertribal relationships throughout the Southwest? Without suitable quantities of early Diné textiles to examine, how might interested researchers approximate the rich results obtained through ethnohistorical studies of more recent Diné weaving traditions?

An archaeological approach is a productive way to engage with such questions. From an archaeological perspective, textiles are the result of a highly technical, multistage production process in which weaving is but the final step.[6] In the case of early Diné woolen textiles, their developmental history and socioeconomic importance can thus be investigated using not only remnant fabrics, but also evidence derived from distinct forms of material culture associated with various prerequisite activities like herding, shearing, cleaning, and spinning. Searching academic texts and grey literature reports for material evidence of these additional activities can result in an expanded body of archaeological evidence for early Diné textile production. In general, the archaeological traces of highly mobile or short-term activities like herding or shearing are frustratingly difficult to pin down; these remain the particular research focus of the author.[7] Notably, however, the identification of fifteen different sets of weaving tools and loom features found at five early Diné defensive site complexes ("pueblitos")[8] provide direct evidence for textile production by Diné communities in the Dinétah heartland during the period between roughly 1710 and 1750 (table 1).

Table 1. Archaeological Evidence for Early Diné Weaving, pre-AD 1800

Site Name	Site Number	Weaving-related Artifacts or Features	Est. Date*	Reference
Split Rock Pueblito Weaving Tool Cache	LA 71599	2 wooden spindle whorls (one decorated) 4 worked sticks	c. 1720s–1730s	Marshall 1991: 83, 281
Largo School Pueblito Weaving Tool Cache	LA 5657	3 worked sticks	c. 1730s	Marshall 1991: 12–17
Frances Canyon Pueblito	LA 2135	1 wooden spindle whorl (split in half) 2 wooden shed rods (incised) 2 sets of vertical loom floor anchors	c. 1710–1740s	Carlson 1965: 35–38, 40
Pueblito Canyon Pueblito	LA 1684	2 ceramic spindle whorls 1 wooden batten (incised)	c. 1730s	Keur 1944: 81
Crow Canyon Pueblito	LA 20219	1 ceramic spindle whorl (reworked Gobernador Polychrome sherd)	c. 1720s–1730s	Marshall 1995: 12

* *Source*: Data from Towner, *Defending the Dinétah* (2003).

Two spindle whorls recovered from early Navajo defensive site complexes in Dinétah. On the left is a fragment of an ~2½-inch (6.1-cm)–diameter disc formed from a reworked Gobernador Polychrome sherd found at Crow Canyon Pueblito. On the right is a complete ~3¾-inch (9.7-cm)–diameter cottonwood disc with a faint, black-painted spiral decoration on one face, recovered from a cache near Split Rock Pueblito. Courtesy of the Maxwell Museum of Anthropology, University of New Mexico. Catalogue nos. 2018.2.283 and 90.26.2.

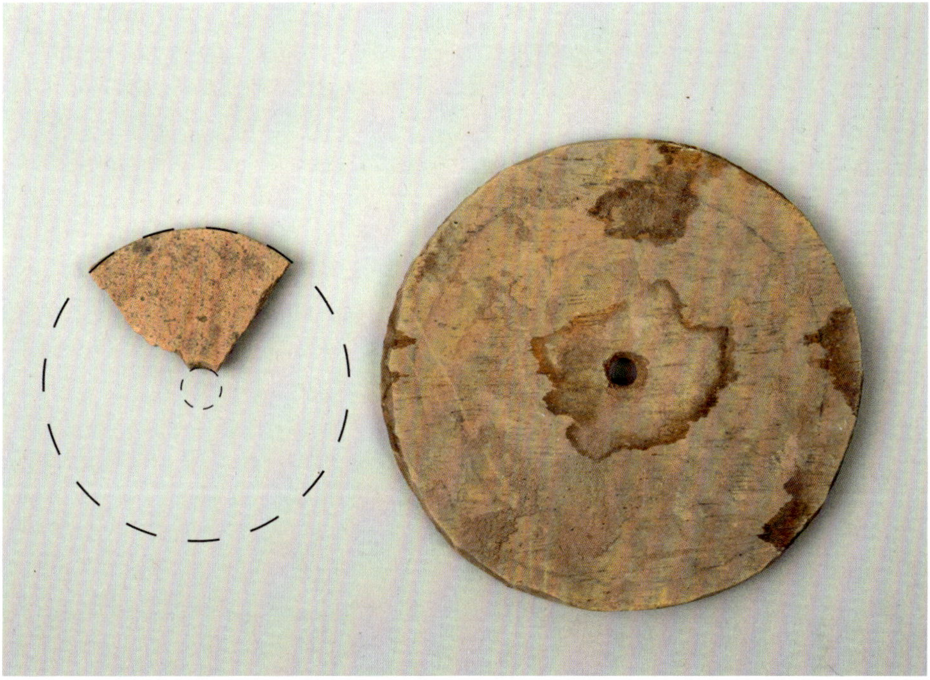

Formal material analyses rooted in archaeological theories of craft specialization have rarely been applied to Diné weaving in general, with the recent work of Diné archaeologist Rechanda Lee being a notable exception.[9] Examining the artifacts listed in table 1 (and potentially others as yet undiscovered) in this manner might allow researchers to explore new questions about technical skill and the *chaîne operatoire* of early Diné weaving independent of remnant textiles.[10] An example of one such worthwhile study would be an analysis of spindle whorls from early Diné archaeological sites. Studies from central Mexico and the US Southwest both suggest that variability in whorl size and weight can reflect specific decisions by spinners related to the choice of fibers being spun or a preference for producing certain thicknesses of yarn.[11] Such information would be invaluable for investigating the early eighteenth-century Spanish colonial references to Diné cotton textile production that are otherwise inaccessible to researchers.

In a similar vein, archaeological weaving-related artifacts and features allow researchers to draw ethnographic analogies with more recent bodies of Diné weaving knowledge. Such connections help to extend the well-developed discussions about post-1800 Diné weavers' embodied experience and economic and cultural agency further into the past.[12] In so doing, these objects have the potential to add incredibly detailed and nuanced insights to understandings of Diné community experiences in Dinétah and elsewhere leading up to and during the Spanish colonial period in New Mexico. This was exemplified at a 2023 symposium in which photographs of the worked wooden tool elements from Frances Canyon, Largo School, and Split Rock

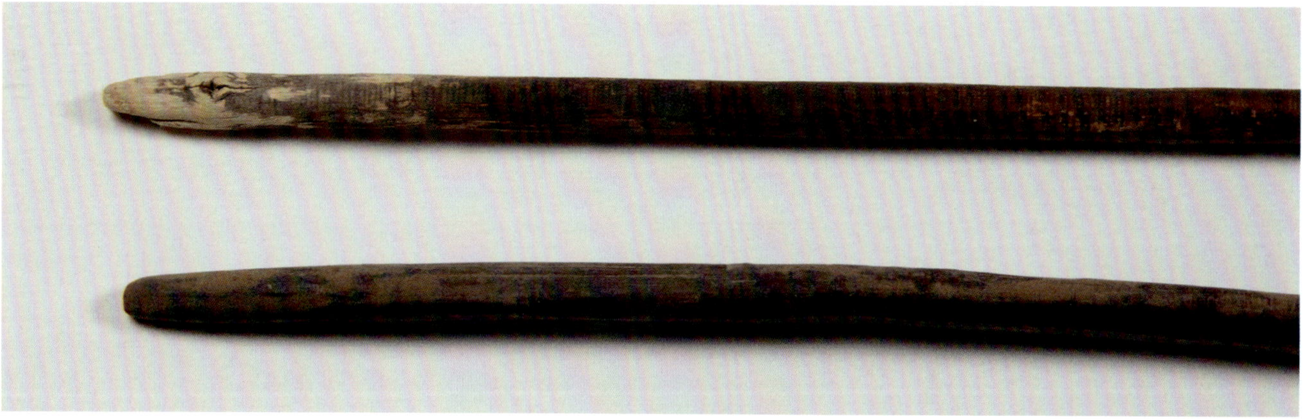

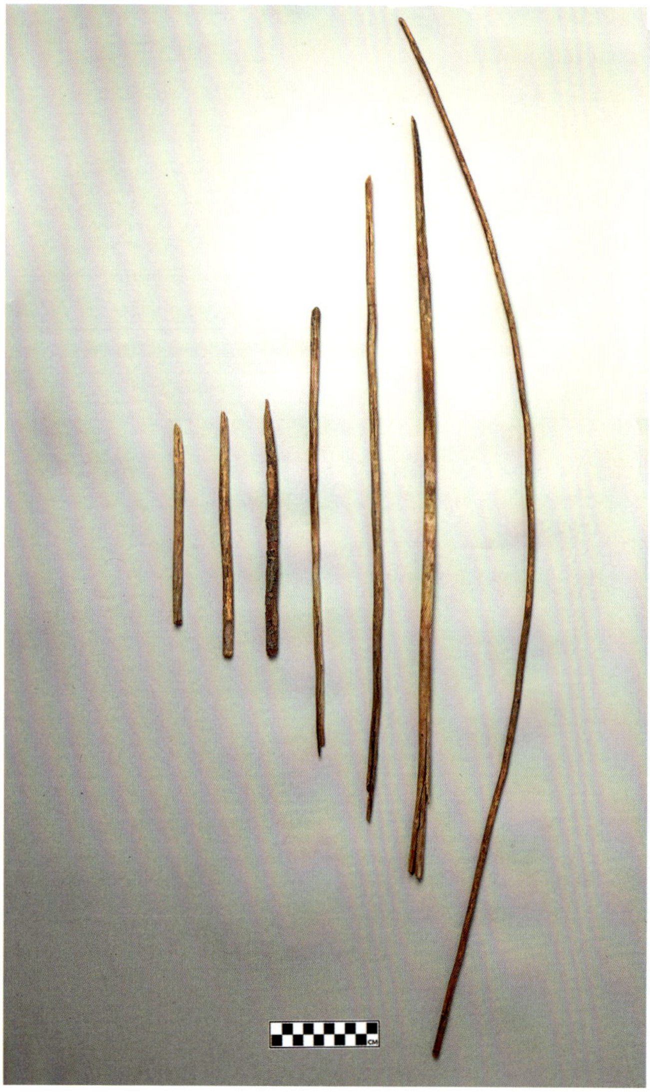

ABOVE

Image showing the worked ends of shed rods recovered from a cache near Frances Canyon Pueblito, Dinétah, New Mexico. The two rods measure 46 ¼ inches (117.5 cm) and 35 ¾ inches (91 cm) long, respectively, and are marked by several hundred shallow incisions caused by the tensioning of the warp threads of a loom. © University of Colorado Museum of Natural History. Courtesy of University of Colorado Museum of Natural History.

LEFT

A collection of likely weaving-related tools recovered from caches near early Navajo defensive site complexes in Dinétah. The three worked sticks on the left are from the Split Rock Pueblito complex and include one spindle that fits into the wooden whorl shown in the figure on page 57. The four worked sticks on the right are from the Largo School Pueblito complex and are likely shed sticks. Courtesy of the Maxwell Museum of Anthropology, University of New Mexico. Catalogue nos. 2018.2.222 and 90.26.3.

Pueblitos triggered a discussion between the author and the Diné weavers Barbara Teller Ornelas, Lynda Teller Pete, Tyrrell Tapaha, and Kevin Aspaas. The weavers drew attention to a variety of themes, including the cultural importance and treatment of weaving tools, the choices that underlie the preparation of textile warps, and how the caching of tools at these defensive sites speaks to their socioeconomic importance to local Diné families in the early 1700s.[13]

Working with archaeological materials also highlights shifts in the history of Diné archaeological research that can help textile researchers rethink the long-term development of Diné weaving in the Southwest. Until relatively recently, the origins of Diné weaving were most commonly conceptualized in acculturative terms that attributed the craft to a unidirectional technological exchange *from* Pueblo people *to* Diné people sometime in the late-sixteenth or seventeenth centuries, perhaps the result of Pueblo refugees fleeing Spanish colonialism along the Rio Grande.[14] These framings clearly reflect the larger state of early anthropological and archaeohistorical thinking about Navajo origins throughout most of the twentieth century. In this literature, the Diné were viewed as recent northern immigrants to the Southwest whose modern political success lay in a presupposed ability to adapt and borrow from features of Pueblo culture such as agriculture, textile and pottery production, the clan system, or ceremonial practices.[15]

During the late 1980s and 1990s, however, an explosion in early Diné archaeological fieldwork driven largely by natural resource and infrastructure development in northwest New Mexico upended the status quo. The documentation and chronological dating of hundreds of early Diné sites including habitations, economic activity areas, and special-use defensive and ceremonial sites revealed that many of the material culture markers did not fit the expected temporal frameworks used to support the most influential of these models, the "Pueblo Refugee Hypothesis."[16] As a result, Diné and non-Diné researchers alike have spent the past two decades developing alternative theoretical models for early Diné history that draw upon these updated datasets and embrace Indigenous archaeology's mission of doing research "with, for, and by" Native communities.[17] These new approaches specifically draw on Diné oral traditions in order to offer a new model for Diné ethnogenesis rooted in arguments for a broad autochthonous Southwestern cultural tradition that is ancestral to both modern Pueblo and Diné communities. Elements from this tradition merge with northern Athapaskan-speaking hunter-gatherers circa AD 1200–1300 to form the core of contemporary Diné society.[18]

In her preface to Joe Ben Wheat's *Blanket Weaving in the Southwest*, Ann Lane Hedlund comments on the general need for Southwestern textile scholars to think more critically about the archaeohistorical models that provide the temporal frameworks for discussions of Indigenous textile traditions.[19] In the case of Diné textiles, if the core of Diné society has its origins in an earlier and more complex Southwestern world where village dwellers maintained complex socioeconomic relationships with hinterland forager-farmer populations, then Diné weaving would presumably have its roots in these interactions as well. From this perspective, features like the floor anchors noted by Earl Morris at Frances Canyon Pueblito, which display clear similarities to loom furniture seen at archaeological sites throughout the Four Corners region,[20] or Kent's suggestion that "Anasazi [*sic*] striped shoulder blankets furnished the model . . . for early Navajo shoulder blankets"[21] should perhaps not be discussed as indications of Diné cultural borrowing, copying, or assimilation, but rather as evidence for the long-term continuity of ancestral Southwestern weaving traditions among diverse descendant communities.

In summary, there are several ways by which archaeology can benefit studies of the Diné weaving tradition. In particular, archaeological approaches deemphasize textile-centric analyses in favor of materials-based assessments of a broader suite of weaving-related practices, thus offering a way to overcome the interpretive challenges posed by the poor preservation of early Diné textiles. Taken together, archaeological studies of early Diné weaving in the centuries before AD 1800 can improve our understandings of Diné lifeways at a critical period of change in Southwestern history and link the legacies of contemporary Diné weavers with those of their ancestors.

BIBLIOGRAPHY

Amsden, Charles A. *Navaho Weaving, Its Technic and History*. Albuquerque: University of New Mexico Press, 1934.

Atalay, Sonya. "Indigenous Archaeology as Decolonizing Practice." *American Indian Quarterly* 30, nos. 3 & 4 (2006): 280–310.

Bellorado, Benjamin A. "The Significance of Structure-14 at Bare Ladder and Its Features in a Local and Regional Context." In *Condition Assessment and Conservation Recommendations for Structure 14 Bare Ladder Ruin (42SA6965), Natural Bridges National Monument*, edited by B. A. Bass, Angelyn Bass, Douglas Porter, Keri Stevenson, Neil Dixon, and Katherine Shaum, Appendix D. Prepared by the Department of Anthropology, University of New Mexico, National Bridges National Monument, Project No. H1200-09-0005, 2016. Manuscript on File at the Edge of the Cedars Museum, Blanding, UT.

Blomberg, Nancy J. *Navajo Textiles: The William Randolph Hearst Collection*. Tucson: University of Arizona Press, 1988.

Bonar, Eulalie H., ed. *Woven by the Grandmothers: Nineteenth-Century Navajo Textiles from the National Museum of the American Indian*. Washington, DC: Smithsonian Institution Press in association with the National Museum of the American Indian, Smithsonian Institution, 1996.

Brugge, David M. "Emergence of the Navajo People." In *From the Land of Ever Winter to the American Southwest*, edited by Deni J. Seymour, 124–49. Salt Lake City: University of Utah Press, 2012.

Bsumek, Erika. “The Navajos as Borrowers: Stewart Culin and the Genesis of an Ethnographic Theory.” *New Mexico Historical Review* 79, no. 3 (2004): 319–51.

Campbell, James W. “Exploring the Early Navajo Pastoral Landscape: An Archaeological Study of (Peri)Colonial Navajo Pastoralism from the 18th to 21st Centuries AD.” PhD dissertation, Harvard University, 2022.

Campbell, Wade, Kerry F. Thompson, and Richard M. Begay. “*Naasgo*: Moving Forward—Diné Archaeology in the Twenty-First Century.” *Kiva* 87, no. 3 (2021): 253–67.

Carlson, Roy L. *Eighteenth Century Navajo Fortresses of Gobernador District*. Boulder: University Press of Colorado, 1965.

D’Alessandro, Jill. “With Beauty All Around Me, I Walk.” In *Anthropology and Beauty: From Aesthetics to Creativity*, edited by Stephanie Bunn, 53–66. London: Routledge, 2018.

Dockstader, Frederick J. *The Song of the Loom: New Traditions in Navajo Weaving.* New York: Hudson Hills Press, 1987.

Dyk, Walter. *Son of Old Man Hat*. Lincoln: University of Nebraska Press, 1967.

“Ecologies of Making: Knowledge and Process in Navajo Weaving.” *Shaped by the Loom* research symposium, Bard Graduate Center, New York, NY, February 17, 2023. https://www.youtube.com/watch?v=iaxHtQIOjCg.

Flad, Rowan K., and Zachary X. Hruby. “‘Specialized’ Production in Archaeological Contexts: Rethinking Specialization, the Social Value of Products, and the Practice of Production.” *Archaeological Papers of the American Anthropological Association* 17, no. 1 (2007): 1–19.

Hackett, Charles W. *Historical Documents Relating to New Mexico, Nueva Vizcaya, and Approaches Thereto, to 1773*, vol. 3. Washington, DC: Carnegie Institution of Washington, 1937.

Hedlund, Ann Lane. “Beyond Beauty: Exploring the Ethnoaesthetics of Navajo Weaving.” *American Indian Art Magazine* 40, no. 3 (2015): 44–59.

Hester, James J. *Early Navajo Migrations and Acculturation in the Southwest*. Museum of New Mexico Papers in Anthropology, no. 6. Santa Fe: Museum of New Mexico, 1962.

Hill, W. W. “Some Navaho Culture Changes during Two Centuries (With a Translation of the Early Eighteenth Century Rabal Manuscript).” In *Essays in Historical Anthropology of North America: Smithsonian Miscellaneous Collections*, vol. 100, 395–415. Washington, DC: Smithsonian Institution Press, 1940.

Ibarra, Thania E., A. López Corral, and R. Santacruz Cano. “The Artisan and the Tool: A Technological–Functional Analysis of Tlaxcallan Spindle Whorls.” *Archaeometry* 60, no. 6 (2018): 1221–36.

Kelley, Klara, and Harris Francis. *A Diné History of Navajoland*. Tucson: University of Arizona Press, 2019.

Kent, Kate Peck. "The Cultivation and Weaving of Cotton in the Prehistoric Southwestern United States." *Transactions of the American Philosophical Society* 47, no. 3 (1957): 457–732.

———. *Navajo Weaving: Three Centuries of Change*. Santa Fe: School of American Research Press, 1985.

Keur, Dorothy. *Big Bead Mesa: An Archaeological Study of Navajo Acculturation, 1745–1812*. Memoirs of the Society for American Archaeology, no. 1. Washington, DC: Society for American Archaeology, 1941.

———. "A Chapter in Navaho-Pueblo Relations." *American Antiquity* 10, no. 1 (1944): 75–86.

Kidder, Alfred V. "Ruins of the Historic Period in the Upper San Juan Valley, New Mexico." *American Anthropologist* 22 (1920): 322–29.

Lee, Rechanda. "'ASHŁ'Ó YÓHOOŁ'AAH (Learning to Weave): The Cultural Transmission of Technological Style in Diné Textiles." MA thesis, Northern Arizona University, 2014.

———. "A Search for Continuity in the Transmission of Technological Styles in Navajo Weaving Traditions." *Kiva* 87, no. 3 (2021): 316–35.

Malcolm, Roy L. "Archaeological Remains, Supposedly Navaho, from Chaco Canyon, New Mexico." *American Antiquity* 5, no. 1 (1939): 4–20.

Marshall, Michael P. "The Pueblito as a Site Complex: Archaeological Investigations in the Dinétah District." In *Rethinking Navajo Pueblitos*, 1–282. Farmington, NM: Bureau of Land Management, Farmington Resource Area, 1991.

———. *A Chapter in Early Navajo History: Late Gobernador Phase Pueblito Sites of the Dinétah District*. OCA/UNM Report No. 185-469B. Albuquerque: University of New Mexico Office of Contract Archaeology, 1995.

M'Closkey, Kathy. *Swept Under the Rug: A Hidden History of Navajo Weaving*. Albuquerque: University of New Mexico Press, 2002.

Miller, Heather Margaret-Louise. *Archaeological Approaches to Technology*. New York: Routledge, 2017.

Reed, Paul F., and Lori S. Reed. "Reexamining Gobernador Polychrome: Towards a New Understanding of the Early Navajo Chronological Sequence in Northwestern New Mexico." In *The Archaeology of Navajo Origins*, edited by Ronald H. Towner, 83–108. Salt Lake City: University of Utah Press, 1996.

Sapir, Edward. "Internal Linguistic Evidence Suggestive of the Northern Origin of the Navaho." *American Anthropologist* 38, no. 2 (1936): 224–35.

Strand, Eva Andersson. “The Textile Chaîne Opératoire: Using a Multidisciplinary Approach to Textile Archaeology with a Focus on the Ancient Near East.” *Paléorient* 38, no. 1/2 (2012): 21–40.

Tanner, Clara Lee, and Charlie R. Steen. “A Navajo Burial of about 1850.” *Panhandle-Plains Historical Review* 28 (1955): 110–18.

Teague, Lynn S. *Textiles in Southwestern Prehistory*. Albuquerque: University of New Mexico Press, 1998.

Thompson, Kerry F., and Ronald H. Towner. “Navajo Archaeology.” In *Oxford Handbook of Southwestern Archaeology*, edited by Barbara J. Mills and Severin Fowles, 481–94. New York: Oxford University Press, 2017.

Towner, Ronald H. *Defending the Dinétah: Pueblitos in the Ancestral Navajo Homeland*. Salt Lake City: University of Utah Press, 2003.

Walters, Harry, and Hugh C. Rogers. “Anasazi and ‘Anaasází: Two Words, Two Cultures.” *Kiva* 66, no. 3 (2001): 317–26.

Warburton, Miranda, and Richard M. Begay. “An Exploration of Navajo–Anasazi Relationships.” *Ethnohistory* 52, no. 3 (2005): 533–61.

Wheat, Joe Ben. “Spanish-American and Navajo Weaving, 1600 to Now.” In *Collected Papers in Honor of Marjorie Ferguson Lambert.* Papers of the Archaeological Society of New Mexico, no. 3, edited by Albert H. Schroeder, 199–226. Albuquerque: Archaeological Society of New Mexico, 1976.

———. *Blanket Weaving in the Southwest*, edited by Anne Lane Hedlund. Tucson: University of Arizona Press, 2003.

Wyman, Leland C., and Charles A. Amsden. “A Patchwork Cloak.” *Masterkey* 8, no. 5 (1934): 133–37.

Yohe, Jill Ahlberg. “The Circulation and Silence of Weaving Knowledge in Contemporary Navajo Life.” *American Indian Culture and Research Journal* 36, no. 4 (2012): 107–26.

———. “What Weavings Bring: The Social Value of Weaving-related Objects in Contemporary Navajo Life.” *Kiva* 73, no. 4 (2008): 367–86.

NOTES

1. Kent, *Navajo Weaving*; M’Closkey, *Swept Under the Rug.*

2. D’Alessandro, “With Beauty All Around Me, I Walk”; Hedlund, “Beyond Beauty”; Lee, “’ASHŁ’Ó YÓHOOŁ’AAH (Learning to Weave)”; Lee, “A Search for Continuity”; Yohe, “The Circulation and Silence of Weaving Knowledge.”

3. Wheat, *Blanket Weaving in the Southwest*, 35–43.

4. Hackett, *Historical Documents,* vol. 3, 381–82; Hill, "Some Navaho Culture Changes during Two Centuries."

5. Amdsen, *Navajo Weaving*, 205 (Canyon del Muerto/Massacre Cave, c. 1750–1804); Wyman and Amsden, "A Patchwork Cloak" (unknown location, c. 1750–early 1800s); Tanner and Steen, "A Navajo Burial of about 1850" (Canyon del Muerto/Antelope House, c. 1850); Malcolm, "Archaeological Remains, Supposedly Navaho," 15–18 (Chaco Canyon/Chacra Mesa, pre-1850); Carlson, *Eighteenth Century Navajo Fortresses*, 113–16 (Dinétah, Frances Mesa Pueblito [Site 6; LA 2135], c. 1710–1745).

6. Flad and Hruby, "'Specialized' Production in Archaeological Contexts"; Miller, *Archaeological Approaches to Technology*; Strand, "The Textile Chaîne Opératoire."

7. For a summary of early Diné herding research focused on identifying corral/enclosure features, see Campbell, "Exploring the Early Navajo Pastoral Landscape," 131–50. Shearing is a pastoral activity that has not been considered in the early Diné context to date. Both published accounts and oral histories indicate that modern bladed hand shears were not common items in Diné households until the mid-twentieth century (e.g., Dyk, "Son of Old Man Hat," 156). Instead, shearing was carried out using everyday knives, ad hoc blades fashioned from sharpened scrap metal (e.g., cans), flaked stone, or by plucking.

8. Towner, *Defending the Dinétah*.

9. Lee, "'ASHŁ'Ó YÓHOOŁ'AAH (Learning to Weave)"; Lee, "A Search for Continuity."

10. Miller, *Archaeological Approaches to Technology*; Strand, "The Textile Chaîne Opératoire."

11. Ibarra et al., "The Artisan and the Tool"; Teague, *Textiles in Southwestern Prehistory*, 41–64.

12. Bonar, *Woven by the Grandmothers*; M'Closkey, *Swept Under the Rug*; Yohe, "The Circulation and Silence of Weaving Knowledge"; Yohe, "What Weavings Bring."

13. "Ecologies of Making."

14. Amsden, *Navaho Weaving*, 128–30; Blomberg, *Navajo Textiles*, 1; Dockstader, *The Song of the Loom*, 15–16; Kent, *Navajo Weaving*, 8.

15. Bsumek, "The Navajos as Borrowers"; Hester, *Early Navajo Migrations and Acculturation*; Keur, *Big Bead Mesa*; Kidder, "Ruins of the Historic Period in the Upper San Juan Valley"; Sapir, "Internal Linguistic Evidence Suggestive of the Northern Origin of the Navaho."

16. Reed and Reed, "Reexamining Gobernador Polychrome"; Thompson and Towner, "Navajo Archaeology"; Towner, *Defending the Dinétah*.

17. Atalay, "Indigenous Archaeology as Decolonizing Practice."

18. Brugge, "Emergence of the Navajo People"; Campbell et al., "*Naasgo*: Moving Forward"; Kelley and Francis, *A Diné History of Navajoland*, 33–114; Walters and Rogers, "Anasazi and 'Anaasází'"; Warburton and Begay, "An Exploration of Navajo–Anasazi Relationships."

19. Hedlund in Wheat, *Blanket Weaving in the Southwest*, xxi. It should be acknowledged, however, that Joe Ben Wheat himself had long been a cautious scholar in this regard, raising questions about the assumed Pueblo origins of Diné weaving in his writing since at least the late 1970s (see Wheat, "Spanish-American and Navajo Weaving, 1600 to Now").

20. Carlson, *Eighteenth Century Navajo Fortresses*, 35. Compare with traditional Southwestern looms described by Kent ("The Cultivation and Weaving of Cotton," 482–89), or the in-situ floor loom anchors identified at Bare Ladder Ruin, a Pueblo III period (AD 1150–1300) site in the Bears Ears region of southeastern Utah (Bellorado, "The Significance of Structure-14 at Bare Ladder").

21. Kent, *Navajo Weaving*, 175.

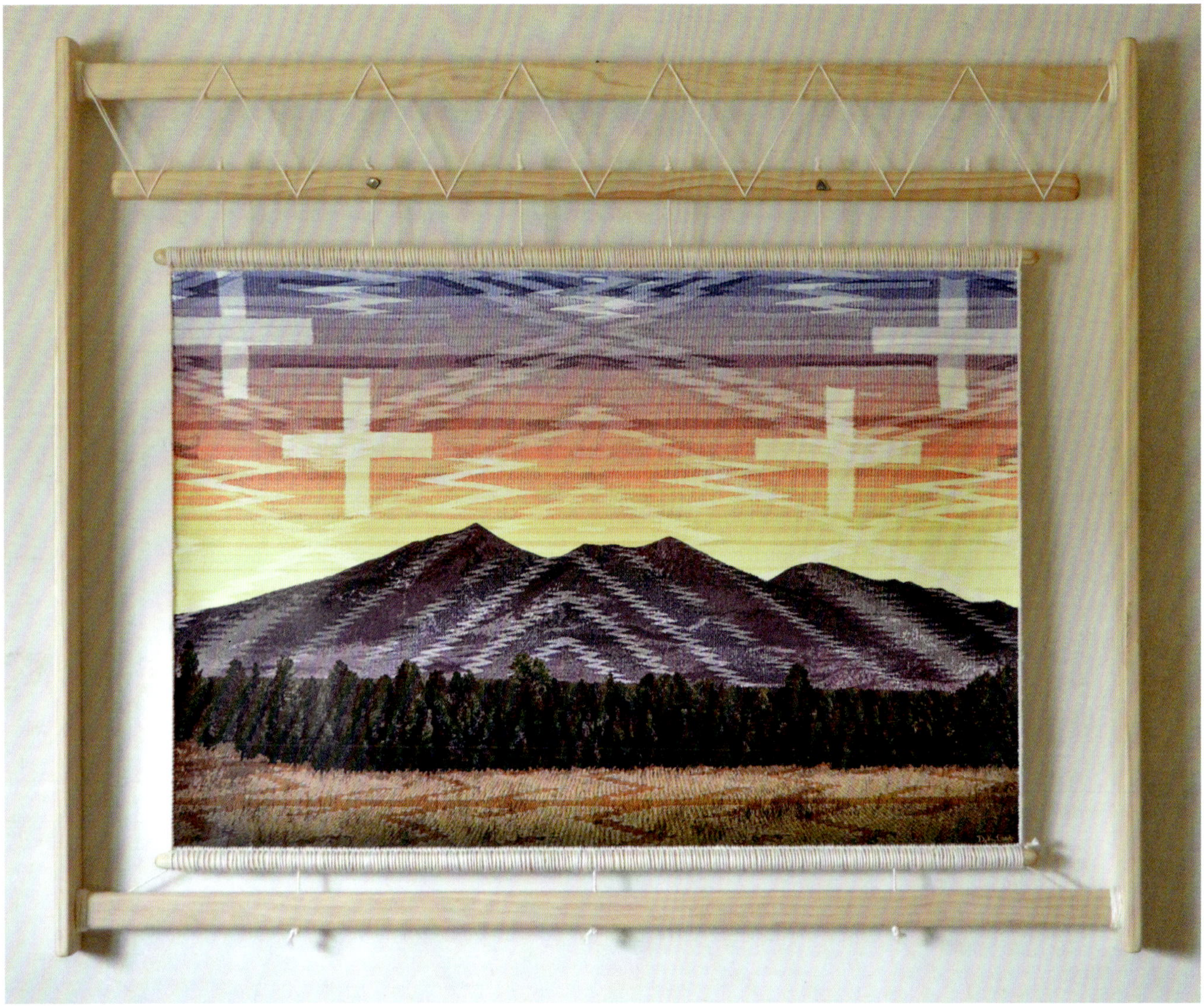

Woven Landscape: Dook'o'oosłííd, August 2022. Darby Raymond-Overstreet (Diné, b. 1994). Mixed media: Digital collage of scanned Navajo textiles and photography on canvas; pine, abalone shell, yarn. 37 ½ × 45 ½ × 2 ½ inches. Courtesy of the artist.

Woven Landscapes *is a series of digital collages that depict views of the Navajo Nation in the visual language of our weaving tradition. These compositions are rendered using digital photography and historic textiles woven at the turn of the twentieth century. On their own, the weavings I work with reflect the environment in a multitude of ways that make them uniquely Diné. This extension of the land takes form in the process, the materials used, and in the values and philosophies embedded in each piece.*

As Diné, our relationship to the places that we call home has been cultivated over generations. We are interwoven with these places through continued stewardship and thriving traditions. This series serves as a visual representation of the relationship between land, art, and cultural identity.

—DARBY RAYMOND-OVERSTREET

5 Interwoven

Portraying Diné People and Homelands

DARBY RAYMOND-OVERSTREET

Yá'át'ééh shí éí Darby Raymond-Overstreet yinishyé. Hooghan łání nishłį́, Bilagáanaa bá shíshchíín, Kinyaa'áanii éí dashicheii dóó Naahiłii éí dashinálí. Ákót'éego diné asdzáán nishłį́. Hello, my name is Darby Raymond-Overstreet. I am Many Hogans and born for White Americans; my maternal grandfather is Towering House, and my paternal grandfather is African American.

I grew up in Flagstaff, Arizona, a border town to the Navajo Nation, which occupies the land at the base of the sacred mountain Dook'o'oosłííd. This mountain is the foundational landscape of my upbringing. It is a sacred place to many local Indigenous peoples, including the Diné, and it is a place of abundance in the region of the Colorado Plateau. The expansive resources and forestry of the area are the basis for the establishment of the city of Flagstaff, and the university that came later helped to attract a diverse community of academics and students pursuing advanced degrees—including my parents. As I was growing up there, my community was made up of folks who came from different tribes, many others who were non-Native, and those of us who were mixed. Not only does the mountain provide the environment for the varied and abundant natural ecosystem in place, but it has also provided and continues to provide a space for a diversified community of people.

I consider growing up in this place—as a Diné person with a mixed background—to be one of the driving forces behind my pursuit of education and art. Here, my inquiries about identity took root and branched out into further curiosity about culture and belonging. One of the main catalysts in the development of my voice as an artist was the recognition and need to address the veil of invisibility that has shrouded Indigenous peoples of the United States in the minds of the greater American population. I experienced the effects of this invisibility even within a community with a large Indigenous presence, and to a greater extent when I left the Southwest to attend college. It became abundantly clear to me that there were significant differences between what I knew was true of the Native American experience and what was so often projected onto Native peoples.

This disconnect can be attributed to the continuing legacy of intentional attempts to expunge the presence of Indigenous peoples and cultures from this continent. Since contact with colonial invaders, our communities have been up against forces of erasure that have manifested very directly through attempts at extermination, removal, forced acculturation and assimilation, and desecration of our sacred places and natural resources. More indirectly, this erasure has been expressed through false narratives of Indigenous histories perpetuated in education, dehumanizing stereotypes of Indigeneity that have flooded American pop culture, and thoughtless cultural appropriation that exploits and degrades our rich cultures down to kitschy consumer goods for profit.

The rampant cultural appropriation by corporate industries of what they have called "Navajo" design emboldened me to start creating art about our weaving tradition. Too often Indigenous peoples are regarded as relics of the past. Like the belongings of our ancestors held in museums and private collections, our communities are often perceived as remaining stagnant in time. Because of the disconnect between what I knew to be authentic to Diné culture and what was callously labeled as "Navajo" and sold to consumers around the world, I became motivated to reclaim the visual language described by our weaving tradition. I saw an opportunity to illuminate the history of strength and resilience of our ancestors and current generations.

My work focuses for the most part on weavings that were created at the turn of the twentieth century and up to the 1950s because of the historical context of these works as it relates to Diné resilience. This era of weaving is the basis of many Navajo textile collections, and these historic pieces are therefore familiar to those who are acquainted with our people through history books and museum exhibits. Through a digital collage process, I merge the artistry of traditional woven rugs with digital portraits of contemporary Diné people and landscapes. The works are suspended inside Navajo looms that frame each piece to convey the concept of being woven into the cultural fabric that is Diné, serving as homage to weavers and the practice of weaving. The tradition of weaving has always been a major facet in the success and longevity of our people. Weaving is an integral component of our collective identity and is one of the cultural practices that has repeatedly seen us through times of immense adversity. Armed with this tradition, our ancestors were able to adapt through the various trials of hardship brought on by a shifting world propelled by colonial ideals and values. Were it not for their adaptability, those on whom I base my portraits may not have been woven into the fabric of Navajo culture at all.

By working with historic Diné textiles held in museum collections and portraying contemporary Diné, I show who these designs come from and who they were made for. This serves as a visual statement that *we are still here*. Our current generations also stand as a living testament to the legacy of our ancestors who made these pieces. Navajo weavings are not just commodities or artifacts. They reflect who we are as a

The Passage, July 2019. Darby Raymond-Overstreet (Diné, b. 1994). Mixed media: Scanned Navajo textiles, canvas print, pine, yarn. 32 × 45 × 2 inches. Courtesy of the artist.

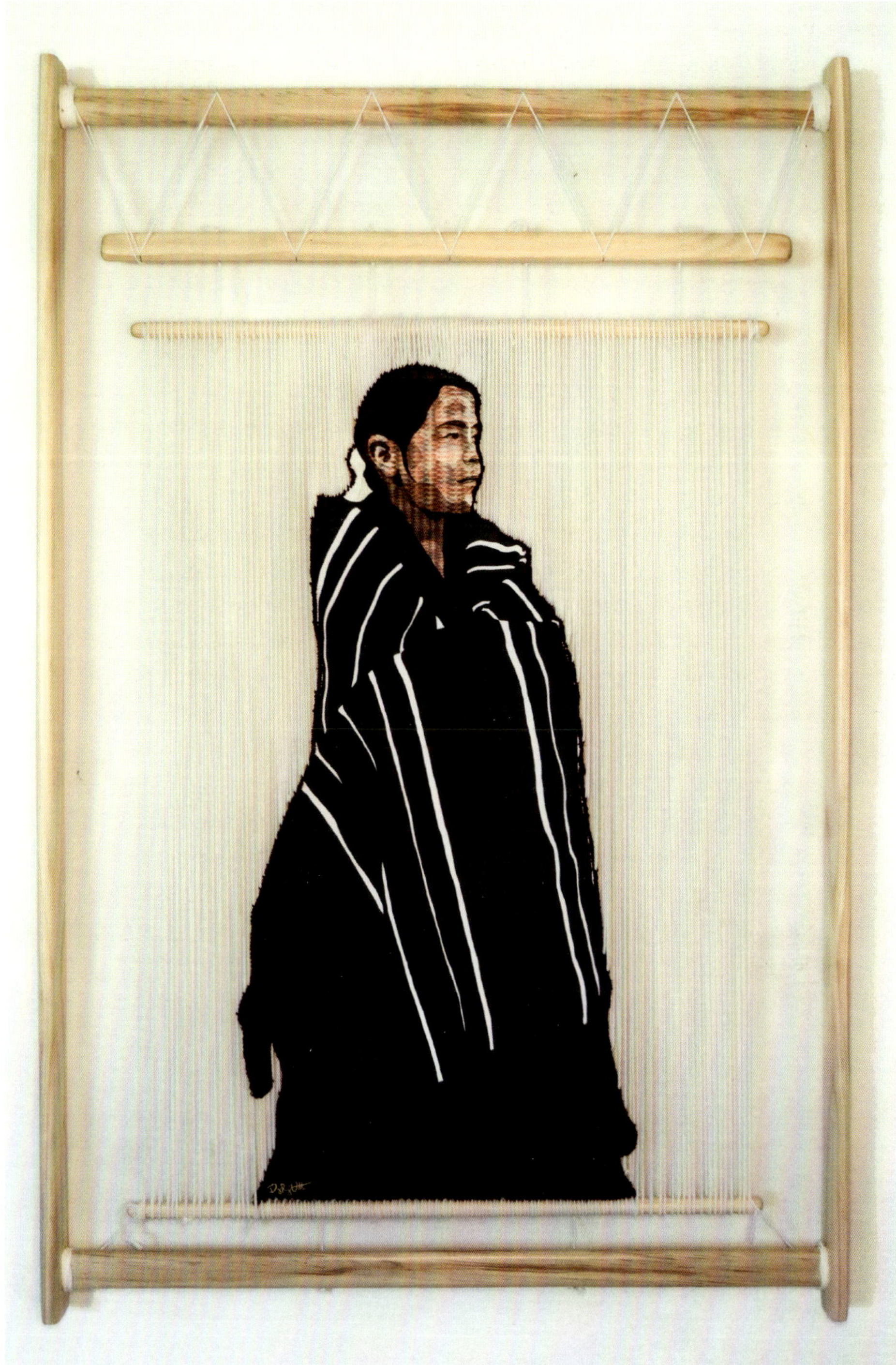

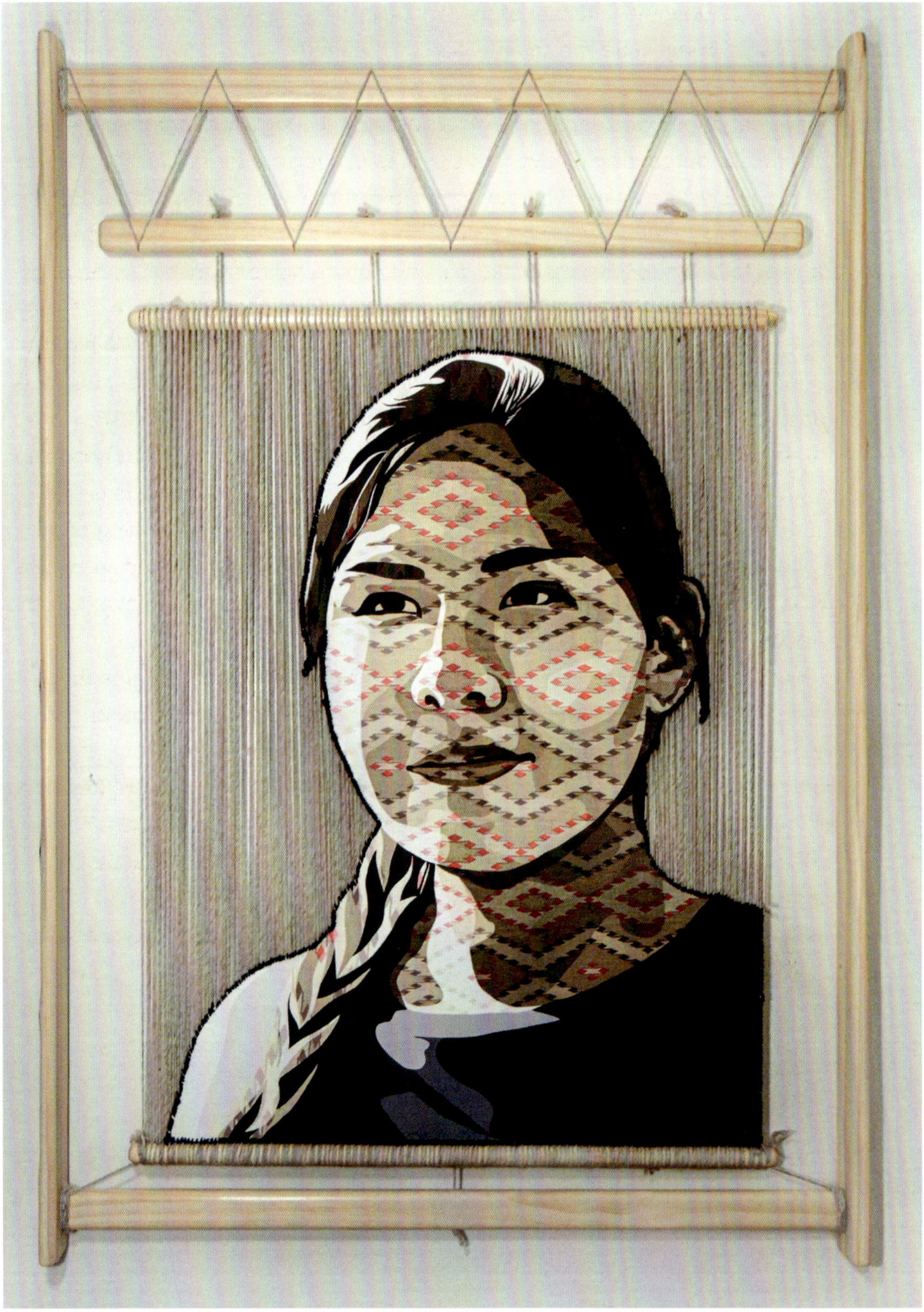

Inherited Legacies, December 2019. Darby Raymond-Overstreet (Diné, b. 1994). Mixed media: Scanned Navajo textiles, canvas print, pine, red coral and pyrite inlay, yarn. 30 × 45 × 2 inches. Courtesy of the artist.

people, and the value they hold cannot be constrained by capitalist monetary conceptions of worth. Their value is also amplified by their cultural significance, which is grounded in their representation of agency, kinship, identity, and traditional values. Equally important, these weavings carry and represent the legacy of a transgenerational and timeless outpouring of love that endured in even the most difficult of times. This legacy serves as the basis of perseverance of which we are a product and is one that our families and communities will continue to sustain for generations to come.

In addition to being extensions of familial and communal relationships, weavings also function as an extension of the lands that we call home. Diné Bikéyah, our Navajo homeland, is described as the region between the four sacred mountains. Within this space, our relationship to the places we call home has been cultivated over countless generations, rendering us interwoven with these places through continued stewardship and through traditions rooted in an ecologically conscious ethos. In studying and working with historic weavings, I find that one of their most valuable aspects is that they are a physical manifestation of this ethos. They reflect the understanding of a beautiful and deeply meaningful relationship that exists between us, the environment, and all living things—a symbiotic relationship whose delicate harmony is valued. In this way, they express a true sense of belonging.

This deep belonging has been threatened, however, by colonial enactments of dominion over this land: violent removal efforts, exploitative relationships, and extractive practices against the Earth that continue to impact communities on the Navajo Nation and on Indigenous lands across the continent. These acts are fueled by ambitions for profit with dismissive attitudes toward their detrimental impacts. These attitudes persist today and threaten the wellbeing of our communities at large.

In the *Woven Landscapes* series, I want to embody a Diné perspective on the environment. We are living in a time in which we need to examine our collective values and reconsider how we relate to the Earth, which affords us all that we have. Seeing the environment as a place of opportunistic exploitation for money and power—rather than as an integral component of life that we are each deeply connected to—is a form of self-harm. Ongoing practices of exploitation have placed us in danger as the reality of climate change manifests with disastrous effects on communities of color. Indigenous ways of living related to natural resources are directly impacted, including accessibility to water, food, medicinal plants, and habitable environments. Through my work, I want to illuminate a perspective in which the environment is a place of sacred beauty, not just a site of extraction to feed capitalist greed.

Our Diné ancestors knew this. They celebrated and acknowledged the landscape through their cultural practices, their ways of living, and through their art, all of which are grounded in notions of harmony and beauty. The weaving tradition of our people is no exception: it embodies this knowledge in all aspects of practice. From taking great care in the responsibility of land stewardship and animal husbandry to imbuing weavings with the values and philosophies that have been cultivated within the site-specific regions of Diné Bikéyah and passed down from generation to generation, this practice

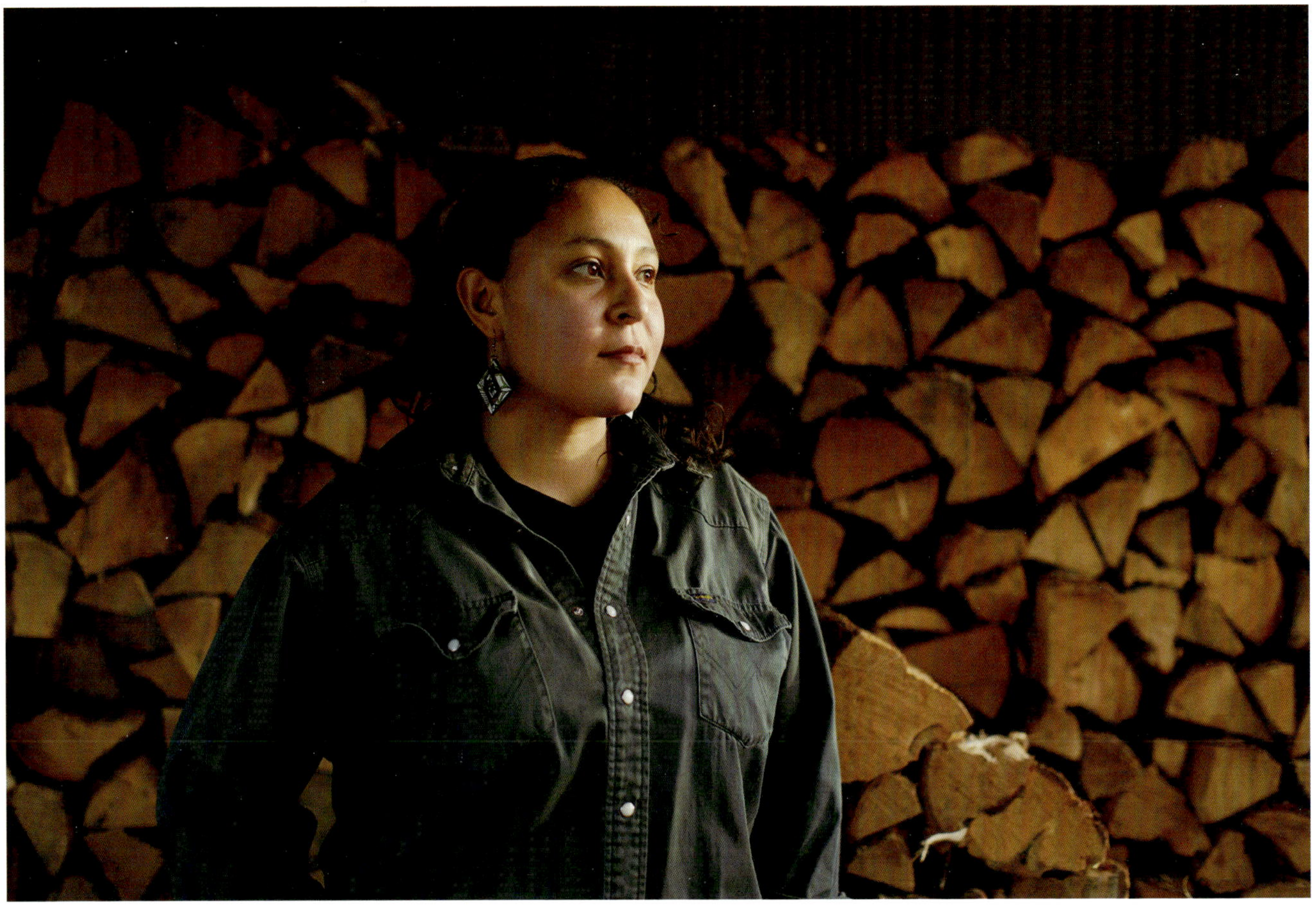

Darby Raymond-Overstreet at her home and studio, Chimayo, New Mexico, 2020. Photograph by Byron Flesher. Courtesy of Hadley Welch Jensen.

embodies the inextricable and interdependent relationships between land, art, and people. The overall wellness and vibrancy of these agents of culture depend on a careful and balanced nurturing.

As I look toward the future and consider the relationships that we cultivate and maintain with the environment, my hope is that we can make our way back to living in a more responsible and respectful way that is based in reciprocity. Collectively, I hope that we can live grounded in kinship, especially with the places that give us the gift of belonging.

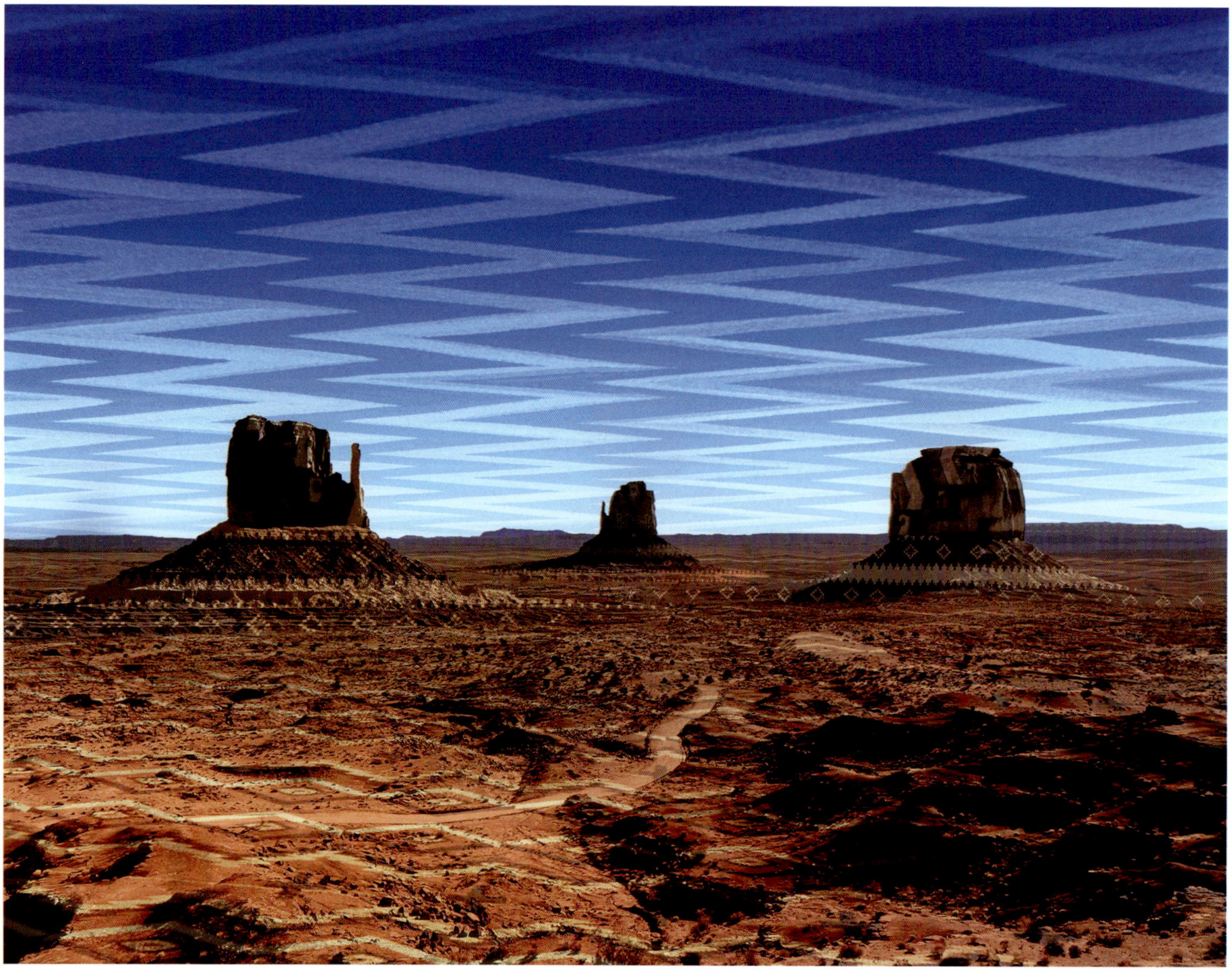

Woven Landscape: Monument Valley, 2023. Darby Raymond-Overstreet (Diné, b. 1994). Mixed media: Digital collage of scanned Navajo textiles and photography. 32 × 24 inches. Courtesy of the artist.

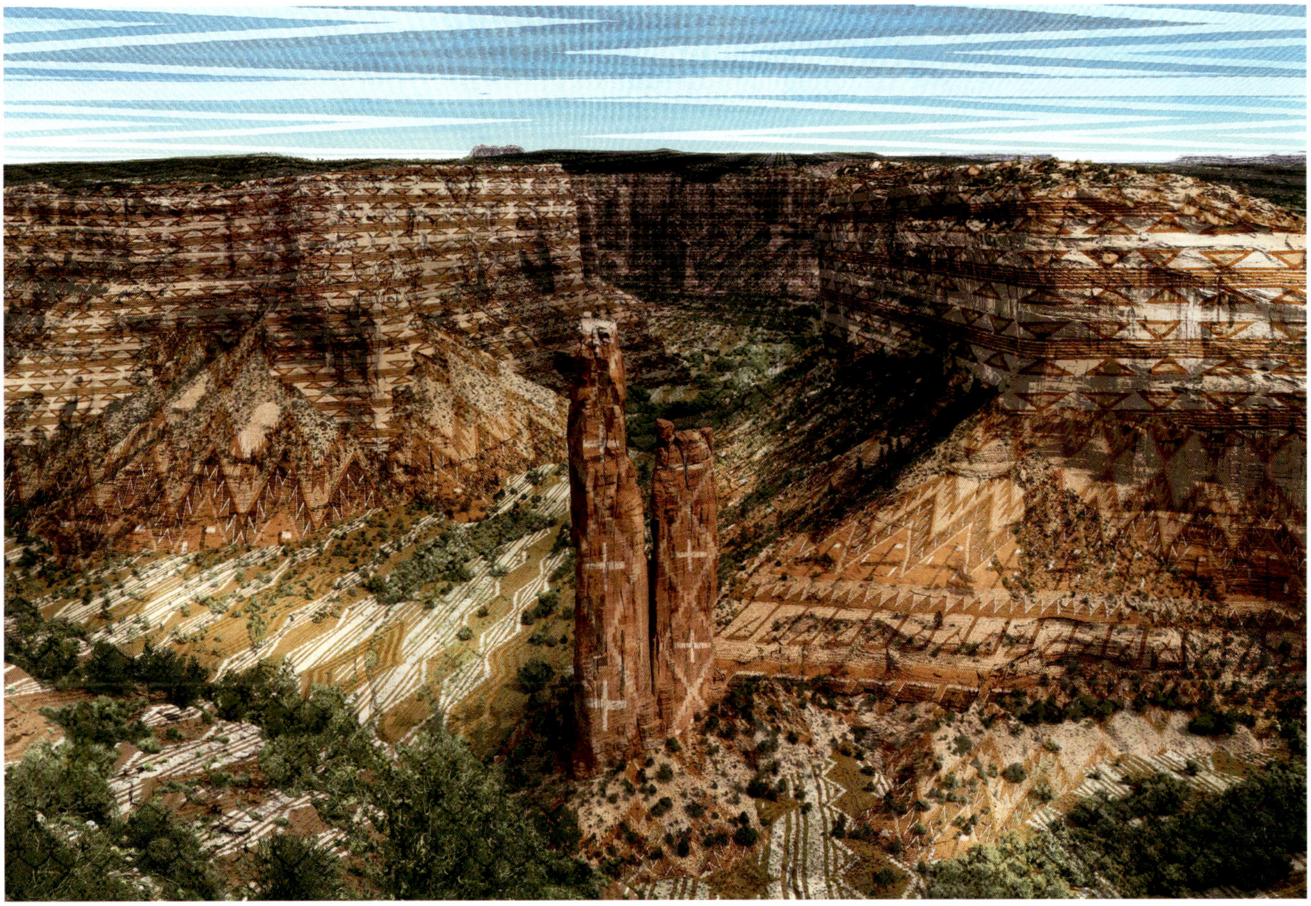

Woven Landscape: Canyon de Chelly, 2023. Darby Raymond-Overstreet (Diné, b. 1994). Mixed media: Digital collage of scanned Navajo textiles and photography. 36 × 24 inches. Courtesy of the artist.

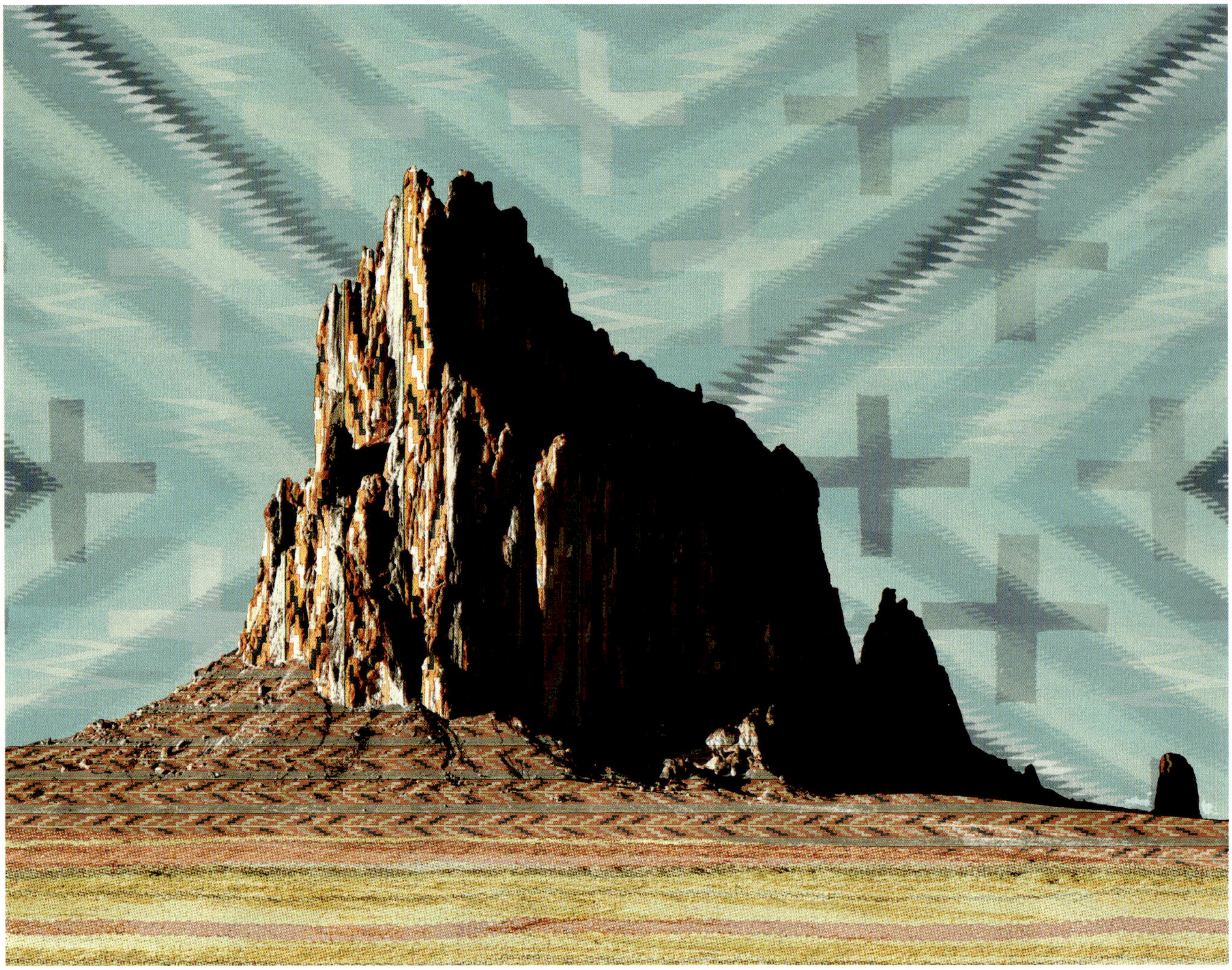

Woven Landscape: Shiprock, 2018. Darby Raymond-Overstreet (Diné, b. 1994). Mixed media: Digital collage of scanned Navajo textiles and photography. 32 × 24 inches. Courtesy of the artist.

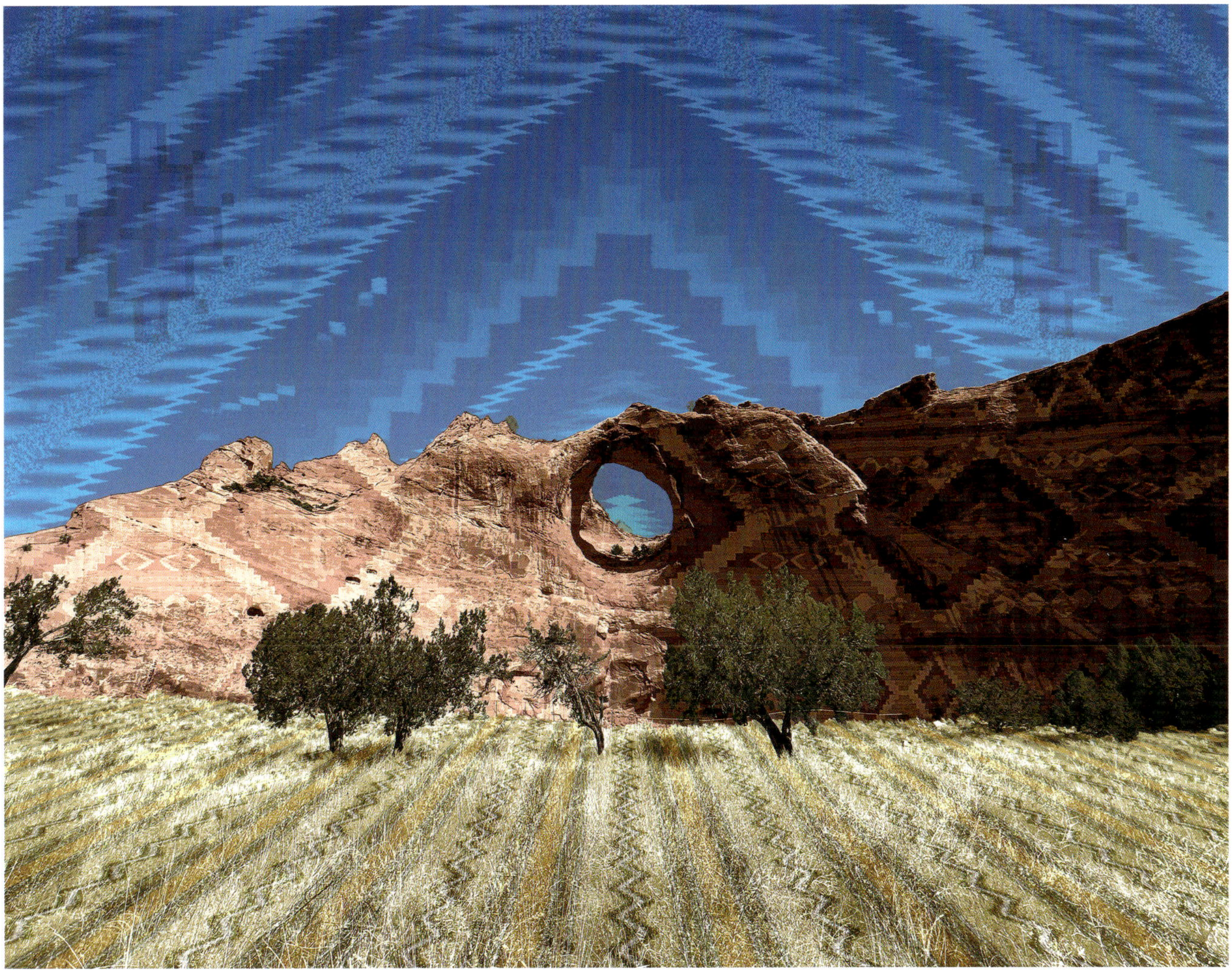

Woven Landscape: Window Rock, 2023. Darby Raymond-Overstreet (Diné, b. 1994). Mixed media: Digital collage of scanned Navajo textiles and photography. 32 × 24 inches. Courtesy of the artist.

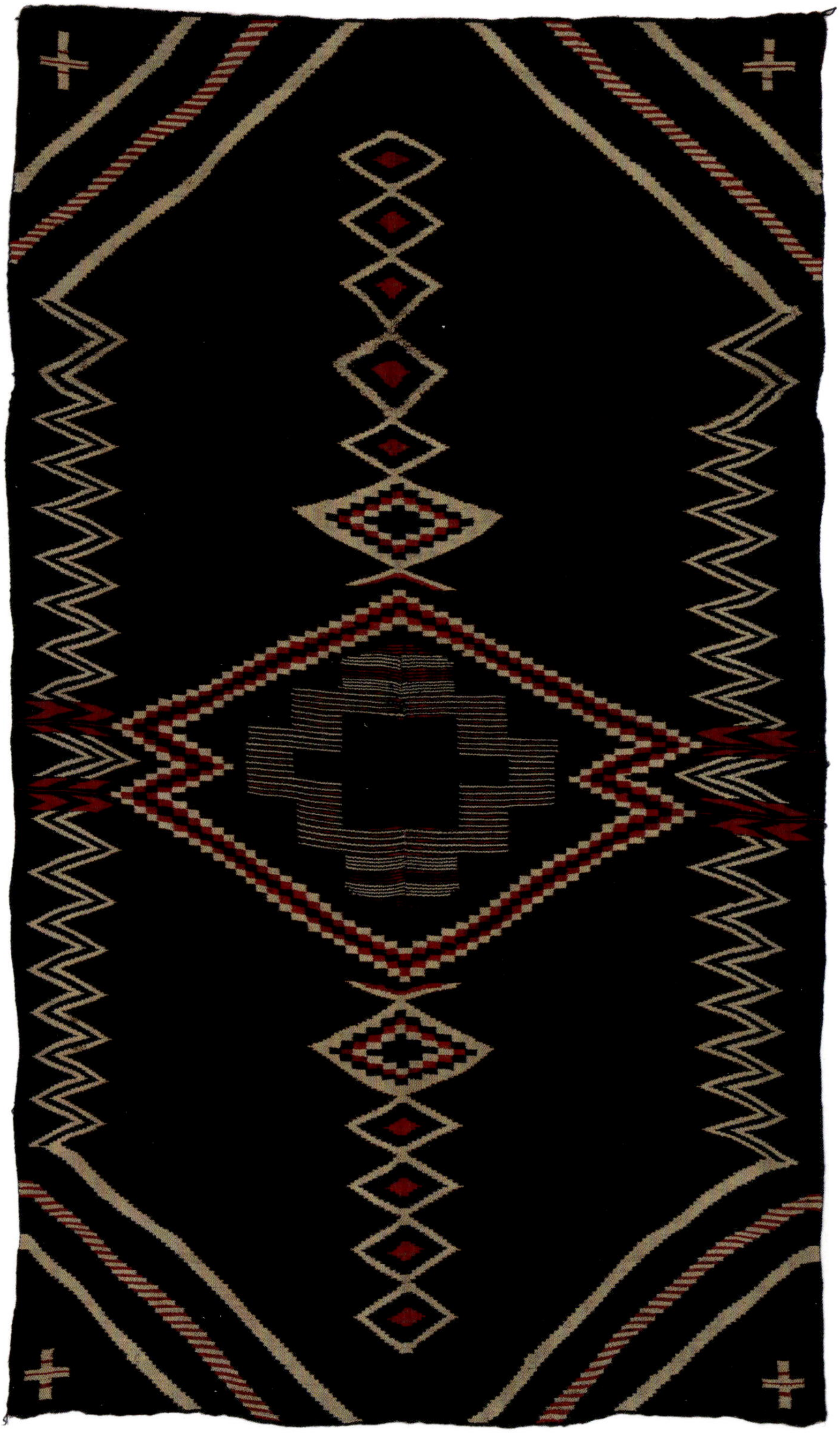

Poncho or serape, 1870–1880. Artist once known (Diné). Handspun wool, bayeta, indigo dye. 84 ¾ × 51 inches. Museum of Indian Arts and Culture/Laboratory of Anthropology, Harry Kelly Collection, 9159/12. Photograph by Addison Doty.

Known as a slave blanket, this Diné poncho or serape was woven using the forced borrowing of Spanish colonial angles. These are not sharp diagonals but small geometric steps, indicating that the piece was perhaps made by an expert weaver. Each corner of the poncho has a white Spider Woman cross variant with thin red stripes. I tend to think these crosses convey the weaver's desire to be safe and that they embody a prayer to return home among our four sacred mountains. As much as the clean lines of the designs suggest master-weaving skills, the variegated handspun brown tells us the wool may have been carded under duress. The design elements may have been copied from an existing Spanish serape or poncho, but the red zigzags were possibly the weaver's creative addition of beauty to the design.

—LYNDA TELLER PETE

6 The Art of Resistance

Diné Textiles Woven in Beauty

LYNDA TELLER PETE

To prepare for this exhibition and book, our committee of curators, weavers, and artists spent many visits examining historic Diné weavings in the collection of the Museum of Indian Arts and Culture in Santa Fe. We selected textiles that offered a glimpse into our shared history and lived experience, focusing on materials and wondering how the weavers might have acquired these supplies. As we pored over each weaving, advisory committee members shared family stories and anecdotes from our own individual weaving practices. We learned from one another and gained deep insight and inspiration from our artistic journeys.

The majority of historical Diné weavings in museum collections lack the names of their creators and the places they were made. Some, however, were identified by past curators and collectors with designations such as “suspected servant blanket,” “slave blanket,” or made by a “Navaho squaw”—abhorrent words that always induced a knee-jerk reaction. As each textile was unrolled for us, we knew instantly when a so-called slave blanket appeared. Conversation would cease, and we would suck in our breath to absorb the pain in our guts. The silence was deafening and overpowering. And then our gloved hands would gently touch the weaving, giving it the reverence that we all held for the textile and its maker. One or two committee members would speak of the beauty we were seeing. After a collective sigh, we would go back to work, evaluating the weave and the design.

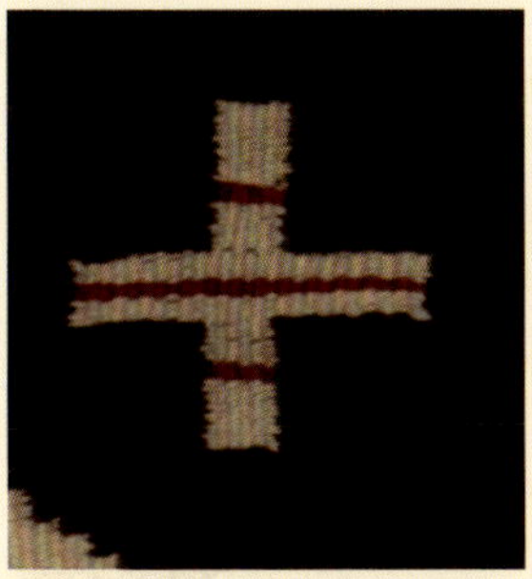

Poncho or serape, 1870–1880 (detail). Photograph by Addison Doty.

Ultimately, as we spent time with each of the textiles made by an enslaved Diné weaver, we would focus on an element of its design: a variant of Spider Woman crosses woven into some part of the textile—a sign of resistance, a sign of hope, a sign of faith.

Each of us was willing and wishing that the weaver had somehow escaped and returned to our sacred homeland—and we noted that now the textile, at least, was in

Saddle blanket or child's wearing blanket (displayed on form), 1850–1860. Artist once known (Diné). Handspun wool, cochineal dye, indigo dye, chamisa dye. 51 1⁄16 × 33 inches. Museum of Indian Arts and Culture/Laboratory of Anthropology, gift of Mrs. Philip B. Stewart, 9123/12. Photograph by Addison Doty.

When I look at this piece, I notice the precision in design, complementary color combination, and the even spin of the weft wools. The cochineal, indigo, and black colors are clear and have lasted for over one hundred years. The clean lines and sharp angles tell me many stories of a master weaver.

The age of this piece (mid-1800s) and the Spanish colonial influence indicate to me that the weaver was enslaved. The Spider Woman variant crosses woven in each of the four corners (not visible here), with four more woven in the center, tell me the weaver is hopeful that she will return to her homeland among the four sacred mountains. The lightning designs speak to her perseverance to weave in beauty, even in captivity. My hope is that she survived to teach her children and grandchildren the art of weaving.

—LTP

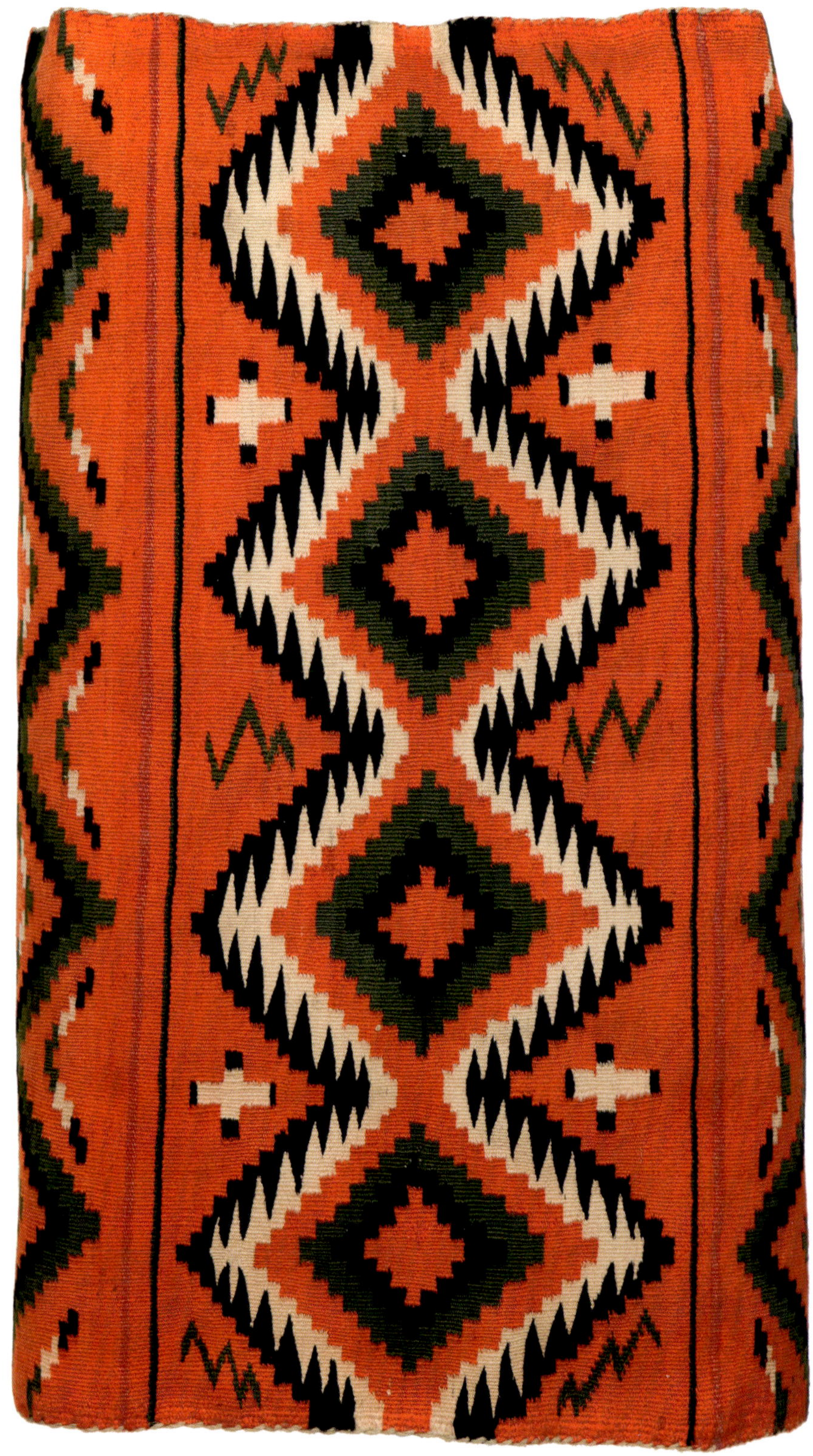

a place where it would be cared for and preserved for posterity. Through these works created by our Diné ancestors, and through our voices as we discuss and appreciate them today, our children and grandchildren will learn the lessons of our history, learn the arts of our people, and will have their genetic memory kickstarted.

Diné weaving is a testament to our connections across the timeline of history to the present day. The varied skill levels of the artists and the stories that could be unraveled in the designs aid in our own quest for excellence in weaving artistry. We are able to identify the beginnings of certain styles and the woven results, originating perhaps in communal living or close relations, that bind our continuing weaving traditions with the innovation of individual artistry. And we are able to see the outcomes of forced assimilation expressed in the creations of enslaved or indentured weavers, which communicate Diné resilience and survivance.

So it was particularly jolting to read that the State of Florida's 2023 social studies curriculum would include lessons on how "slaves developed skills" that could be used for "personal benefit." Enslavement was not a jobs program—either for Africans and African Americans in the United States or for Indigenous peoples impacted by settler colonialism. In our own history, Diné weavers were targeted for slavery precisely *for* their weaving skills—skills that created products used by the families of the enslavers but also exploited for capitalistic greed. We can still see today how generational wealth has grown among prominent families that participated in the Native slave trade, the results evident in particular areas inside Dinétah, its border towns, and several Southwestern cities near the Navajo Nation.

The abuse and genocide perpetrated on Native people in the Americas began in 1492. More than a century later, in 1619, Spanish and Mexican colonizers were stealing the women, children, and livestock of the Diné in the American Southwest. Throughout the fraught and ugly history of slavery and human exploitation in this nation, many euphemisms and softening phrases have been used to justify or elide the inhumanity of slavery—words like "servant trading" or "adopting" (stolen) Indian children into settler households. Those stolen children were baptized, given colonizer names, and absorbed into settler homes as *genizaros*, a Spanish term generally translated as "indentured servant." The linguistic softening designated most enslaved Native children as *criados*, a word implying that they were trained as servants willingly—one translation of criados is "guest servants"—whereas in fact these young people were considered and treated as personal property.

This practice continued well into the time that what is now New Mexico came under the control of the United States in 1850. We know about the enslaved Diné in Hispanic households because of the baptismal rolls of the Catholic Church, which anthropologist David M. Brugge used to track the flow of enslaved Diné. His research shows that Native slavery in the Southwest reached its peak during the 1860s, when more than 2,400 Diné—most of them children—were baptized.[1]

The United States government had long turned a blind eye to the existence of Native slavery, allowing the slave trade in American settlements to expand from as early as the 1840s. When war broke out with the Diné in the early 1860s, the United

States Army in New Mexico Territory weaponized slavery, encouraging raids and paying mercenaries—Native and non-Native alike—in captured women and children. Ironically, the trade in Native slaves by American settlers, Hispanic settlers, and Christopher "Kit" Carson's band (condoned by the US Army) was in full swing while the Union was fighting a Civil War in the east to free the enslaved. The Long Walk of the Navajos to Bosque Redondo in the mid-1860s—the forced removal from our homelands—also occurred during this time.

The tasks of Diné weavers in Spanish and Mexican households before the Long Walk included unraveling Hispanic-made Saltillos, Rio Grande blankets, ponchos, and other woven textiles and reweaving them Diné-style in a weft-faced plain weave and in tight twill and wedge weaves. The warp of these weavings would be continuous, with four laced-in selvages for the outside edges and tasseled corners. The enslaved weavers were also given access to imported indigo and cochineal dyes that were hard to come by prior to Bosque Redondo but readily available in Hispanic households.[2] The Diné weaving style was much more desirable among non-Native collectors and consumers than the looser Saltillo style, and some Diné items were so tightly woven as to be watertight. Sectional lines, a material signature of Diné weaving techniques, were also incorporated into these large, rewoven textiles. The serrated diamonds and angled patterns seen during this period are Spanish and Mexican designs that were imposed upon the enslaved Diné, a process known as "forced borrowing," but were taken up by later generations of weavers.

In 1852, before the Long Walk, Diné headman Armijo spoke with William Greiner, the Superintendent of Indian Affairs, about the ongoing slave raids:

> Three of our chiefs now sitting before you mourn for their children, who have been taken from their homes by the Mexicans. More than 200 of our children have been carried off and we know not where they are. The Mexicans have lost but few children in comparison with what they have stolen from us . . . Eleven times have we given up our captives, only once have they given us ours. My people are yet crying for the children they have lost. Is it American justice that we must give up everything, and receive nothing?[3]

Greiner forwarded Armijo's heartbreaking words to Washington, DC, and added this note:

> There is too much truth in what these Indians complain of—it was the custom of the Mexicans to fit out expeditions against them, everyone claiming what he stole as his plunder. They [the Navajos] own large flocks of sheep, goats, horses, mules, and cattle. They are a very industrious, hard-working people. They not only till their lands themselves, but they manufacture their own clothing—and a Navajo blanket will at any time command the price of a mule. It is not to be wondered at if they should retaliate when they so repeatedly suffered by these marauding expeditions. These Indians are now what the

> U.S. Government is striving to make of all the Wild Indian tribes—a farming community. I was so well convinced with the truth of the remarks of Armijo, that I confess I had but little to say.[4]

Greiner's message fell on deaf ears in Washington. The slave raids continued, often under the guise of American military campaigns.

When Euro-American settlers moved westward into the Southwest in the mid-1800s, the Diné and other tribes resisted this encroachment on their lands—yet another invasion after those of Spain and Mexico. The Diné fought passionately to live within the four sacred mountains, the territory known as Dinétah. Indeed, the Diné were strong warriors because they fought for their homelands and their families. When Maj. Gen. James H. Carleton gave orders to Kit Carson to force the Diné off their homeland, he said, "The men are to be slain whenever and wherever they can be found. The women and children may be taken as prisoners." Carson led a scorched-earth military campaign that involved burning homes and grazing lands, slaughtering livestock, destroying crops, and contaminating water sources to starve out the Diné. Carson hired mercenaries from other tribes, trackers, New Mexico volunteers, and Mexicans to participate in what amounted to genocide and gave slave traders the opportunity to enslave hundreds of women and children.[5] As Diné scholar and historian Adam Teller has said, "we feel about Carson the way Jews feel about Hitler."[6]

Following the people's surrender at their last stronghold in Canyon de Chelly, Arizona, they endured forced marches to the Bosque Redondo Reservation at Fort Sumner, New Mexico. Over ten thousand Diné in fifty-three different groups marched more than four hundred miles—starving, suffering family losses, many dying of exposure. Once at the fort, they lived in horrific conditions. The "reservation" was, in reality, a prison camp, guarded by US soldiers.

Even in captivity at Bosque Redondo, the Diné continued to weave. A census of the Navajo Indians at Bosque Redondo on the 31st day of December 1864, taken by Capt. Francis McCabe of the 1st Cavalry, New Mexico Volunteers, reported:

> Number of lodges, 1[,]276. Number of families 1,782, total population 8,354. Number of horses, 3,038, mules 13, sheep 6,962, goats 2,757 and number of looms, 630.[7]

Six hundred and thirty recorded looms in 1864. Imagine the number of looms left behind after the return from Bosque Redondo in 1868. Where did all the finished textiles end up? There were no tourists to buy them.

The 1864 census report on Bosque Redondo, "Condition of the Indian Tribes: Report of the Joint Special Committee, Appointed Under Joint Resolution of March 3, 1865," describes the work of the weavers at the prison camp:

> They fabricate a strong and durable cloth and elegant blankets of a variety of patterns and brilliant colors, for which purposes the Navajoes [*sic*] value the wool they obtain from their sheep. These fabrics are made in hand looms of

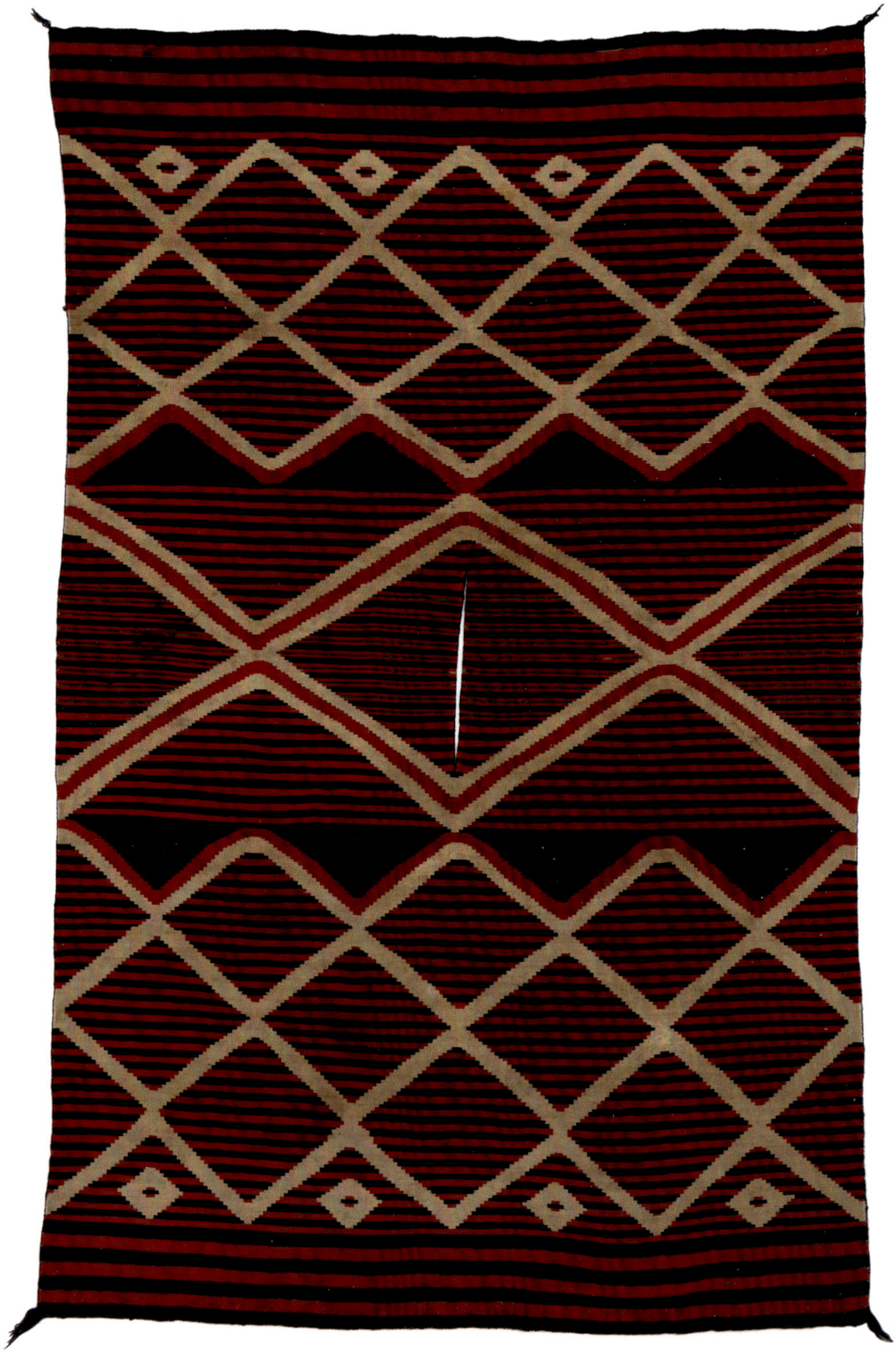

Poncho blanket, c. 1840–1860. Artist once known (Diné). Handspun churro yarn, lac dye, indigo dye, bayeta, vegetal dye. 81½ × 54½ inches. Museum of Indian Arts and Culture/ Laboratory of Anthropology, H. C. Yontz Collection, courtesy of John and Linda Comstock and the Abigail Van Vleck Charitable Trust, 9051/12. Photograph by Addison Doty.

Our journey to tell the stories of the weavers of these textiles has been inspiring. These weavers faced the violence of settler colonialism, which included executive orders for extermination, forced relocations, livestock reduction, conversion to Christianity, government boarding schools, and trading post directives that could have stifled individual artistic creativity. These weavers created incredible works of art during these times.

I voice my gratitude that the prayers and songs of my matriarchs have allowed me to gather strength every day to live my life in balance. I now carry their resiliency, their warrior spirits, and the power of our Diné language to weave with creative freedom.

—LTP

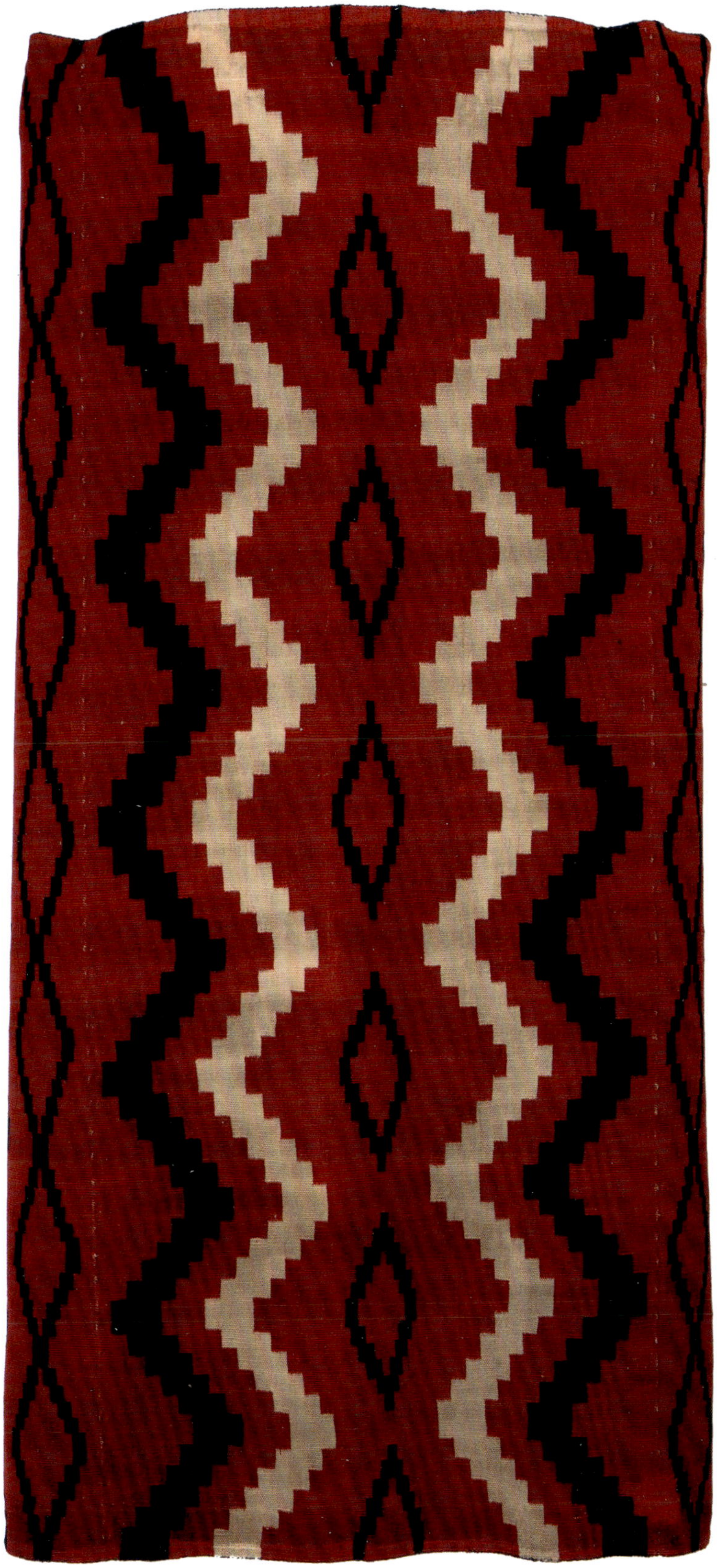

Shoulder blanket (displayed on form), 1850–1860. Artist once known (Diné). Handspun wool, cochineal dye, indigo dye, bayeta, lac dye. 80 × 55 inches. Museum of Indian Arts and Culture/ Laboratory of Anthropology, Museum purchase, 9091/12. Photograph by Addison Doty.

Outwardly, this blanket's prominent tie-down lines signal that the loom was too small for this piece, and the uneven edges show that it may have been woven in tumultuous times. Maybe the loom had to be moved often, with prolonged exposure to the elements.

Made by a master weaver, this shoulder blanket features clean design lines. The clear red of lac and cochineal (from bayeta) is paired with indigo and natural white, spun for evenness. The geometric designs seem to float and, from afar, look like serrated angles, achieved without modern measuring tools. The blanket tells a story of perseverance to create a textile of beauty and harmony, woven under difficult conditions. Today, this piece provides inspiration for Diné weavers.

—LTP

> simple construction by the women of the tribe. One industrious female can finish a blanket in three weeks, which will wear for ten years, is perfectly waterproof, and will command a price as high as $50 to $200. The garments of the men and women are principally formed from the strong woolen cloth above mentioned, those of the women being often tastefully bordered by a combination of colors representing all the hues of the rainbow.

Prior to enslavement—and before Bosque Redondo—Diné textile designs were geometric, terraced blocks woven into complex patterns and gender-identifying stripes. The most prominent styles woven during this period are the large men's blankets called First Phase, Second Phase, and the ever-popular Third Phase, also referred to as Chief blankets. Women's mantas and other functional textiles were also woven and had been since at least 1650.

While the Diné were at Bosque Redondo, four thousand Rio Grande blankets were acquired for distribution by the army, of which about a thousand were given to the prisoners. Inspired by the Hispanic design elements on these blankets, weavers merged them with their Navajo designs.[8] The combined designs—brought home by brave warrior weavers who escaped or returned at the end of their incarceration and continued to weave to provide for their families—remain fully incorporated in Diné weaving styles today. We are the descendants of these weavers, and it is our responsibility to keep this tradition alive.

The slave raids subsided in 1868, one year after the 1867 Peonage Act went into effect, making slavery illegal in the territory of New Mexico, and the same year the treaty of 1868 was signed, allowing the people to return to Dinétah. Navajo leader Barboncito (Hastiin Dághaa'), a signatory to the treaty, had made a point of raising the issue of stolen children during the treaty negotiations. I believe these things—the new law, the new peace, and the ability of the Diné to defend themselves and to seek protection under the law—all came together to stop the slave raids in 1868. Just one abduction was reported during all of 1869, and none the following year.

It should be noted that in the American Southwest, slavery was never technically legal. Spain had outlawed slavery in New Spain in 1543 (except for the taking of "war captives"); slavery was outlawed in Mexico since its independence in 1821; and slavery was illegal in all American states and territories following the Emancipation Proclamation of 1863. Eventually, the Peonage Act achieved some local compliance, but discrimination did not stop. Consider the significant differences in the (equally appalling) histories of Black and Indigenous inhabitants of the United States: formerly enslaved African Americans received citizenship in 1868; Navajos became citizens in 1924. Formerly enslaved African Americans were able to vote in 1870; Navajos could legally vote in 1924. In both cases, many states and local municipalities found ways to avoid compliance with the law. And finally, mission and government boarding schools, which violently separated Indigenous families and enforced "assimilation" of hundreds of thousands of Native children beginning in 1869, did not close until almost 1980.[9]

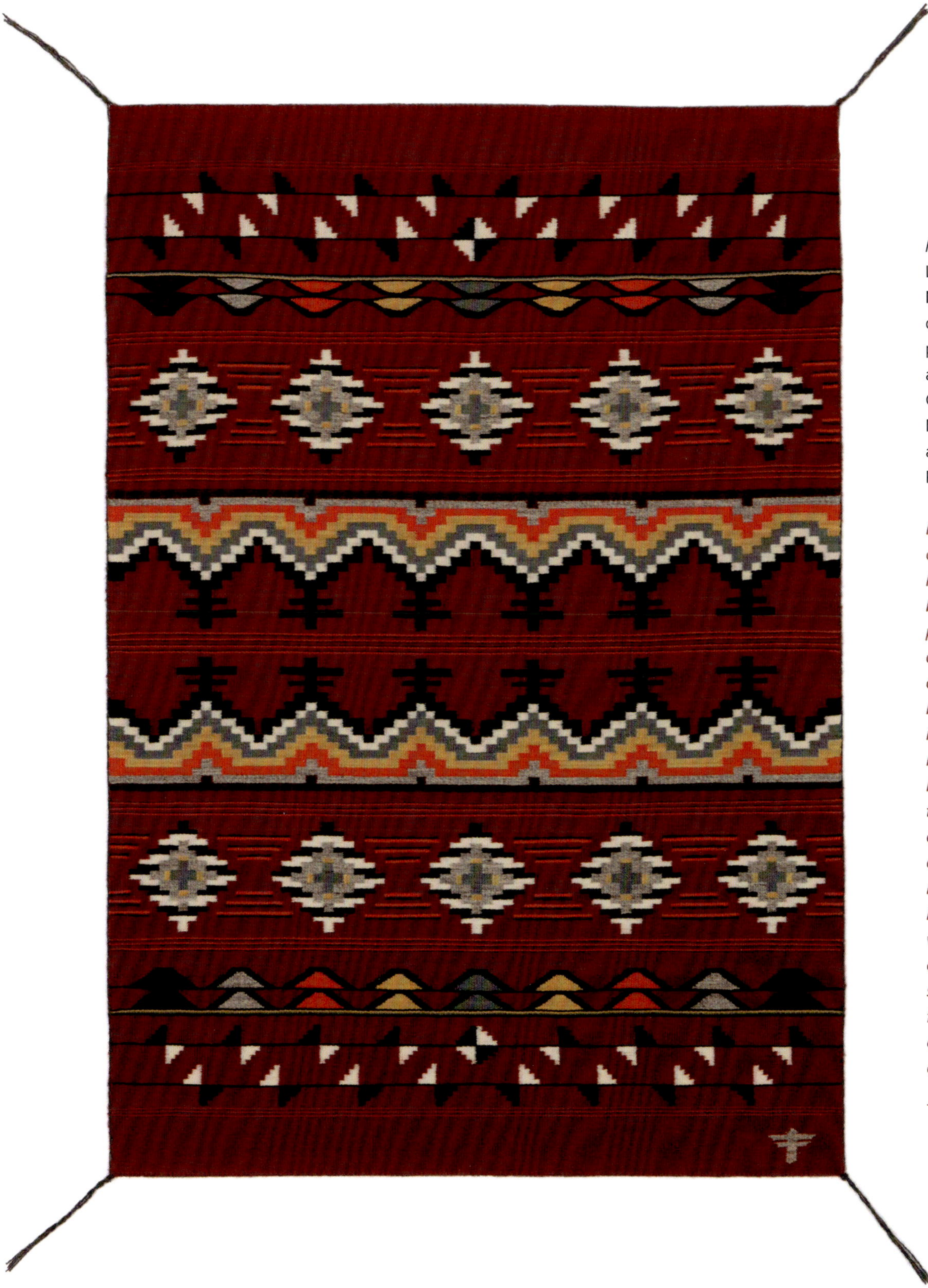

Migration of Dragonflies, 2015. Lynda Teller Pete (Diné, b. 1958). Natural blended wool, aniline dye (aniline-dyed wool purchased as commercial weft and re-spun by Barbara Teller Ornelas). 36 × 26 inches. Heard Museum Collection, gift of Mark and Julie Dalrymple, 4951-57. Photograph by Addison Doty.

Migration of Dragonflies is a child's blanket revival (now known as a small-format blanket), a style originally produced in the 1800s. A dragonfly necklace, earrings, and bracelet commissioned by my family for my birthday inspired me to weave a story of migrating dragonflies. The small black-and-white design fans on the top and bottom of the textile are the dragonfly embryos; after they mature, they fly back north over the mountains. The black-and-white diamonds with inset grey crosses are depictions of frozen ponds, as some dragonflies can be seen flying under the ice. The center of the textile depicts mature dragonflies atop colorful foliage.

—LTP

The Diné returned home from Bosque Redondo to their newly designated reservation lands in the Four Corners in June of 1868. More than a century later, most of us carry the generational trauma of this time of imprisonment, and we are still addressing the atrocities that were committed during this period of our history. But one hundred and sixty years later, we are still here. We remain resilient Diné, performing our ceremonies, practicing k'é[10] in our families and communities, conducting traditional protocols for puberty, and speaking our language—a language that won a world war for the Americans in 1945—despite the forced assimilation of boarding schools that sought to eradicate Diné language and cultural arts.

Today, we are creating works of art in basketry, pottery, silverwork, and weaving. We exist by the sheer audacity of our ancestors' prayers, their determination to survive and to return home to our four sacred mountains. That will to survive is evident in the historic blankets made by formerly enslaved Diné women and children. These are not only "slave blankets"—they are textiles of resistance, of hope, and of faith.

We are still weaving in beauty.

BIBLIOGRAPHY

Abel, Anna Heloise. *The Official Correspondence of James S. Calhoun while Indian Agent at Santa Fe and Superintendent of Indian Affairs in New Mexico*. Washington, DC: Government Printing Office, 1915.

Brugge, David M. *Navajos in the Catholic Church Records of New Mexico, 1694–1875*. Window Rock, AZ: Navajo Nation, 1968; 3rd ed. Santa Fe, NM: School of Advanced Research Press, 2010.

Child, Brenda J. *Boarding School Seasons: American Indian Families, 1900–1940*. Lincoln: University of Nebraska Press, 2000.

Fisher, Nora, ed. *Rio Grande Textiles*. Santa Fe: Museum of New Mexico Press, 1994.

Fitzsimons, Matt. *The Counterfeiters of Bosque Redondo: Slavery, Silver and the U.S. War Against the Navajo Nation*. Charleston, SC: Arcadia Publishing, with The History Press, 2022.

Hedlund, Ann Lane. "Recycled Reds: Raveled Insect-Dyed Yarns in Blankets of the American Southwest." In *A Red Like No Other: How Cochineal Colored the World, An Epic Story of Art, Culture, Science, and Trade*, edited by Carmella Padilla and Barbara Anderson, 146–57. Santa Fe, NM: Museum of International Folk Art and New York: Skira/Rizzoli, 2015.

McCabe, Capt. Francis. "1865 Census of Navajos at Fort Sumner." In United States War Department, *The War of the Rebellion: A Compilation of the Official Records of the Union and Confederate Armies*, ser. 1, vol. 48, pt. 1: *Reports, Correspondence, etc.*, 523. Washington, DC: Government Printing Office, 1880–1901.

Sides, Hampton. "The Place Where Two Fell Off." *Outside* online, October 2, 2006. https://www.outsideonline.com/adventure-travel/destinations/north-america/place-where-two-fell/.

"US Indian Boarding School History." The National Native American Boarding School Healing Coalition. https://boardingschoolhealing.org/education/us-indian-boarding-school-history/.

NOTES

1. See Brugge, *Navajos in the Catholic Church Records of New Mexico*.

2. Before Bosque Redondo, Diné weavers had access to bayeta, a term referring to red flannel cloth imported from England, which they unraveled, and in some cases, re-carded and re-spun to match the weight of their own yarn, resulting in colors ranging from pink to shades of coral and deeper reds. *Editorial note*: While bayeta is most often associated with red, the term refers to trade cloth in general. Various reds found in Diné weavings were also made with yarn from a cochineal-dyed trade cloth that arrived from Mexico through El Camino Real de Tierra Adentro (the Spanish colonial "Royal Road of the Interior," which ran from Mexico City to just north of Santa Fe). See Hedlund, "Recycled Reds."

3. Abel, *The Official Correspondence of James S. Calhoun*, 467–69.

4. Ibid.

5. See Fitzsimons, *The Counterfeiters of Bosque Redondo*.

6. Quoted in Sides, "The Place Where Two Fell Off."

7. McCabe, "1865 Census of Navajos at Fort Sumner," 523.

8. See Fisher, *Rio Grande Textiles*.

9. "Though we don't know how many children were taken in total, by 1900 there were 20,000 children in Indian boarding schools, and by 1925 that number had more than tripled" ("US Indian Boarding School History"). For a more general history of Native American boarding school experiences, see Child, *Boarding School Seasons*.

10. In Diné culture, *k'é* refers to affective action and solidarity, including such concepts as love, compassion, humility, kinship, kindness, community-mindedness, friendliness, generosity, and peacefulness.

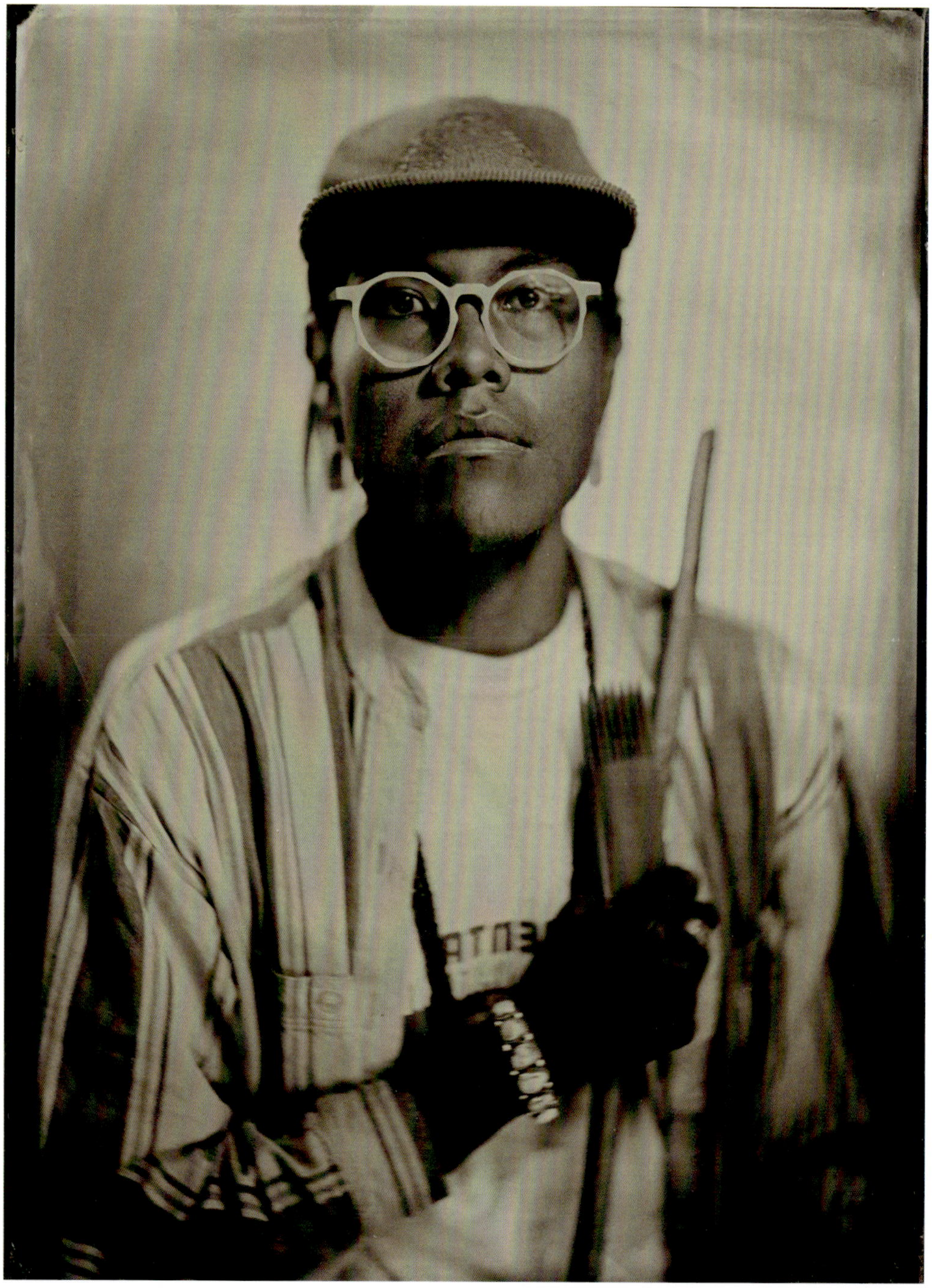

Portrait of Tyrrell Tapaha, 2021. Tintype. Photograph by Eric Retterbush.
Courtesy of Tyrrell Tapaha.

7 Tangible Memories

Sheep, Weaving, Walking

TYRRELL TAPAHA with Hadley Welch Jensen

The following conversation between Diné weaver, fiber artist, and sheepherder Tyrrell Tapaha and *Horizons* exhibition co-curator Hadley Welch Jensen was recorded on April 14, 2023. It has been lightly edited for length and clarity. —HWJ

Tyrrell Tapaha (TT): Yá'át'ééh shí éí Tyrrell Tapaha yinishyé. Shídóóné'e éí Tł'ízíłaní nishłį́. Bít'ahnii báshíshchiin. Tábą́ą́hą dáshícheii. Naakaí Diné'é dáshínálí. Áádóó, Tł'ízí Dahádlą'dę́ę́ náshááá. Ndí, Átł'óhí níshłį́, Ná'niiłkaadí níshłį́, dóó ba'oltá'í níshłį́. Hello, my name is Tyrrell Tapaha. I am of the Many Goats Clan. I am born for the Folded Arms People. My maternal grandfather is of the Water's Edge People. My paternal grandfather is of the Mexican People. I'm from Goat Springs. Also, I am a weaver, I am a sheepherder, and I am an educator.

Hadley Welch Jensen (HWJ): To begin, I'd like to ask how you position your work as a mode of contemporary storytelling. Can you expand on that idea?

TT: For context, all my storytelling is really just refining a set image and/or lens that I'm currently looking through with my life, and a lot of the visuals either stem from familial ties or have some other story that is outside of myself. My work is kind of collage-esque. A lot of the narratives that work in my type of design layout are asking, where's this information coming from? How am I using it? And how am I tailoring that to the end product, whether that be through the message, through the materials, or through the visuals of the work? So, I focus a lot on the fundamental components of storytelling. Where is it coming from? Who's telling it? And where is it going?

HWJ: Can you talk about the tradition of pictorial weaving?

TT: Diné weaving has always been documentary. It has always correlated with pop culture and actively critiques it. In some sense, it has allowed us to be visual scribes of our lives. Historically, our weavings were solely utilitarian and very simple in design. Precontact works were striped bands with natural colors, but even that had purpose in terms of what the weavers were trying to capture. And because I have access to a lot of different resources, my work takes that shape. I try to replicate a model of living that has given my people its livelihood.

HWJ: What are some of the things that stand out to you about the pictorial weavings that we chose for *Horizons*?

TT: What I like about the *Horizons* pictorials is that they're very outright funky, in the sense that they were created during a time when there was a formal standardization of what Navajo aesthetics are and what that *should* look like. What I love about the pieces that were chosen is that they go outside of that box, they work with that, and they play with that. This innovation really took off despite limited exposure or accessibility to different spaces. And the fact that they were able to fabricate these beautiful images blows my mind, because I see myself doing that. But I'm spoiled in the sense that I can look in any direction and find something new or something to talk about. They're doing the same thing, and I admire that they did that in a different time.

HWJ: Could you talk about the importance of materials in your weaving practice?

TT: I've described myself as a big ball of feeling. So much of my everyday life—and walking through my world—is feeling, interacting, and giving purpose to objects and items and people in my life. I've realized that I picked that up from the culture I've been immersed in. This medium in particular is very spiritual, everything has a connection, everything has a story, and it's a microcosm of our universe. The attention to materials is always part of the discussion. I am in a unique position of being one of the few weavers who still does sheep-to-loom processing. There's such a high caliber of standards that exists, and there's already a perfect model to work with. I guess all this is to say, if it ain't broke, don't fix it. At least with my materials, I look at it the same way. They've lasted this long, they have functionality.

Navajo weaving is multifaceted. Being able to understand your materials and how you interact with them as an artist, as a creator—it speaks and adds to your work. I have recently ventured into making my own tools, for the sake of knowing that I can do that. I don't have to be relying on other people. We love supporting toolmakers, but I should know how to make a comb, I should know how to make a batten. And I should know how to choose what wood is best for that.

OPPOSITE
Adá Nítsíį́kees: Think for Yourself, 2020. Tyrrell Tapaha (Diné, b. 2001). Handspun and commercial vegetal-dyed Navajo-Churro and alpaca wool. 54 × 42½ inches. Tia Collection, Santa Fe, New Mexico. Photograph by Addison Doty.

Diné textiles have always been used for documentation. In this piece, the chaos in the lower portion is like the "TV-static" that comes with the overstimulation of our time. I incorporated the Female and Male lightning designs to pay homage to my community and my family. The middle portion is a glimpse of the roots in my life. To the left is my great-grandmother Mary Kady Clah, the third generation that allowed me to learn from our family's practice. To the right is my other great-grandmother, Fannie Yazziee, a renowned weaver and livestock holder.

It also expresses the vulnerability that I don't often give myself time to assess. It lived and breathed through every moment of what I was navigating. I wrapped all of this up with the Diné philosophy of "Ádá Nítsíį́kees," which is a deeper way of saying, "Think for yourself."

—TYRRELL TAPAHA

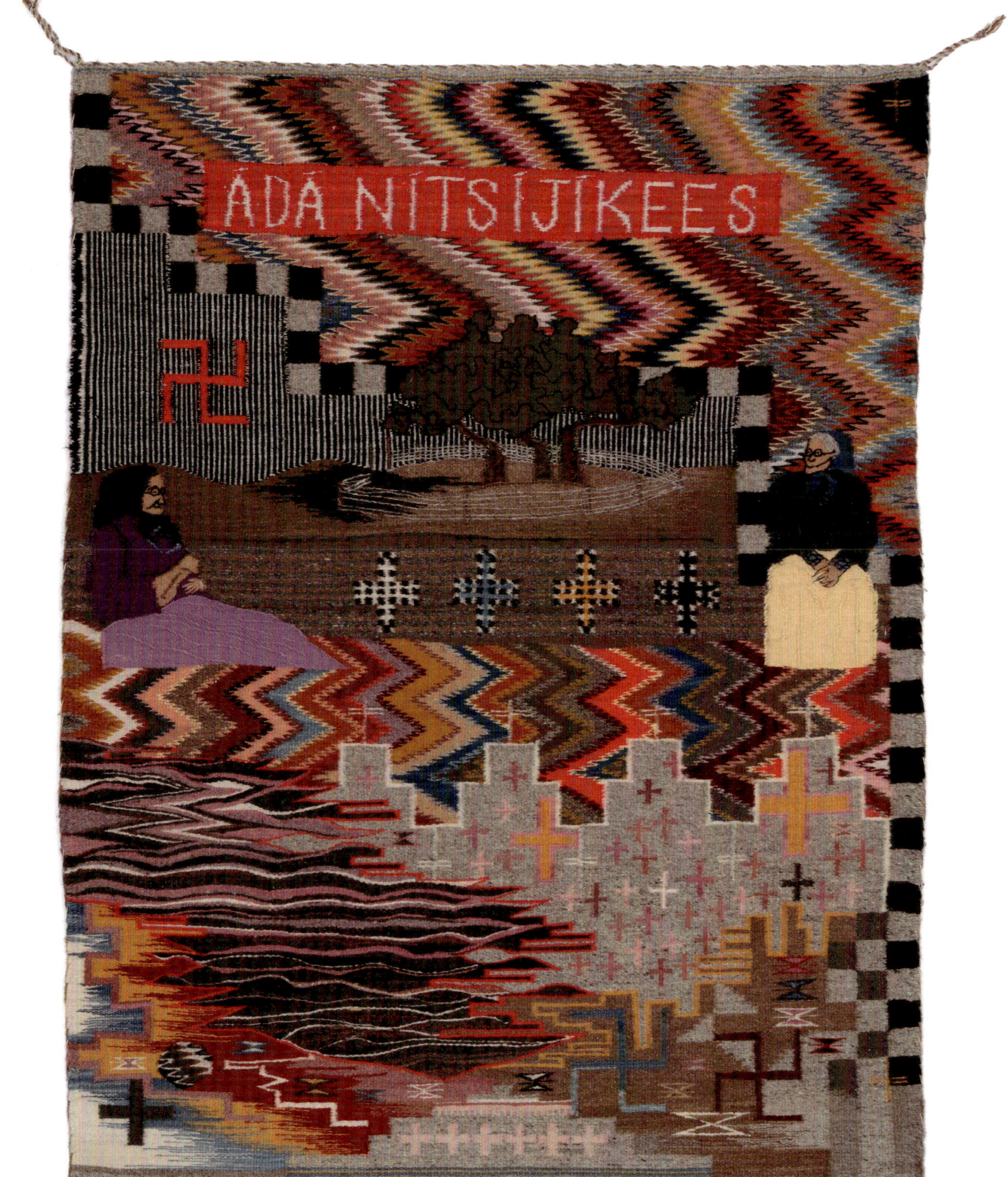
ÁDÁ NÍTSÍJÍKEES

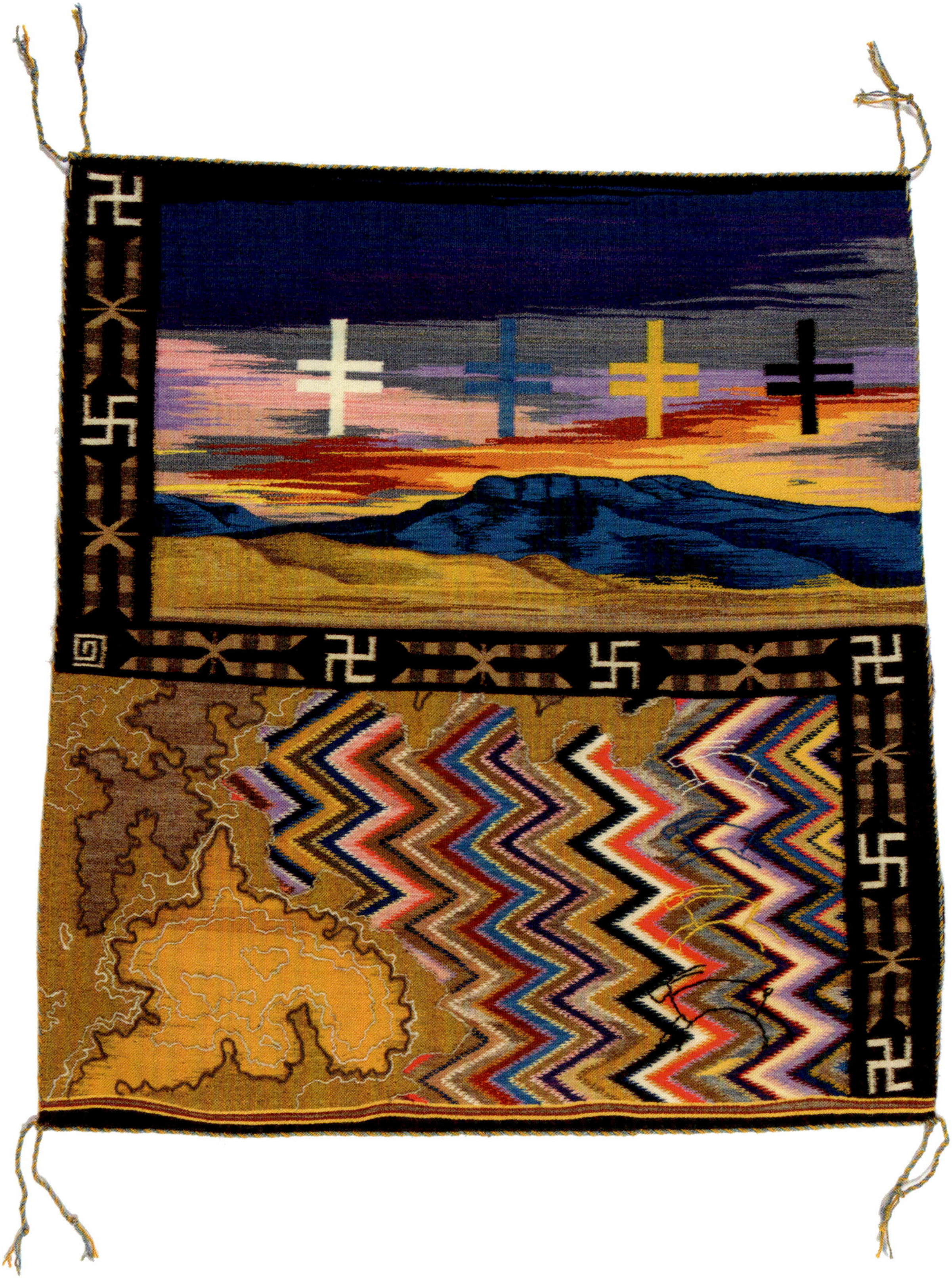

Just a Sheepherder, 2022. Tyrrell Tapaha (Diné, b. 2001). Handspun and vegetal-dyed Navajo-Churro, alpaca, merino, and mohair wool; tapestry weave. 46 × 48 inches. Gochman Family Collection, New York. Photograph by Alon Koppel. Courtesy of Tyrrell Tapaha.

Untitled, 2022.
Photograph by Tyrrell Tapaha.
Courtesy of the artist.

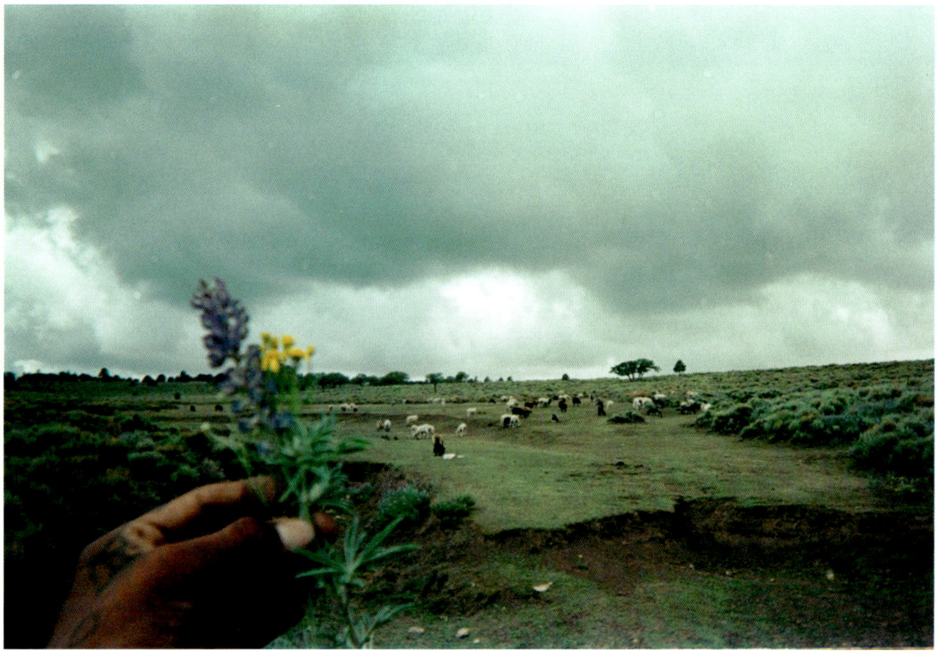

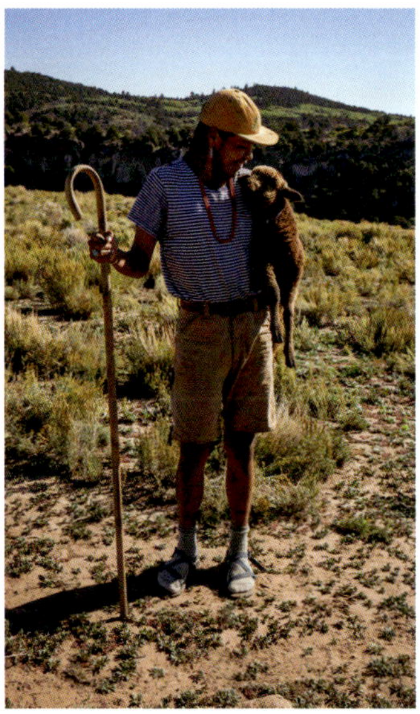

Tyrrell Tapaha with Chloe, a Navajo-Churro lamb, 2021.
Photographby Dawson Peters.
Courtesy of Tyrrell Tapaha.

HWJ: When we've looked at pieces together in collections, I remember asking you whether weavers adapt to the agency of their materials. And if, as you're weaving, you are responding to what the material has to give or offer. That has stayed with me when I look at a weaving.

TT: Fiber arts in particular are just a really rigid system. There are fundamental rules and mechanical limitations that you have; you can only do so much. In some sense, by understanding a system, I'm allowed to play and experiment within the parameters of the medium. It's what I love about it. It's personal, you can dissect it as visual thinking and problem solving, not only in a mechanical sense but as people living their lives. Going back to my idea of storytelling, so much of why my work looks the way it does is because I'm feeling a whole assortment of things. I want the imagery to pair with that. If it doesn't make sense, and if it's cluttered, it's because that's how I'm feeling.

HWJ: That raises another question about textiles as a kind of archive. I don't know if you think of them in that way, or if that language is how you would describe what you do. But in a way, even if you don't know who the individual artist was, there's so much you can learn about a weaver just based on their choice of materials, designs, and techniques.

TT: You can see and feel it. I like that thought—one of the first comments I had when we were viewing collections together was that you can tell the beginning of a weaving just by the feeling of how densely it's packed. It's being familiar with how that medium works. It's a lot easier to break that down and make it digestible for assessment, if that makes sense. I've described it as weaving being a tangible bank of feeling experiences that have been lived. And in all honesty, in museum collections the catalogue records almost never have anything about the weaver. It's always about when the weaving was purchased and its life after the fact. And it's funny because every conversation *we* have about work is about the conversation *prior* to that. Again, being a person who works in that medium, you see that life, and you can't disregard that. It's intoxicating. It's *life*.

HWJ: As a weaver, what is one of the most interesting things about looking at some of the older pieces in museum collections? What are you drawn to?

TT: I'm drawn into the stylistic choices that have been made and, more specifically, the technicalities of certain designs and motifs. It doesn't really look like it with my work, but a lot of the motifs that I've spent time doing are family-related designs that only exist in my part of the reservation, and currently only exist within my family. So having the opportunity to spend time to dissect and to learn, and to integrate that into my works, it's really fun: to see new flavors that I haven't seen before.

Some of my work documents my great-grandma. It's really crazy that I still learn so much from her techniques and styles, just from the evidence that she left behind. She didn't read or write, but she would weave small samplers. Whether they were like the twill counts or those outlines that I do (specifically, "tsídii bídaa'," or the "bird's bill")—she made those and documented it so she could remember the count. And now that she's been long gone, I can come back and still learn and experience and *feel* how she set that up. Again, being a creator, and specifically a maker, you can feel how that is done. I know her counts off the top my head, I know why she chose them for that specific reason. And when you're in collections, you can't help but think and look with that lens.

HWJ: Of the individual choices that were made?

TT: Exactly. With this specific medium, it's so bare. It is, in some sense, very rudimentary. But the beauty in that is the sky's the limit. There's so much you can do, and there's so much that can be accomplished. And it *has* been done—you just need to decide who you want to be, which story you want to be listening to, as you look at that.

HWJ: It seems that the process of each weaver is exposed in a way that—at least if you know what you're looking at or looking for—is specific to this medium.

TT: I've described it as just fiber. That's the weird part of having tangible thinking like this—you can backtrack and source this. It leaves a trail in a lot of different ways, and because this history is somewhat well documented, you can trace that. If you deep-dive and listen to the stories on the family end, these go back centuries—like, all my outline designs came from slavery within the Rio Grande region, and that was pre–

Bosque Redondo. How did that end up in a weird pocket in the San Juan River Valley, with only one family weaving that now? As I said, with all of these designs and motifs and exposure in their given time periods, you can find out a whole world of living just from feeling a piece.

HWJ: In thinking about an exhibition on Diné textiles, it seems like a worthwhile challenge, as a curator, to consider how to (or if you can) represent embodied practice in the context of a gallery. How do you give visitors a sense of the embodied knowledge related to weaving? How do you invite viewers to see the artist in the art—to see those material traces of the weaver's process?

TT: It's a communal conversation. Are we ready to be talking about those things? And even if we are, is anyone listening? And I say that in terms of my whole career, which has been based in, and flourished during, the pandemic. It feels like currently, within the art world, there is always a resurgence of some minority group, whether it's Middle Eastern art or Black art having multiple resurgences. Right now, it feels like Native art is the topic. And when pop culture gets ahold of something, the imagery and the receptiveness within the community changes completely. So it's odd to know that my work that lives and breathes can exist in—and wants to strive to live in—these white-walled spaces. But what does that matter if no one's listening? If no one is ready to receive that?

HWJ: You're part of a group exhibition that opened at James Fuentes Gallery in New York in September 2023. Could you talk about that work?

TT: In that show, I'm trying to craft the sheepherding narrative that I've been working on, as a series, for the past couple of years. I know that weaving as a medium for storytelling, without any context whatsoever, is very, very limiting. Because—at least within how pop culture consumes work—it's not a medium that the general public is familiar with. It's not "valid," in some sense. But I'm learning to tailor my message in a way that it can be received. I'm learning to branch out into structural or sculptural works; I'm wanting to weave more in three dimensions. Whether that's doing a loom sculpture and having projections on that of my life, or doing a darker series of butchering in which I'm docking lamb tails, wielding a bloody tail and a knife. Again, giving people a stark or in-your-face image of what this way of life looks like. I don't think that you can really do that by being coy. There need to be people in these spaces who know and work with these things. We need more people to live their lives in these spaces.

HWJ: When you talk about "these spaces," what do you mean?

TT: Like, US institutions? It's the only vehicle we have, you know; it's galleries, collections, museums. All of which are functioning institutions that don't interact in the same way but in some sense have the same structure. Ultimately, they are the vehicles of consumption for the masses. If we don't have a relationship with them, how can we effectively communicate what we're wanting to talk about?

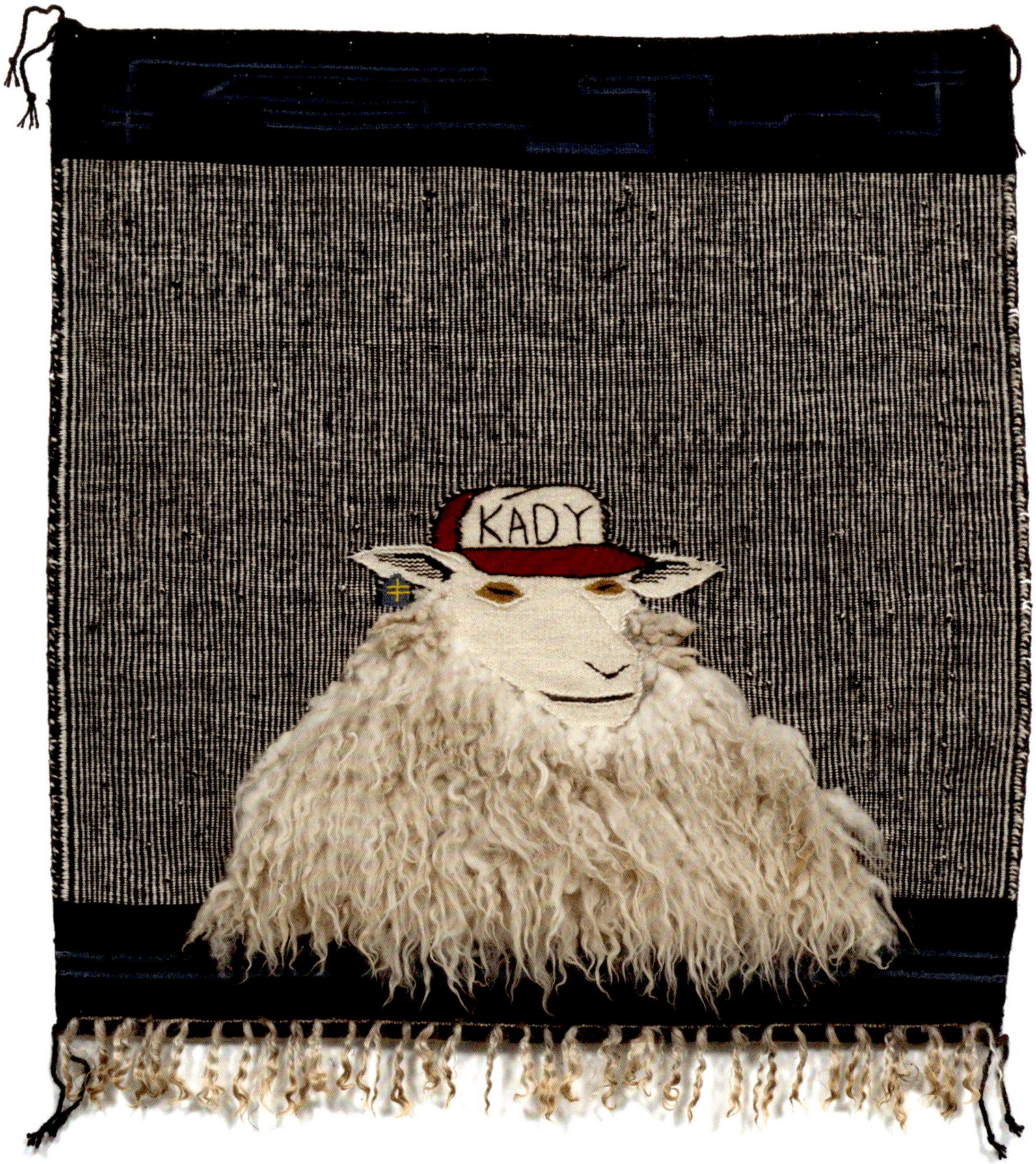

Cheii Nasty, 2023. Tyrrell Tapaha (Diné, b. 2001). Handspun and acid-dyed Navajo-Churro and mohair wool. 40 × 42 inches. John and Susan Horseman Collection, St. Louis, Missouri. Photograph by Jason Mandela. Courtesy of Tyrrell Tapaha and James Fuentes Gallery.

HWJ: I think museums (or exhibitions specifically) used to be more about teaching. As someone who's engaged in exhibition making, I see it more as a way to shape an experience for someone, create a space for contemplation, offer something, and then ultimately, it's up to your visitor if they choose to engage. As you said, are people listening? Are they receiving what you have to offer?

TT: I've been fortunate that my work has been well received. And all the spaces that I've been included in have been just great and phenomenal, especially for the community. But I guess the cynic in me knows that those spaces are few and far between. In terms of working with institutions, the structure in such spaces is not designed to include and have these voices readily accessible. That's something that we need to look at, if we're wanting to talk about art not being created in a vacuum. How do we create spaces to be truly transparent and critical?

HWJ: How do you see your work contributing (or not) to a larger conversation about Indigenous and Native art that could be specific to the Southwest, where we are, or more broadly?

TT: I've taken to describing it as a spectrum, with the fine art world being on one end and folk art/craft on the other. My work exists within that spectrum in a lot of different ways. I know we have perfectly symmetrical stuff, the standards and ideas that have been set in stone. That is everything that I want to work against. I feel like this art movement that's going on right now loves my work because it understands that spectrum and sees it in my work. This is me living my life and using my medium as documentation of sorts. But how do we expand critical thinking to the *origins* of the work? And to the audience consuming it?

HWJ: How do you see Indigenous aesthetics and lifeways on and within the Navajo Nation relating to contemporary art?

TT: They're the same damn thing! I'll answer it this way: Everything that I've talked about is my idea of what makes art *art*; it has substance no matter what the message may be. And I think that's what's interesting about this Native art movement. It's focusing on artists, it's focusing on trauma, it's focusing on systemic problems, and the work and the people who are living that, who have lived that.

I'm a sheepherder. I'm a weaver. And that's my reality. That's who I am. I've never really been exposed to anything that's *not* that. It boggles my mind to know that in a crowd of people, should I have a conversation with one of them, to that outside person who doesn't know me, I'm the most interesting person in the room. And I live life with the intent of living *my* life. I guess this is to say that this art movement that I keep referring to is putting attention on Native art because it's been built and flourished and designed on oppression. In some sense, we're the cultural cockroaches. My work shouldn't exist in a contemporary sense, but the fact that it does speaks to something. And in my mind, that's why this consumption of Indigenous and Native art is so

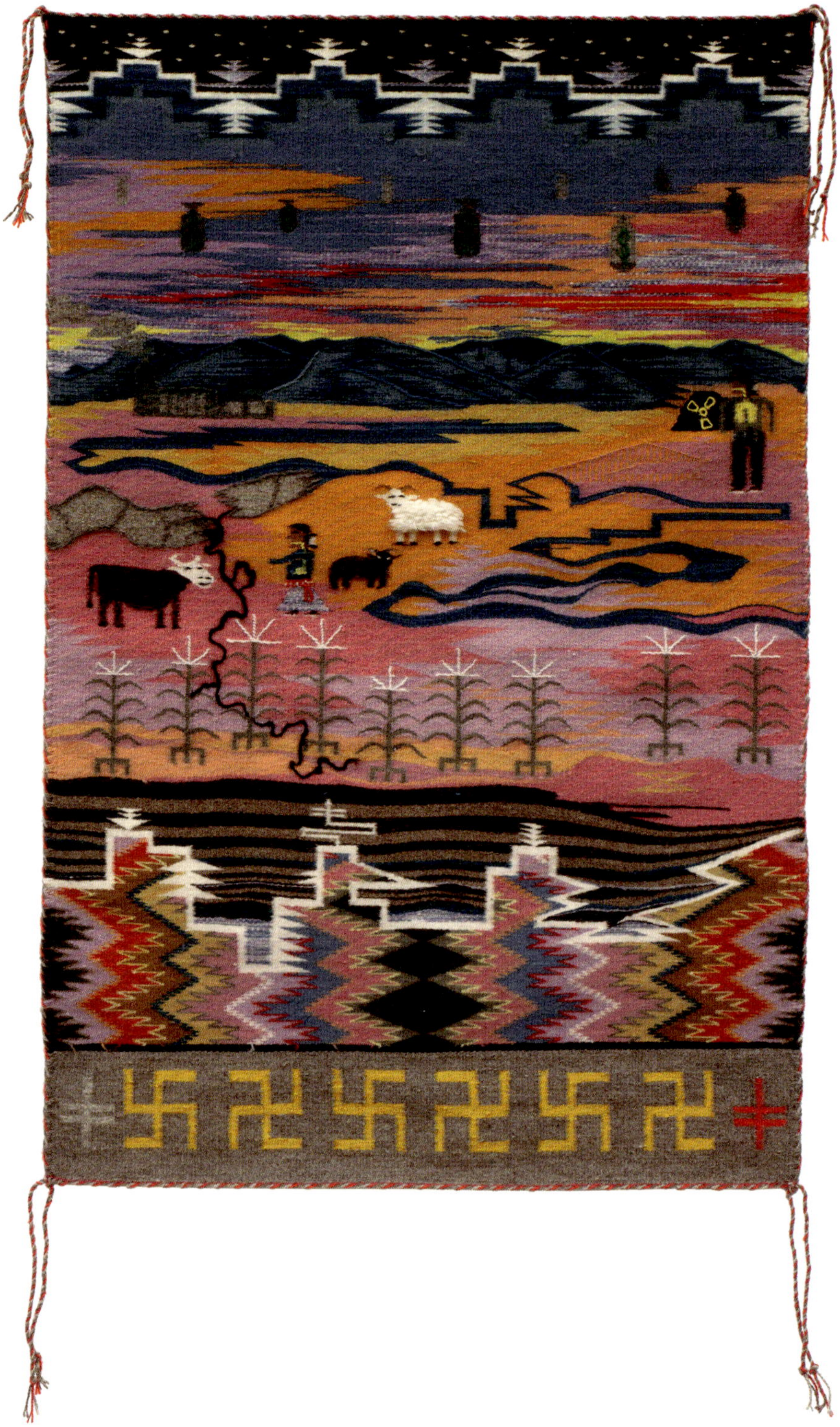

Chaos at Four Kornerz, 2024. Tyrrell Tapaha (Diné, b. 2001). Tapestry weave, vegetal-dyed Navajo-Churro wool. 51½ × 34¾ inches. Tia Collection, Santa Fe, New Mexico. Photograph by James Hart Photography. Courtesy of Tia Collection.

organic, because it has a reference and it has place—you can see and feel it in the work. Native art is made from the societal scraps.

This is a difficult question to answer in an abstract way. It's better to be specific to my own experience. I was answering in terms of what I see in my work, and what I see in the work of other people who are successful right now. Think about the Tlingít artist Rachel Martin. Rachel has beautiful work, and she's just using colored pencils on paper. Her work is amazing because it talks about her life, it *shows* her life. I don't know anything about the motifs because I'm not from that part of the world, but I can see that it radiates. And I see that in her. I feel like so much of Western art has been jumping through hoops for the pop movements, for the consumption of the masses. What I like about this wave now is it's entirely not that.

HWJ: What do you think the future of Diné weaving looks like? Or what do you imagine for the future?

TT: I've tried to avoid that question. I think people look at me and expect an answer because they see that in my work—in terms of things moving in a direction that feels familiar, but different. And I understand why I'm placed there. I'm in a unique position within my own family, who thought that Roy Kady was going to be the last one to do the sheepherding thing, to be a weaver, and to have a tie to this. My great-grandma did that prior to him because she's the only one of her eight siblings who didn't go to school. Her parents exempted her to be this herbalist-sheepherder-weaver person. And now I'm in a position where I'm the torchbearer. I didn't think of it that way until I was asked the question, what do you think is next? I don't think anyone knows. I don't see myself as the face of anything. I am a placeholder and a stepping stone in a long history that's going to keep going. So, whatever the future looks like, it's going to be different. And it's going to make sense to the people who are living their lives in that way.

It's funny seeing the older generation look at my work, because they understand and their question is not, why are you the way that you are? It's more, why are you choosing to talk in this way? Why are you continuing the conversation? It's a question mark, not a period. I think that relates to something that I find people are fixated on when it comes to categorizing Indigenous and Native art more generally. It's about this relationship between historical and contemporary—it's this binary. And it feels unnecessarily forced because it doesn't seem that it's experienced in that way. It's more of a continuum.

HWJ: In your own work and your own life, where are you finding inspiration right now?

TT: That's the funny part of being in your twenties. Everything is overly dramatic, and it seems like everything is pressing. I had a really, really shitty winter. I had a lot of growing pains and a lot of learning opportunities. Great, felt awful. But it needed to happen, and it's a conversation that I'm really proud to have and to have my work be a vehicle for.

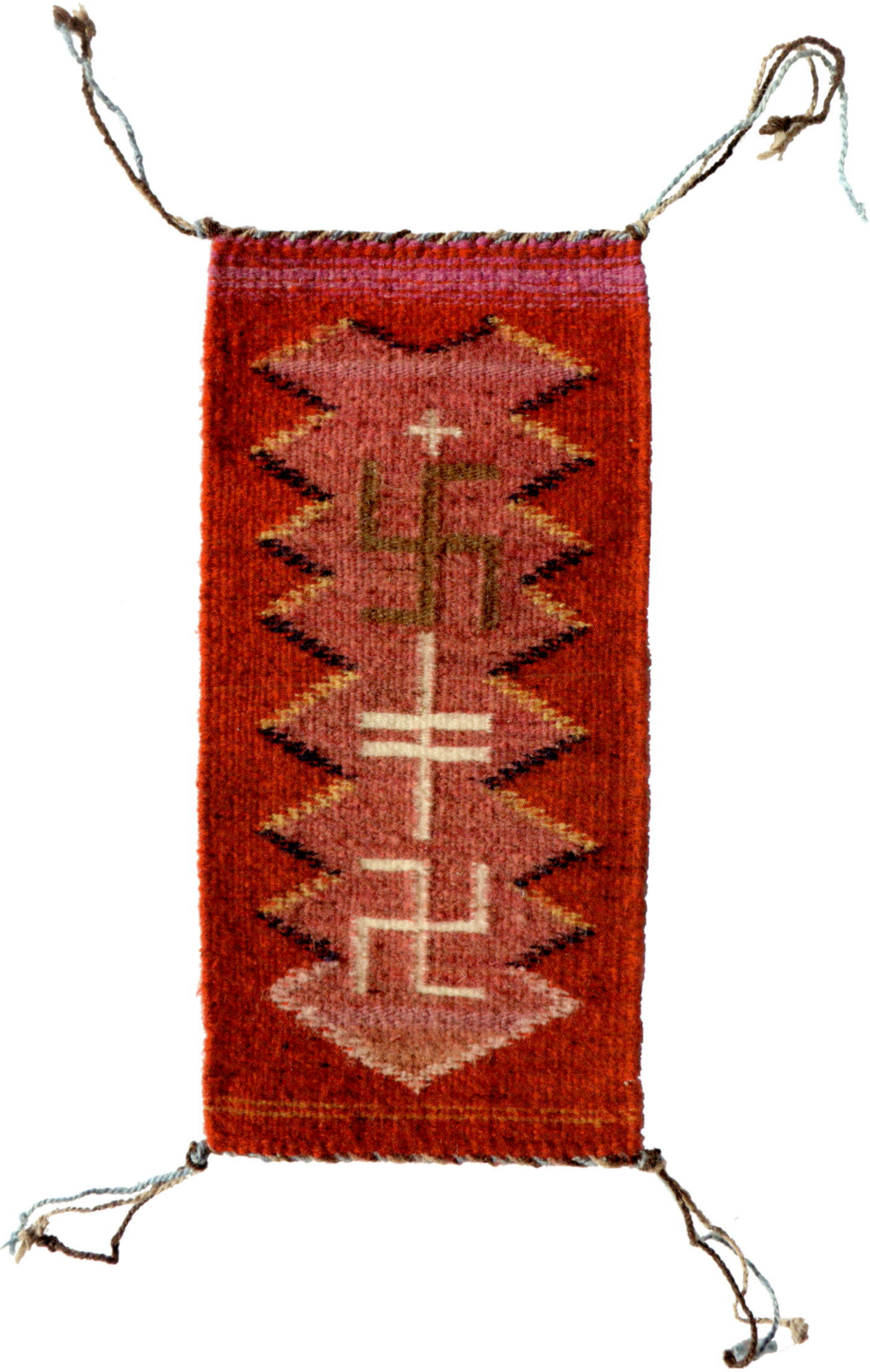

A Bird's Eye View, 2021. Tyrrell Tapaha (Diné, b. 2001). Handspun vegetal-dyed Navajo-Churro wool. 15 ¾ × 9 ¾ inches. Private collection. Photograph by Dawson Peters. Courtesy of Tyrrell Tapaha.

So in being frazzled this winter, I realized I was just paying attention to the worldly things, like boys, finances, whatever it may be. But I already know what makes me happy. I am a firm believer that the soul knows what it wants. And I can list that on my hand: *sheep, walking, weaving*. And I know that whatever has blessed my life has stemmed from those three things. No matter what I do, that's always going to be the right answer.

It's really funny talking to creators because we'll talk about all this fluff in our lives. And I always like to be the smart ass, and be like, we already know the right answer! Go back to your work. It doesn't always feel great in the moment, which makes sense. But that's been my best tool that has gotten me as far as I am. I think people look at it more as a work ethic kind of conversation, but I realized that it's just, I know what I want, and I know how to get it. And it'd be a disservice if I didn't.

HWJ: I think it's really powerful to be able to name those things. Sometimes it's so hard to do the things that we know we can do to help ourselves. But you can always lean on those things and allow your practice to be that continuum.

TT: Yeah, I am the conversation, and it flows through me. It's always going to be happening. I keep referring to myself today, in particular, as being this ball of feeling, and that's something that I learned a lot about this winter—that I need to appropriately dose where I put my time and energy. I love that my works are as intimate and passionate as they are, but they eat away at me because I give so much of myself to them. And one, I can't do that anymore, for the sake of it's not sustainable, but two, it raises the question of where did I come from, where am I now, and where am I going? Knowing that I have those three pillars that make my existence what it is, the answer seems a lot easier. I have played with my humanity enough, in my short time on this earth, that I can see where my time needs to be put. It aches, and I don't like it.

But something that really resonated with me comes from having Roy Kady in my life [see pages 116, 117]. He's my granduncle, and our usual emotional expression, especially with older Navajos, is very much like talking to a wall. And so he's never really told me to my face that he's proud of me or that he is impressed with my work. He'll always tell someone behind me, or whatever it may be, and they come back and they're like, "Wow, your grandpa's so proud of you!" One of these times he had some visitors up at the mountain, just evening-time story sharing. He referenced me in this story, and someone asked him the question, how and why are you living this life? And he kind of gave a pause and was like, "You know, I think about when I see Tyrrell sitting in the corral. I think about my time at his age, the world was opening up to me, everything was accessible, and I could go any route." And Roy would spend his evenings in the corral with the sheep, crying because he knows that he wants to be somewhere else. And he *could* be somewhere else and that would be wonderful, but he knows that he needs to be where he is right now. He wasn't explicitly talking to me, but the fact that I could feel what he was feeling, and see that within my life, really resonated with me. It was one of my first affirming statements of, like, I know what I need to be doing.

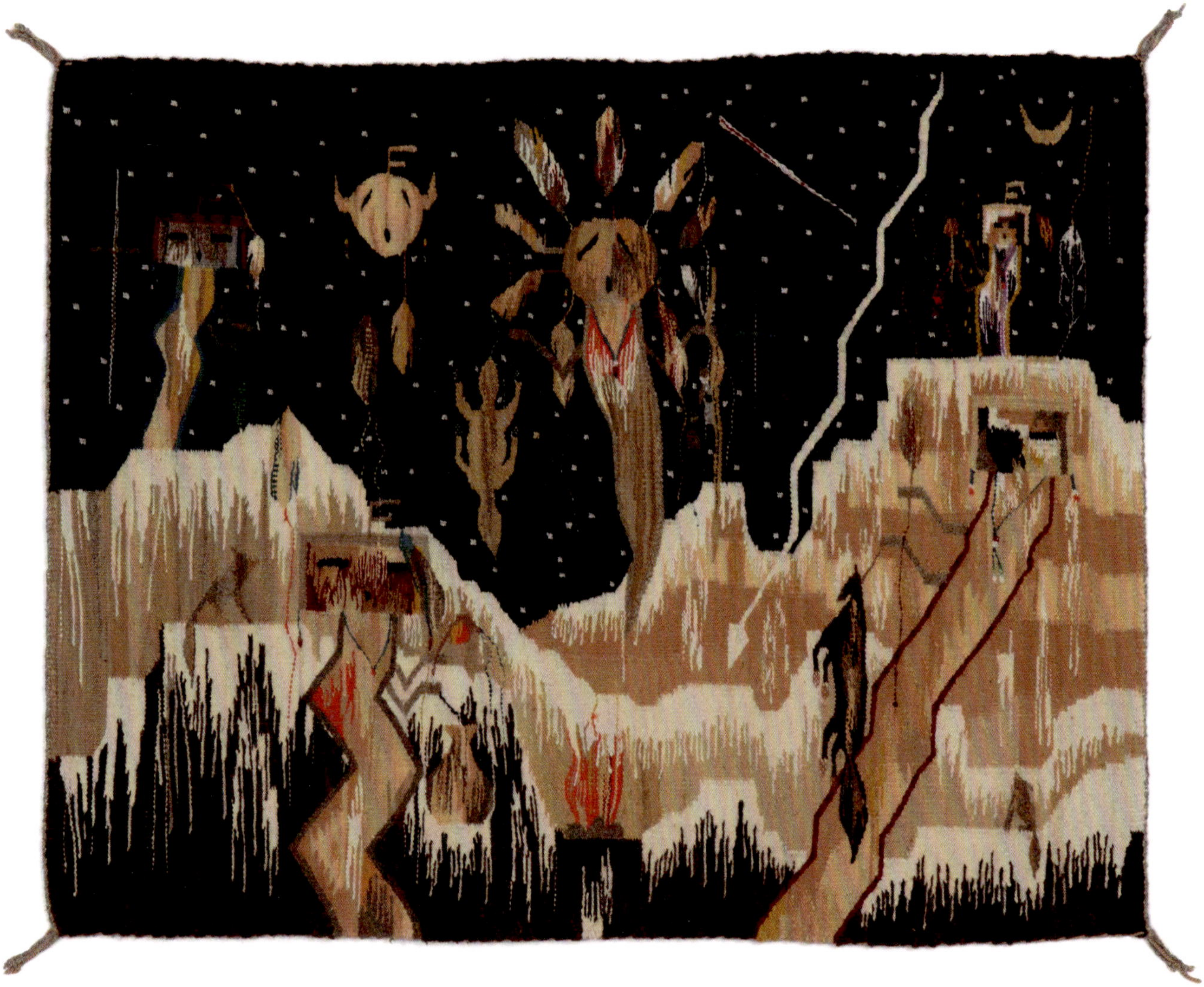

Winter Scene, c. 2010. Titus Steiner Cody (Diné). Wool, natural dyes. 30 × 40 inches. Museum of International Folk Art, gift of Reba and Dave Williams, A.2022.8.1. Photograph by Addison Doty.

Navajo weaving and pop culture have always interacted with each other. Yet an outside viewer to Diné culture often doesn't understand this context, which leads to the undervaluing of contemporary works. I greatly admire our community of contemporary weavers because we all have our own fields of expertise and backgrounds to contribute to the conversation.

Steiner Cody is one of those artists whose works absolutely blow me away. His use of texture, attention to detail, landscape imagery, and portrayal of our Diyin Dine'é (Holy People) is so refreshing and inspiring to see.

—TT

You know, as a maker, I'm a coper. Not a solver. And this winter, I was so excited about this house project. I was like, man, that's my coping. If I can build a house and make a home for myself, it's better than being sad about a person. I know that if I follow through with this house, this house will exist way longer than I will. I know that this means something because my great-grandma's house that they built—my great-great-grandparents' house—is right there, as evidence for that.

HWJ: Could you talk about where you're from?

TT: Where I say I'm from when I introduced myself was Goat Springs, Arizona. That was where my great-grandma moved to after she was married. But prior to that, the era that her parents were around, and when she was young, there was movement everywhere. This was the heyday of traders, post–Long Walk, so we had a lot of settlements. We had maybe six or so settlements on Utah side, Arizona side, on top of the mountain, and across the river on the Utah side. But this place that I'm talking about, Yellow Point Rock on the Utah side, that area is one of our original homesteads and that's our winter camp. My great-great-grandpa used to be a boat person for Hatch Trading Company just across the river, maybe a few miles away. So he had a big old raft and would just go back and forth on the river. And that's where they came from. Like I said, after my great-grandma got married, she moved to the Goat Springs side, closer to Teec [Teec Nos Pos], the actual community, and closer to the mountain [Carrizo Mountain]. At least my exposure to this life has always been there. When I think about home, I think about my great-grandma's home. That's where I'm from. It's a strong tie to my mom's side of the family. So, it's Goat Springs, Arizona, Oak Springs, New Mexico, and then I went to school in Kirtland, New Mexico. And my dad is all Utah Navajo. So my life is the Four Corners.

HWJ: Do you imagine leaving?

TT: Yes. I mean, I'd like to. I brought up that Roy Kady story of longing for a place because I could live in Brooklyn and be really comfortable and very happy. But I know as much as I want that, and can have that, it doesn't serve me right now. So yeah, I live everywhere. I've been going with this weird sheepherding schedule and seasonal flow of working, teaching, and exhibiting throughout the summer. And then in the wintertime I spend it weaving and hunkered down somewhere. In the past it's been Flagstaff and central Utah. Herding in the winter occasionally. But I want to keep working like this until this house is finished. I'll feel more free because I'll have a place of my own to come back to. So that's how I'm choosing to look at where my place is with my work—it's the beauty of nomadic weaving. You can live anywhere. It's atrocious what my vehicle looks like—yarn everywhere, spindles—I buckle my spinning wheel into the seat. When I was carrying my Heard piece [for the annual Heard Museum Guild Indian Fair and Market], it was like an eight-footer weaving as my armrest as I'm flying down the 40. But that's what I think my life will look like—movement, documentation, and sheep. Nomadic, like my ancestors.

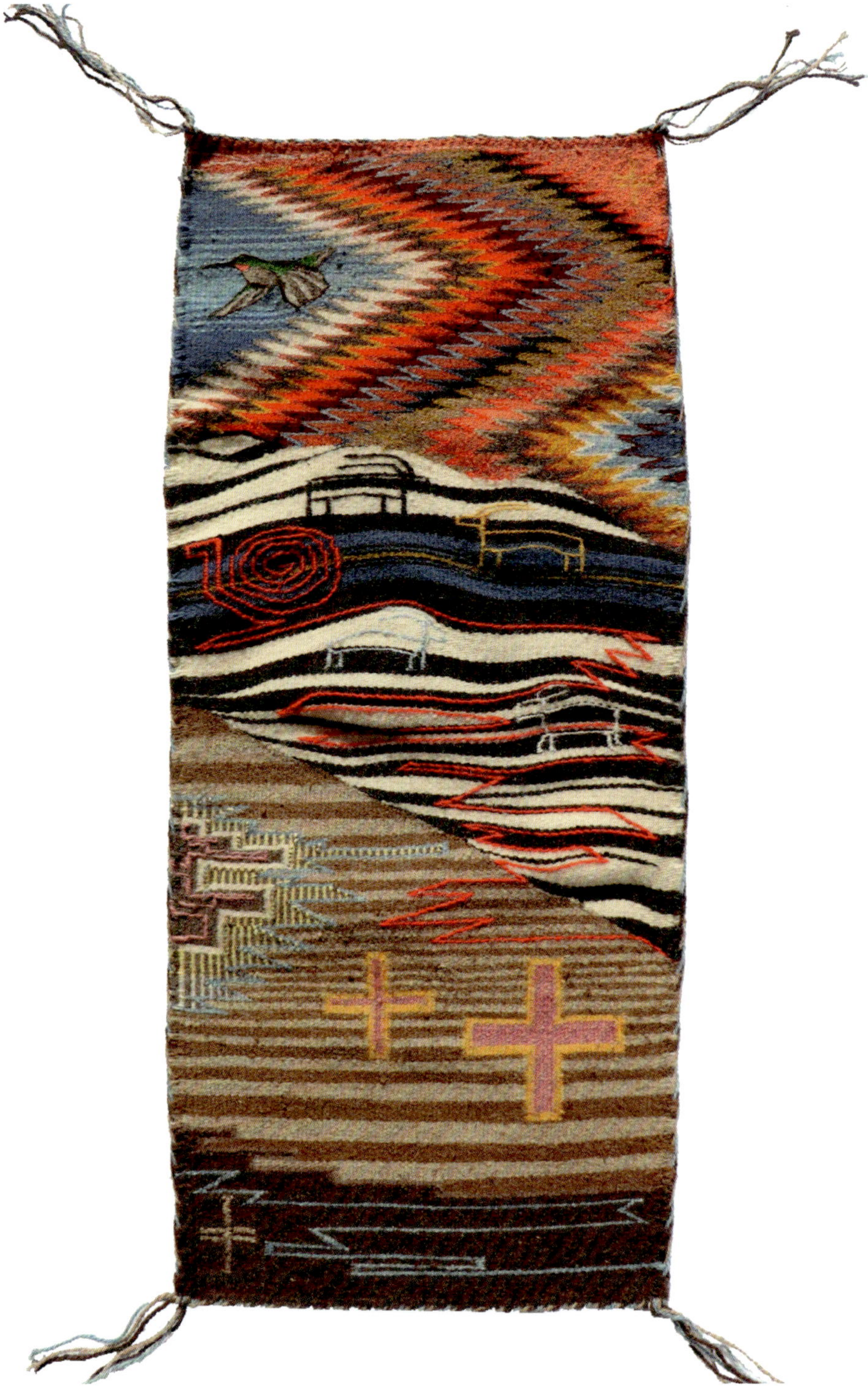

Carrizo Mountain Dance, 2021. Tyrrell Tapaha (Diné, b. 2001). Handspun and commercial vegetal-dyed Navajo-Churro wool. 35 ½ × 15 ¾ inches. Private collection. Photograph by Dawson Peters. Courtesy of Tyrrell Tapaha.

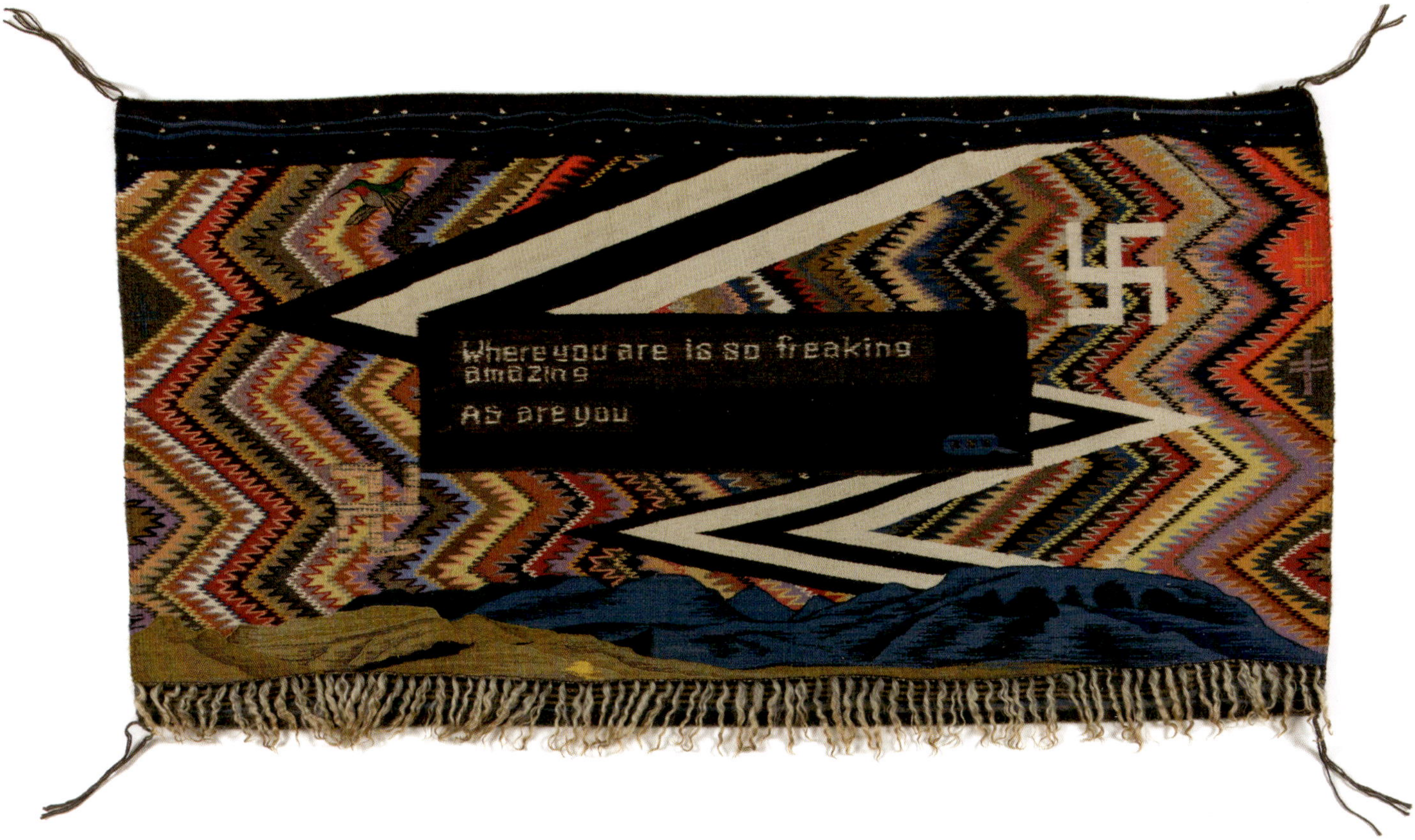

Diné Rhapsody, 2023. Tyrrell Tapaha (Diné, b. 2001). Handspun and commercial vegetal-dyed Navajo-Churro, mohair, and alpaca wool. 38 × 66 inches. Gochman Family Collection, New York. Photograph by Alon Koppel. Courtesy of Tyrrell Tapaha.

HWJ: Before we end, I wanted to give you an opportunity to talk about some of your current or forthcoming projects.

TT: I think they're all in the same vein of work. In some sense, I keep labeling it as a series, but I feel like series are always done in one set flow or go, and I'm a very skewed person on that plane. *I want people to see what I see*. I feel like so much of the pain, discomfort, and joy that I've felt in my life is people wanting to express and to share that with me. I don't mean to toot my own horn, but the life I live is so beautiful, and beauty taking so many different shapes. Navajo weaving is really nitty and gritty. It's really atrocious at times, and it's plagued with alcoholism, substance abuse, domestic violence. I have all of that in my family, and it runs through my veins, and it terrifies me. But that's the imagery that I think of when I think of home, and when I think about the livelihood that I have right now, that's what it's come from. So this work that I'm wanting to do in the future, as well as what I'm working on now, is taking a deeper look at what that is. I want to do loom diagrams and have projections of the 35mm photographs that I've taken while sheepherding and just have that projected on this in-progress blank weaving. I print and paint on a lot of hides that I tan, so having that as part of the installation, you know, physical, tangible ephemera that is tied to me and to

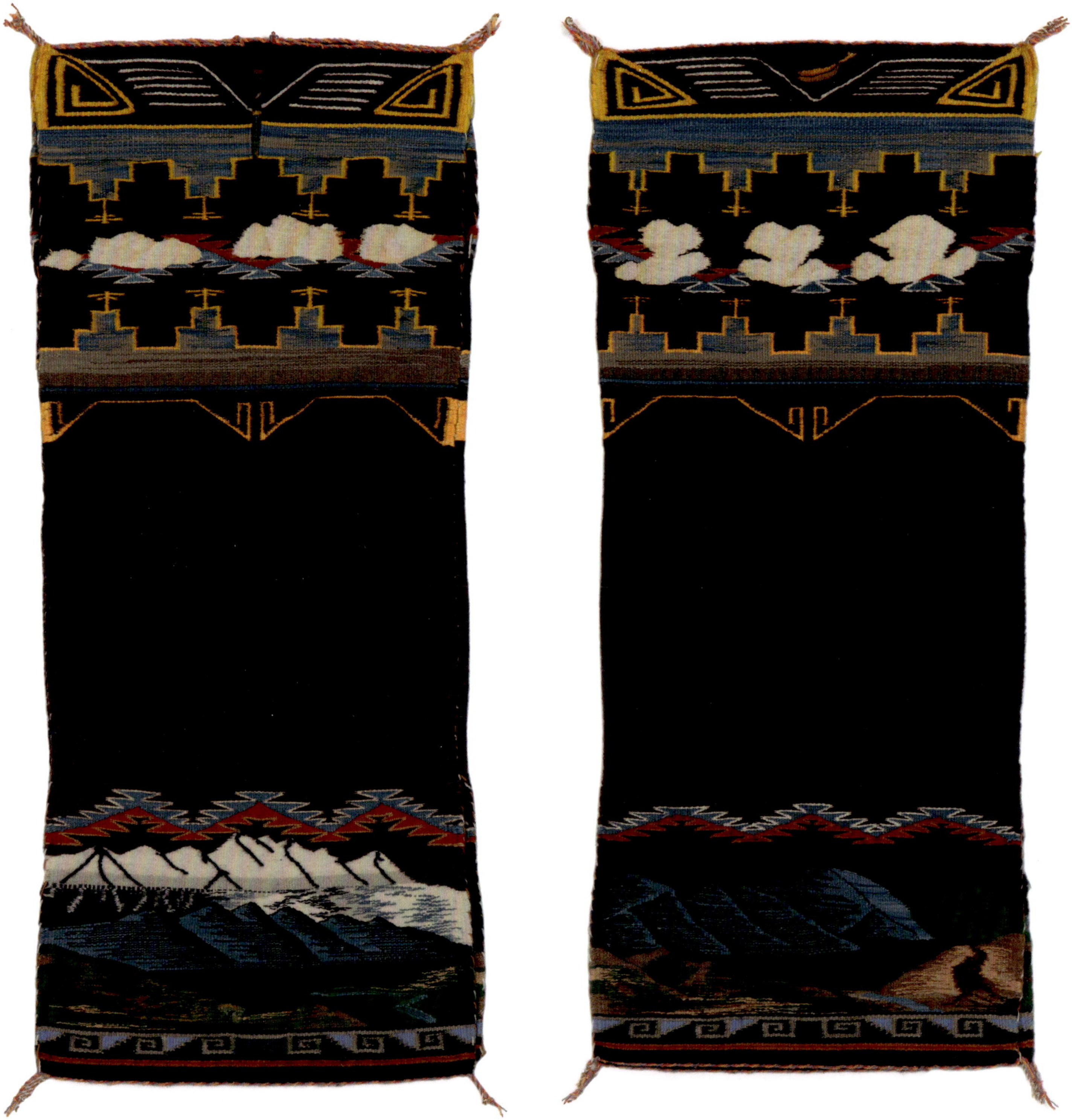

OPPOSITE

Child of the Natural World, 2020. Tyrrell Tapaha (Diné, b. 2001). Two-panel dress, front (left) and back (right). Handspun and commercial and vegetal-dyed Navajo-Churro, mohair, and merino wool, and silk. Each panel: 58 × 28 inches. Collection of the artist. Photograph by Addison Doty.

This two-panel dress was inspired by the beautiful San Pete Valley in Utah, which has become a home away from home. This dress is supposed to be viewed on an east-west axis, with the mountain scene in the front—Mt. Nebo—facing the west rim of the valley. The back panel faces east and depicts the Wasatch Plateau on the eastern half of the valley. The design follows a theme of the natural world present in our lives—the break and coexistence between Mother Earth and Father Sky. The bottom of the dress represents the colors and warmth of our Mother and her expansiveness. The top represents the free and near-electric energy of Father Sky. I was blessed to weave most of this project within the bounds of San Pete Valley. I wanted to commemorate that chapter in my life and bring those blessings wherever the dress goes.

—TT

a place. All this is to say, fine tuning the imagery of what it means to be a sheepherder is what I'm wanting to work on in the near future. It's romanticized out the wazoo, but it's the one thing no one knows the imagery of.

HWJ: It seems so specific to your own lived experience.

TT: Yeah, I went from book-thumping college student to docking lamb tails at five in the morning with my cup of coffee, you know. All within the same month. So, I want to talk about that. It's so often referred to, but I want to be a person who contributes to that conversation.

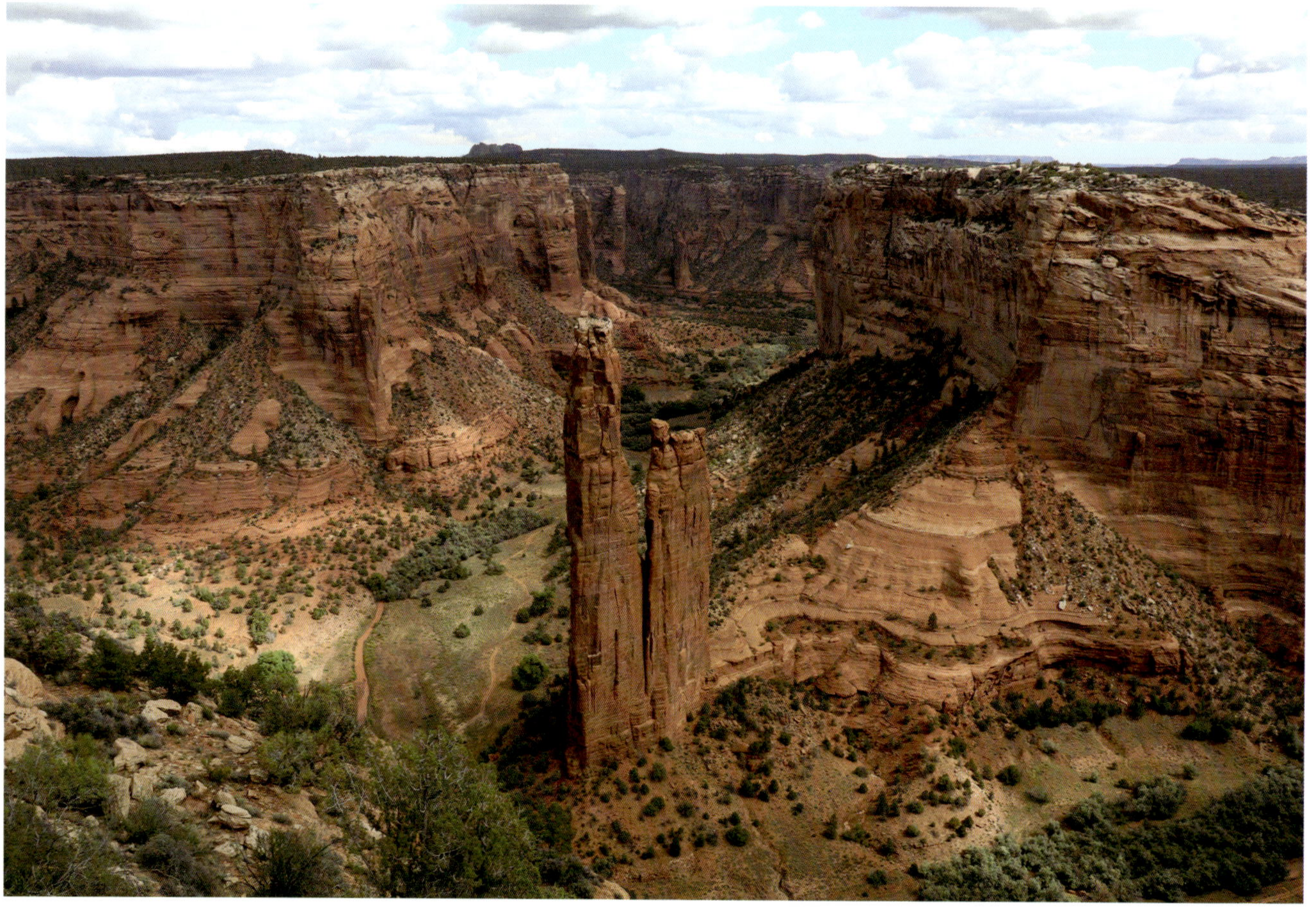

Spider Rock (Tséyi'—Canyon de Chelly, Arizona), 2021. Rapheal Begay (Diné, b. 1991). Courtesy of the artist.

As forms of visual storytelling, Diné weaving and photography are created in collaboration with one's surroundings. Diné Bikéyah is not only our home but is also a source of inspiration for design, color, and connection to the past, present, and future. Our reciprocal relationship to land, language, and memory reflects our creativity and resilience as five-fingered beings.

—RAPHEAL BEGAY

8 Diné Weavings

Bringing Light to Diné Thought and Practice

JENNIFER NEZ DENETDALE

In our origin stories, the deity Spider Woman offered weaving and its tools to the Diné, and Spider Woman's teachings have proven resilient in the face of vast life changes for the people. Generations of weavers and fiber artists have been endowed with her gift, ensuring that our people retain—through weaving—the means to guard against hunger and other difficulties. But a knowledge of Diné history is crucial to appreciating the continuity of weaving.

As a Diné woman and scholar whose experience with our textiles has been limited to research and observations, I am able to imagine the world of our ancestors through my appreciation of the weavings showcased in this volume and to participate simultaneously in the cultural revitalization of this art form. By juxtaposing historic and contemporary textiles with photography and other media, the weavers, fiber artists, and curators of this project demonstrate a versatility in their vision as they move across media. *Horizons* also draws attention to the continuity of oral traditions about weaving from the past to the present, reminding us of the vitality of the wisdom of our Diné ancestors. I am reminded especially of my own grandmother, my late mother's mother, whose maiden name was Louise Manuelito. Louise was the last weaver in our extended kin network. In our possession as a family, we have but one textile made by Louise. I keep it carefully wrapped, for it reminds my family of our grandmothers whose memories live on.

Over twenty years ago, Diné language educator Roseann Willink with Paul Zolbrod brought Navajo weavers to the Laboratory of Anthropology in Santa Fe and shared the textile collection with them. The weavers' stories were published in *Weaving a World: Textiles and the Navajo Way of Seeing*.[1] They offered many narratives in relation to the textiles that brought fresh vision to the collection and, importantly, pointed to the textiles as holding an element of the sacred. One of the items featured in that book is

“Wearing blanket with spider design” (see page xiv). The weavers examined the textile and connected it to a ceremonial piece used in the now-extinct Spiderway ceremony and associated with the Spider People of the Lower World in Diné creation stories. It is the Spider People who brought the loom from one of the lower worlds as the beings moved upward through the worlds to escape the flood, emerging into the present world.[2] Seeing this piece in *Horizons* reminded me of the stories shared by these weavers, reinvigorating an appreciation for the traditional knowledge that they possess.

As weaver Wesley Thomas writes, “My matrilineal and patrilineal grandfathers were instrumental in the construction of my weaving loom and some of my tools . . . They taught me how Spider Woman and Spider Man constructed the first loom in the third underworld, as well as many other weaving stories.”[3] The teachings and the tools—the loom, combs, battens, and warp strings—are our Mothers; they provide sustenance, love, and compassion. Women weavers have always been held in high esteem because of their knowledge and practice. They hold authoritative roles in our society and are seen as Mothers who nurture our people. As I read Thomas’s words, I am reminded of my own grandmother, of whom I have only faint images because I was young when she died, and how she must have relied on her weaving talents for the welfare of her family.

In this book, contemporary weavers engage once again with these textiles and bring forth fresh remembrances of our ancestors. They reflect on living according to our philosophy of Sá ah naagaaghą́í bik’eh hózhóón—meaning that our ancestors endeavored to walk on the Path of Beauty to Old Age. The array of textiles created in the nineteenth century, prior to American occupation of Diné Bikéyah, and into the early reservation period of the mid-to-late nineteenth century, speak to an enduring tradition of weaving. Wearing blankets and biil, the traditional dress worn by Diné women, remind us that textiles were once created largely for our own use. While wearing blankets became coveted throughout the Southwest and into the Plains region by other Indigenous peoples, Diné also utilized and wore them.

The colonial conditions of life under American occupation often sought to sever Diné knowledge and practices around weaving. A watershed moment in our history is American claims to Diné Bikéyah, beginning in the mid-nineteenth century and continuing into the present. This history has led to the loss of our knowledge around weaving and simultaneously the determination of our relatives to learn and relearn the ancestral art of weaving. The attempts to sever Diné connections to the past are resisted when we remember the cultural teachings that are part of the process of creating textiles. This book is part of that resistance, reinforcing a determination to remember the value of teachings embedded in Diné textiles and other forms of culture.

Beginning in the early reservation era, from 1868 and into the early 1900s, trade replaced Navajo reliance on their own manufactured material culture. It also fed their need for items such as canned peaches, coffee, potatoes, and shoes, which they received in return for Diné products such as textiles and livestock. Trade blankets

OPPOSITE
Second Phase Chief blanket, 1850–1865. Artist once known (Diné). Handspun wool, indigo dye, bayeta, commercial wool yarn. 38 × 50 inches. Museum of Indian Arts and Culture/Laboratory of Anthropology, gift of Mrs. Philip B. Stewart, 9129/12. Photograph by Addison Doty.

This weaving displays the conventional design elements of a Second Phase Chief blanket, but its unique color palette reflects the weaver’s creative use of indigo dye. As one of four sacred colors in Diné culture, dootł’izh (blue) represents the directional color of the sky during the day and evokes the horizon line. The layered striation visible within the light blue indigo bands, typically derived from natural (undyed) white yarn, is reminiscent of cirrostratus clouds that indicate advancing precipitation. The weaver’s intentional use of alternating light and dark bands suggests the duality present in day and night. In creating this balanced composition, the weaver may have been inspired by the natural elements found above, below, and within the horizon line.

—RAPHEAL BEGAY AND HADLEY WELCH JENSEN

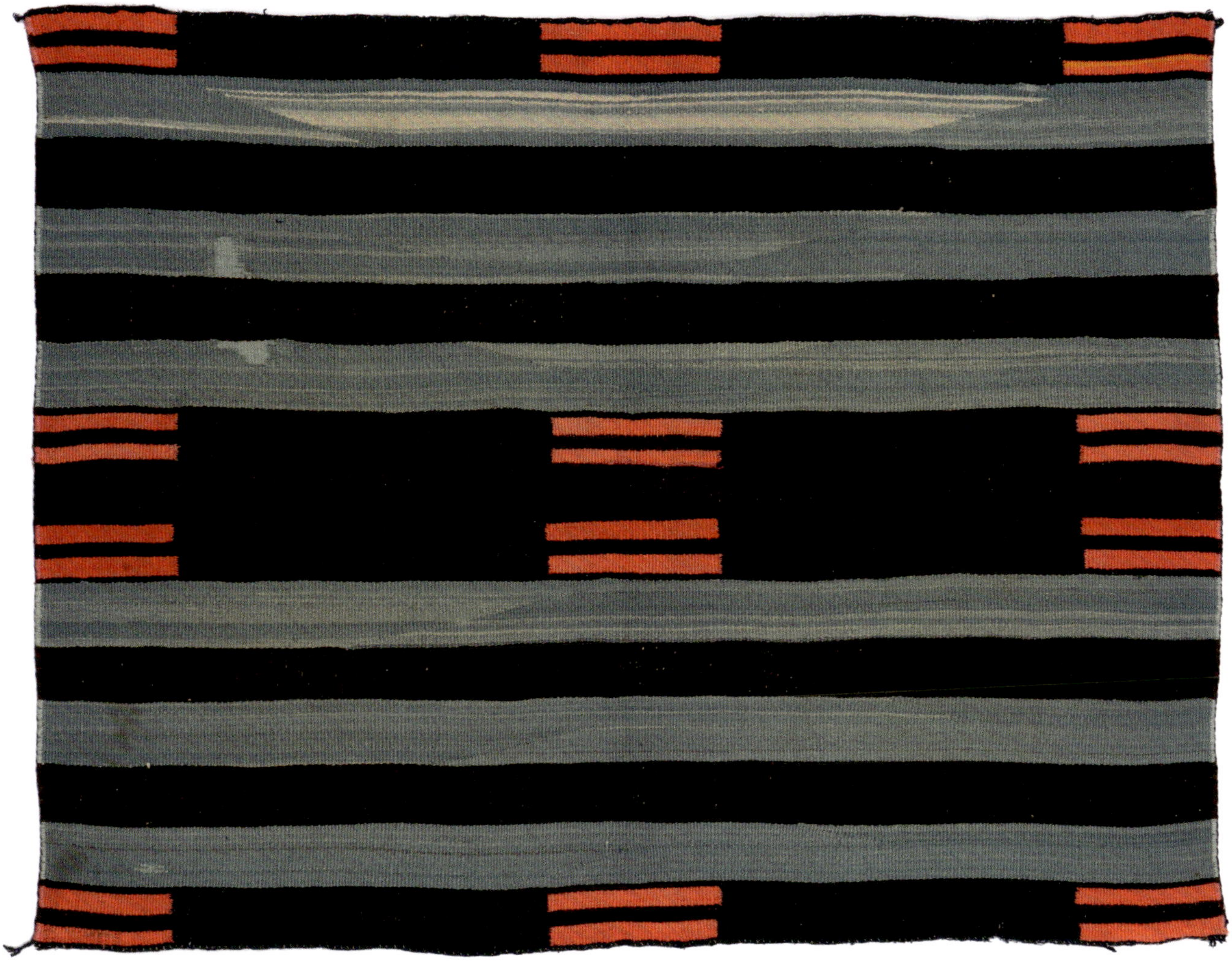

like Pendletons began to replace Diné-made blankets for our own use. Even today, in border towns like Gallup, New Mexico, that dot the boundaries of the Navajo Nation, thousands of Diné flood into stores, restaurants, and pawn shops each weekend to obtain the most basic of necessities as the Navajo Nation still struggles to establish a viable infrastructure. In a store that boasts a long relationship with its Diné customers, Diné wait patiently to speak to the clerks standing behind long wooden counters reminiscent of a romanticized bygone era of trading posts. The walls are decorated with textiles of all sizes and jewelry that Diné favor. Barbara Teller Ornelas's rug (see page 114), with its intricacies in shades of beiges and browns, and its serrated diamonds, triangles, and straight lines, reminds us of the era in which textile experts and scholars tell us that traders influenced weaving styles and patterns.

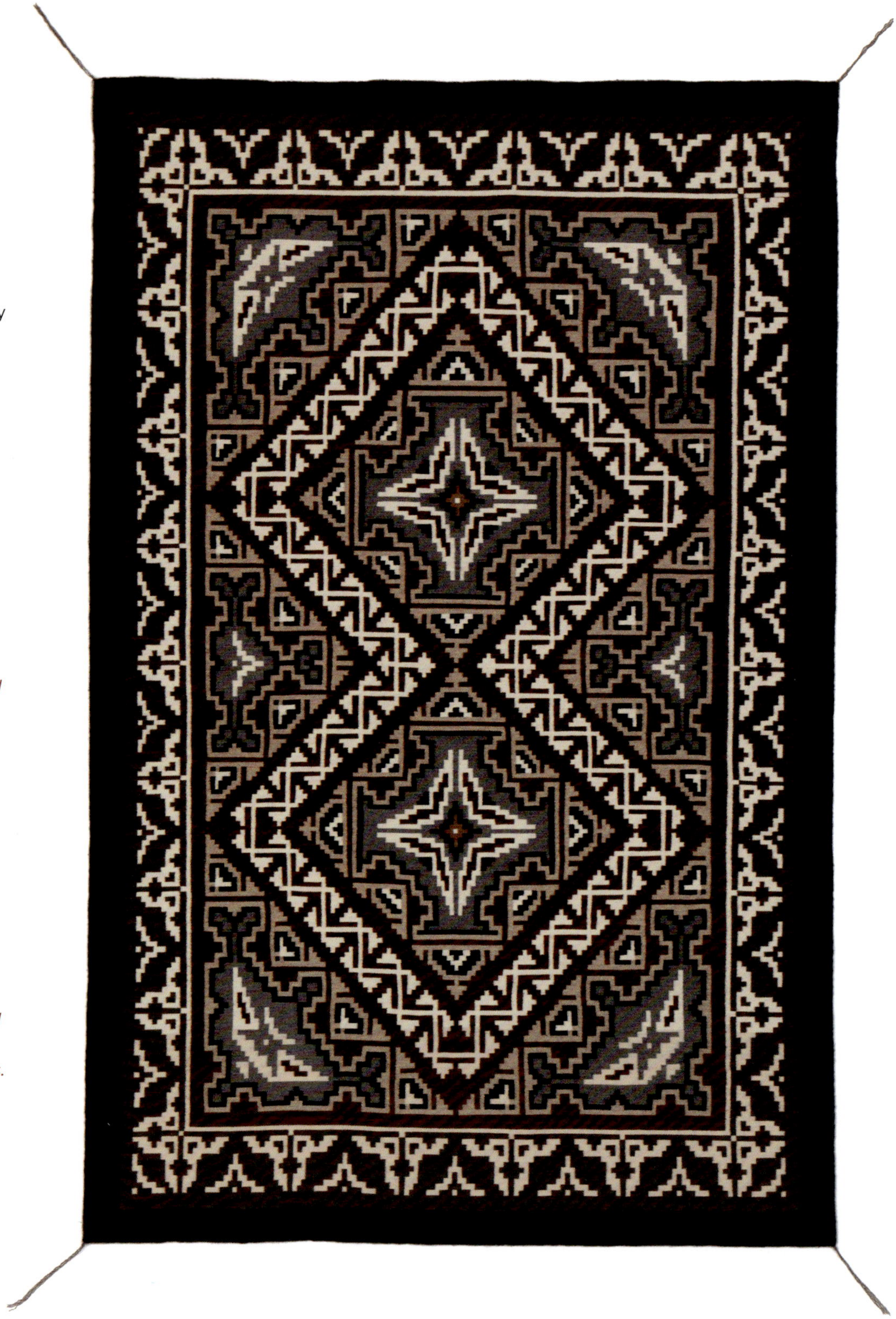

Rug, 1996. Barbara Teller Ornelas (Diné, b. 1954). Handspun, hand-carded warps and naturally blended merino wool from Aunt Margaret Yazzie's sheep. 72 × 48 inches. Heard Museum Collection, Santa Fe Collection of Navajo Rugs, donated by Dr. Charles and Linda Rimmer, 4650-31. Photograph by Addison Doty.

This magnificent Two Grey Hills weaving was made by my sister, Barbara Teller Ornelas. She shares that "our family's commitment to preparing our own wool, including selvage cords and wool warp, is a standard that was set by our elders." When Barbara was small and sitting at the loom that her paternal grandmother, Nellie Peshlakai Teller, set up for her, her grandmother would watch her weave and say, "You were born to be a weaver. I had a dream that you will travel the world and tell people about our work."

This rug features design elements passed down from the weavers in our family—our grandmother Susie Tom, mother Ruth Teller, aunt Margaret Yazzie, and sister Rosann Lee, showing our intergenerational links. As Barbara says, "My work, my ideas, my processes, and my weaving materials are ever evolving but stay true to the standards set by my elders. I take the responsibility of carrying on our family's tradition by teaching my [own] family and mentoring others to help preserve this cultural legacy."

—LYNDA TELLER PETE

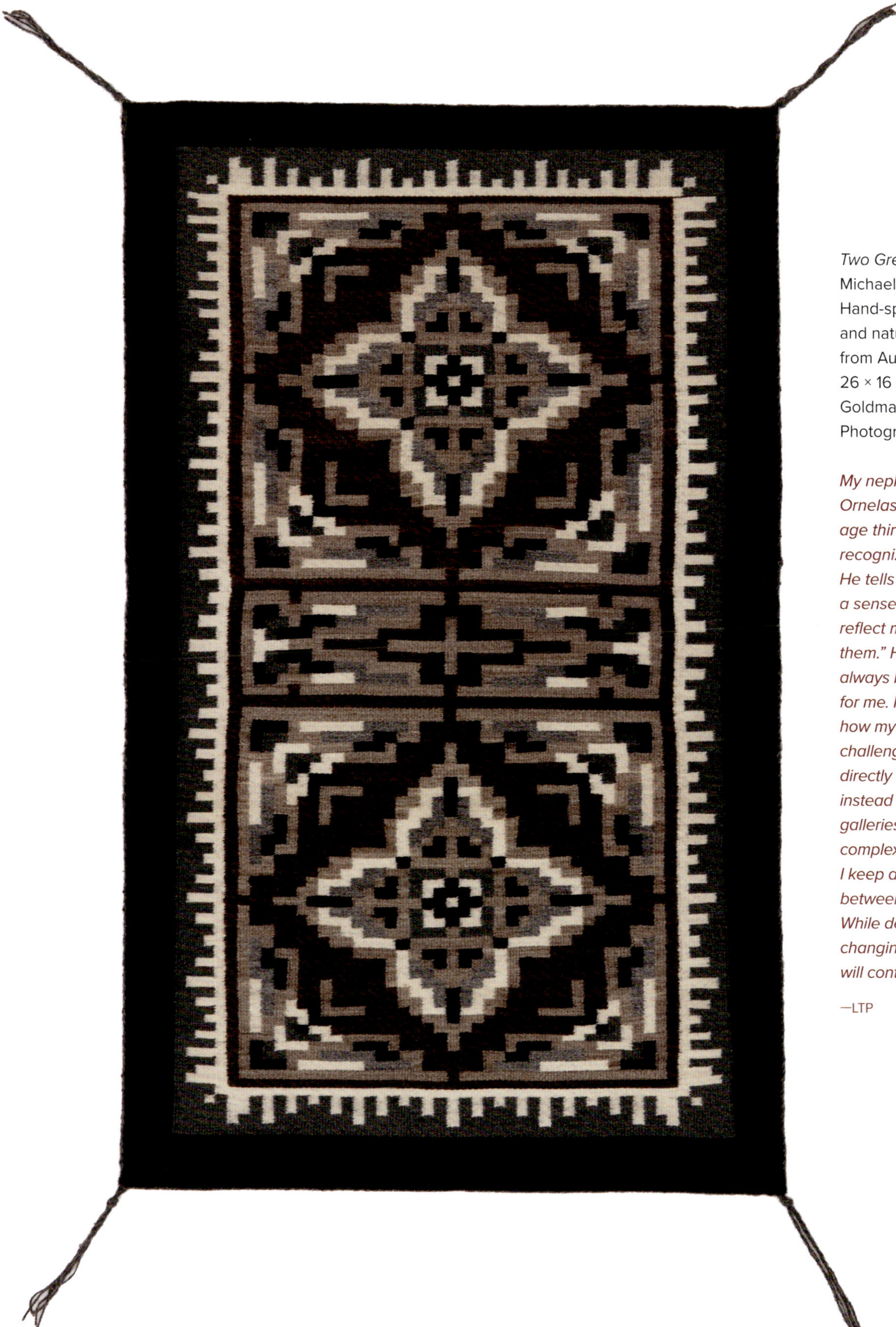

Two Grey Hills Tapestry, 2015.
Michael Teller Ornelas (Diné, b. 1985). Hand-spun, hand-carded warps and naturally blended merino wool from Aunt Margaret Yazzie's sheep. 26 × 16 inches. Collection of Peter Goldman and Beverly Werber. Photograph by Addison Doty.

My nephew Michael Teller Ornelas has been weaving since age thirteen and is now widely recognized for his tapestry weavings. He tells us that "Weaving gives me a sense of balance in life. My pieces reflect my life at the time I create them." He continues, "Weaving has always been about breaking barriers for me. I grew up with stories about how my mom [Barbara Teller Ornelas] challenged the status quo, selling directly to customers and museums instead of going through dealers and galleries. My focus is more on the complexity of my designs. How do I keep a good rhythm and balance between all the elements of the rug? While designs have always been changing, the challenges of weaving will continue to connect us."

—LTP

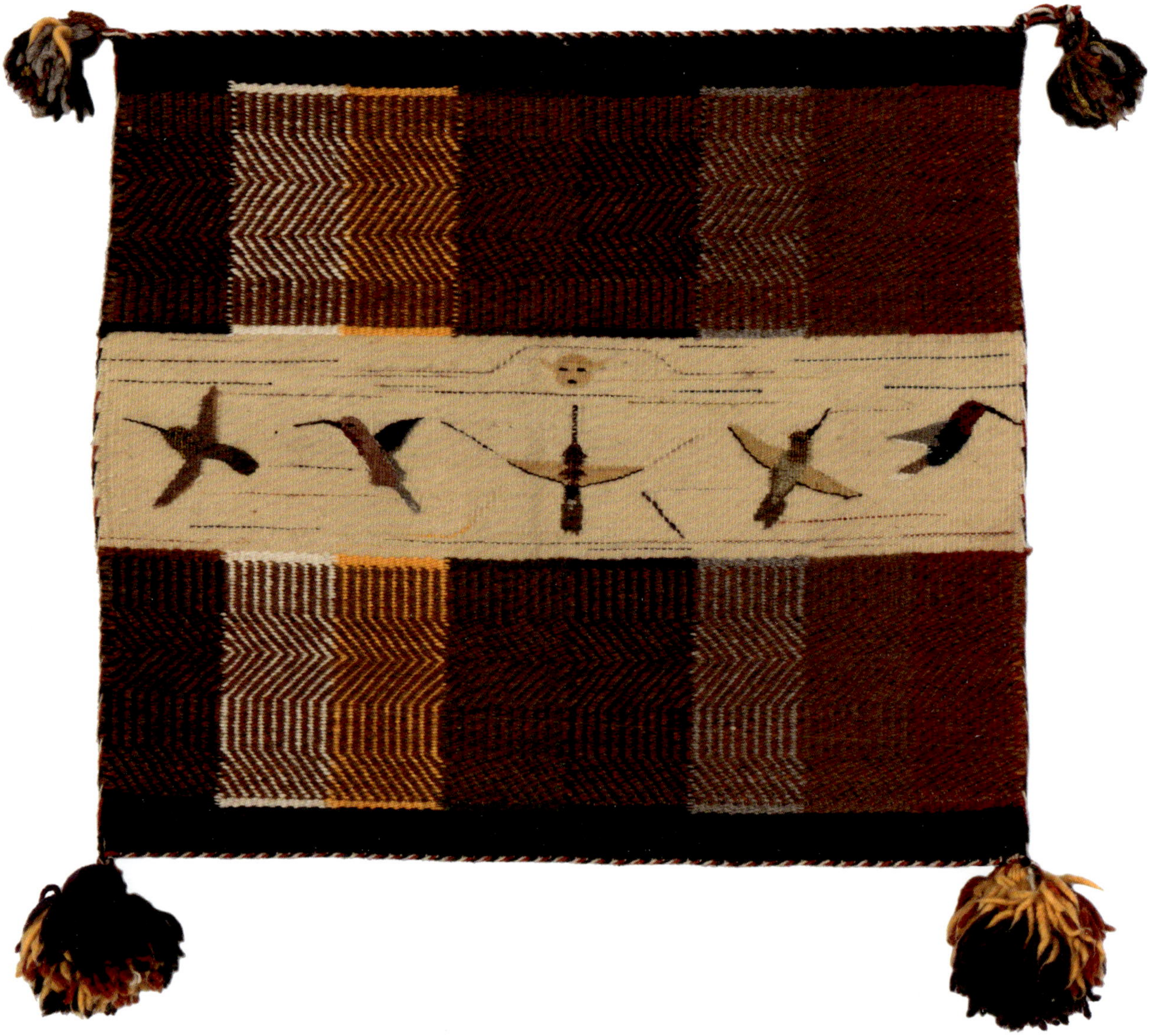

Northern Lights, 2012. Roy Kady (Diné, b. 1966). Saddle blanket. Vegetal-dyed Navajo-Churro wool, cotton thread, tinsel. 37 × 40 inches. Museum of Indian Arts and Culture/Laboratory of Anthropology, Museum purchase, 58345/12A. Photograph by Addison Doty.

Intention is a prerequisite for creation. We give ourselves to our work and it gives itself to us. Particularly with utilitarian ware, the end product is alive and is meant to protect the owner or wearer.

From a technical perspective, this piece showcases a feat of creative innovation. The composition of this work is an intimate glimpse into the potency of what this medium is capable of. Capturing a story, a place, a people, and a family legacy into tangible form.

We believe that everyone and everything strives for beauty. Even our horses want to wear beautiful things. I'd like to think that this saddle blanket is some horse's Louis Vuitton.

—TYRRELL TAPAHA

According to history, once the Navajo leadership limited extortionist interest rates for pawn, the traders moved into towns outside the borders of the Navajo Nation and continued their often-exploitative practices. Today's traders rely on the pawn industry to make a profit; they cater to art markets and to tourists seeking high-end Indian jewelry. This history is part of a structure that underlies the ongoing determination to reclaim weaving as integral to Diné life.

Textiles are about the process of remaking Diné life. The revival of weaving elicits memories of livestock reduction and our relationship to sheep, including activities such as sheep raising and shearing, wool spinning and dyeing, buying and selling yarn, and creating art using that wool. Diné teachings associated with sheep and livestock are vibrant with life, and the fiber artists featured in *Horizons* demonstrate the ongoing cultural work of weaving.

Roy Kady has been part of the efforts to return the resilient Navajo-Churro sheep, whose wool weavers prized, to Navajoland. The livestock reduction era of the 1930s and '40s, and subsequent federal government laws and policies mandated by US Indian Commissioner John Collier, still reverberate throughout our homeland. Families and their kin networks resisted the policies that sought to reduce livestock by fifty percent. The government's devastating mandates also included the replacement of the prized Navajo-Churro sheep with Merino and Rambouillet breeds, which were not as hardy as the churro.

Kady has written about the roots of his connection to the place that he and other weavers, as well as their relatives and ancestors, have inhabited for generations. Kady writes, "Dibé éí binahj i' kéyah bee nidziil í, binahji' kéyah hól ó, éí binahj i'": "The land is strong because of the sheep, the sheep are the reason we have land, because of the land and the sheep."[4] Kady's saddle blankets are renowned and speak to the ongoing efforts to reclaim our weavers' creations for our own use. His *Northern Lights* saddle blanket evokes a whimsical air with its hummingbirds set against a background of subtle shades of brown, reminding us of our relationship to the natural world and other beings beyond the human.

While the wearing blanket represents a period in which weavers wove for their own families and relatives, the biil, the dress worn by women, has seen a revival among Diné in the last forty years. Worn by women and our nonbinary relatives who identify as feminine, the biil represents womanhood and its values rooted in the creation stories about female deities. As told to girls coming of age, the biil represents our most revered deity, Asdzáá Nadleehí, or Changing Woman. Today, the biil is worn for special occasions such as weddings, graduations, and pageant contests.

The weavers and artists featured in *Horizons* also demonstrate the gender diversity of our weavers, all of whom bring knowledge, talent, and skills important to the perpetuation of our Navajo Nation, communities, and kin-based networks. Weaving and fiber art is—and has always been—practiced not only by women but also by our men and nonbinary relatives. Gender is not simply a matter of biology but a way of being that enriches our kin relationships.

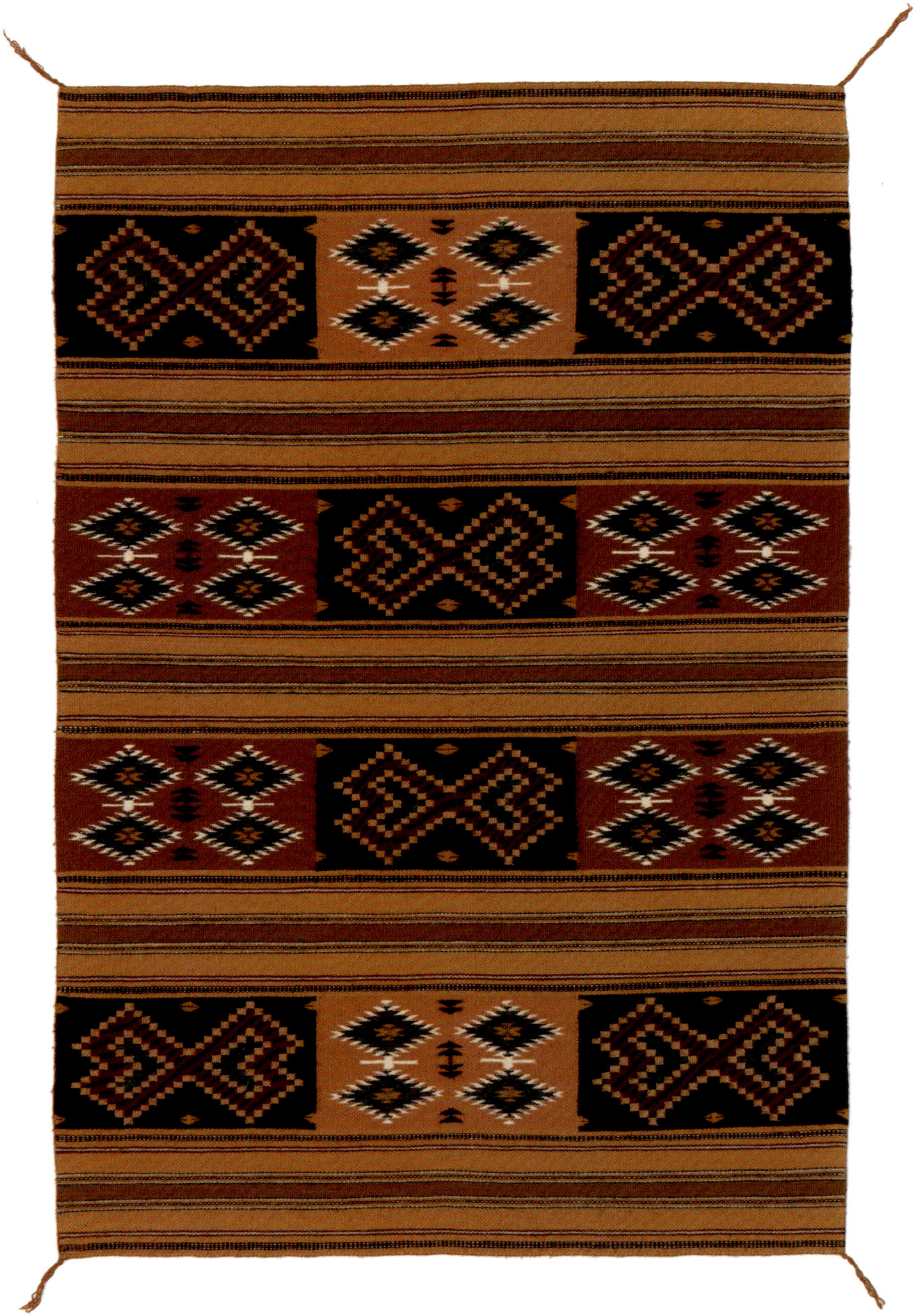

OPPOSITE
Wide Ruins rug, 1995–1998. Minnie Lee (Diné). Re-spun commercial wool yarn, tapestry weave. 49 × 34 inches. Museum of Indian Arts and Culture/ Laboratory of Anthropology, gift of Robert W. Uphaus, 56509/12. Photograph by Addison Doty.

Purchased at the Museum of Northern Arizona, this Wide Ruins rug is attributed to Diné weaver Minnie Lee. It features a selection of natural dyes and a balanced placement of design elements. Lynda Teller Pete reflected during a collections visit that viewing this piece is like "looking at a quilt." Tyrrell Tapaha noted, "It gives me a classic image of a Wide Ruins/Central Agency vibe. Due to the overall consistency of the work, it was made by a well-established weaver."

As an example of a Diné weaving from the late twentieth century, this piece also demonstrates the horizons of time visible in the Museum of Indian Arts and Culture's textile collection, particularly the wide range of periods, designs, and styles.

—HADLEY WELCH JENSEN

Such representations of gender diversity in weaving are offered by Kevin Aspaas, Rapheal Begay, Tyrrell Tapaha, and Roy Kady. Begay envisions his gift of weaving as part of his discourse as an artist utilizing photography of Diné landscape to appreciate the connection between land and weaving. His photograph of the grand Spider Rock speaks to the relationship weavers and fiber artists express in their creations (see page 110). Kady's mentorship of the coming generations of young Diné is demonstrated by his relative Tyrrell Tapaha's weavings, which reflect the importance of intergenerational knowledge. As with Kady's creations, Tapaha's vision of the meaning of the land is woven into his two-panel biil *Child of the Natural World* (see page 108). Kady, Tapaha, and Aspaas affirm the persistence of creating woven wear for our own use, reminding us that weavers' skills and talents were—and are—critical to the perpetuation of the people.

Horizons offers a unique glimpse into the Diné world, a world that Diné bring into being through thought and practice. The textiles selected from the museum's vast collection offer space to reflect on the history of Diné weaving. Considered in conversation with textiles created by contemporary weavers, they not only illuminate long-standing practices but offer hope that someday we Diné will become the target audience and will reincorporate these textiles into everyday use.

BIBLIOGRAPHY

Clahchischiligi, Sunnie R. "According to Custom." *Arizona Highways*. https://www.arizonahighways.com/index.php/article/according-custom, n.d.

Thomas, Wesley. "Shił Yóółt'ooł: Personification of Navajo Weaving." In *Woven by the Grandmothers: Nineteenth-Century Navajo Textiles from the National Museum of the American Indian*, edited by Eulalie H. Bonar. Washington, DC: Smithsonian Institution Press in association with the National Museum of the American Indian, Smithsonian Institution, 1996.

Willink, Roseann S., and Paul G. Zolbrod. *Weaving a World: Textiles and the Navajo Way of Seeing*. Santa Fe: Museum of New Mexico Press, 1996.

NOTES

1. Willink and Zolbrod, *Weaving a World*.
2. Willink and Zolbrod, *Weaving a World*, 38.
3. Thomas, "Shił Yóółt'ooł: Personification of Navajo Weaving," 35.
4. Clahchischiligi, "According to Custom."

Suggested Reading

Arthur, Claudeen, Sam Bingham, and Janet Bingham. *Between Sacred Mountains: Navajo Stories and Lessons from the Land*. Tucson: University of Arizona Press, 1984.

Belin, Esther G., Jeff Berglund, Connie A. Jacobs, and Anthony K. Webster, eds. *The Diné Reader: An Anthology of Navajo Literature*. Tucson: University of Arizona Press, 2021.

Bonar, Eulalie H. *Woven by the Grandmothers: Nineteenth-century Navajo Textiles from the National Museum of the American Indian*. Washington, DC: Smithsonian Institution Press in association with the National Museum of the American Indian, Smithsonian Institution, 1996.

Campbell, Tyrone D., and Steven Begner. *Navajo Pictorial Weaving, 1860–1950*. Atglen, PA: Schiffer Publishing, 2018.

Campbell, Tyrone, Joel Kopp, and Kate Kopp. *Navajo Pictorial Weaving, 1880–1950: Folk Art Images of Native Americans*. Albuquerque: University of New Mexico Press, 1991.

Campbell, Wade. "Na'nilkad bee na'niltin—Learning from Herding: An Ethnoarchaeological Study of Historic Pastoralism on the Navajo Nation." *Kiva* 87, no. 3 (2021): 295–315. DOI: 10.1080/00231940.2021.1893456.

Color Riot! How Color Changed Navajo Textiles. Exhibition catalogue. Phoenix, AZ: Heard Museum, 2019.

Denetdale, Jennifer Nez. *Reclaiming Diné History: The Legacies of Navajo Chief Manuelito and Juanita*. Tucson: University of Arizona Press, 2007.

Faris, James C. *Navajo and Photography: A Critical History of the Representation of an American People.* Albuquerque: University of New Mexico Press, 1996.

Hedlund, Ann Lane. *Navajo Weaving in the Late Twentieth Century: Kin, Community and Collectors*. Tucson: University of Arizona Press, 2004.

———. "Beyond Beauty: Exploring the Ethnoaesthetics of Navajo Weaving." *American Indian Art Magazine* 40, no. 3 (2015): 44–59.

———. *Reflections of the Weaver's World: The Gloria F. Ross Collection of Contemporary Navajo Weaving*. Seattle: University of Washington Press, 1993.

———. *Beyond the Loom: Keys to Understanding Early Southwestern Weaving*. Boulder, CO: Johnson Publishing Company, 1990.

———. *Contemporary Navajo Weaving: Thoughts that Count*. Flagstaff: Museum of Northern Arizona, 1994.

Her Many Horses, Emil, ed. *Identity by Design: Tradition, Change, and Celebration in Native Women's Dresses*. New York: HarperCollins Publishers in association with the National Museum of the American Indian, Smithsonian Institution, 2007.

Kelly, Klara, and Harris Francis. *A Diné History of Navajoland*. Tucson: University of Arizona Press, 2019.

Kent, Kate Peck. *Navajo Weaving: Three Centuries of Change*. Santa Fe: School of American Research Press, 1985.

Kimmerer, Robin Wall. *Braiding Sweetgrass: Indigenous Wisdom, Scientific Knowledge, and the Teachings of Plants*. Minneapolis: Milkweed Editions, 2013.

Lee, Lloyd L. *Diné Identity in a Twenty-First-Century World*. Tucson: University of Arizona Press, 2020.

Lee, Lloyd L., ed. *Diné Perspectives: Revitalizing and Reclaiming Navajo Thought*. Tucson: University of Arizona Press, 2014.

———. *Navajo Sovereignty: Understandings and Visions of the Diné People*. Tucson: University of Arizona Press, 2017.

———. *Nihikéyah: Navajo Homeland.* Tucson: University of Arizona Press, 2023.

Lee, Rechanda. "A Search for Continuity in the Transmission of Technological Styles in Navajo Weaving Traditions." *Kiva* 87, no. 3 (2021): 316–35. DOI: 10.1080/00231940.2021.1906495.

Lonetree, Amy. *Decolonizing Museums: Representing Native America in National and Tribal Museums*. Chapel Hill: University of North Carolina Press, 2012.

Mark, David M., David Stea, and Carmelita Topaha. *An Illustrated Dictionary of Navajo Landscape Terms*. New York: Peter Lang, 2019.

M'Closkey, Kathy. *Swept Under the Rug: A Hidden History of Navajo Rugs.* Albuquerque: University of New Mexico Press, 2002.

McLerran, Jennifer. *A New Deal for Navajo Weaving: Reform and Revival of Diné Textiles.* Tucson: University of Arizona Press, 2022.

Mithlo, Nancy Marie. *Knowing Native Arts*. Lincoln: University of Nebraska Press, 2020.

Rodee, Marian E. *Weaving of the Southwest: From the Maxwell Museum of Anthropology, University of New Mexico*. Atglen, PA: Schiffer Publishing, 1987.

———. *One Hundred Years of Navajo Rugs.* Albuquerque: University of New Mexico Press, 1995.

Tapahonso, Luci. *A Radiant Curve*. Tucson: University of Arizona Press, 2008.

Teller Pete, Lynda, and Barbara Teller Ornelas. *Spider Woman's Children: Navajo Weavers Today.* Atglen, PA: Schiffer Publishing, 2018.

———. *How to Weave a Navajo Rug and Other Lessons from Spider Woman.* Atglen, PA: Schiffer Publishing, 2020.

Tohe, Laura. *Tséyi'/Deep in the Rock: Reflections on Canyon de Chelly*. Tucson: University of Arizona Press, 2005.

Tselani/Terrain: The Tapestries of D. Y. Begay. Exhibition catalogue. Flagstaff: Museum of Northern Arizona, 2018.

Valette, Jean-Paul, and Rebecca M. Valette. *Navajo Weavings with Ceremonial Themes: A Historical Overview of a Secular Art Form.* Atglen, PA: Schiffer Publishing, 2017.

Valette, Rebecca M., and Jean-Paul Valette. *Weaving the Dance: Navajo Yeibichai Textiles (1910–1950).* Albuquerque: Adobe Gallery, 2000. Distributed by University of Washington Press.

Webster, Laurie D., Louise Stiver, D. Y. Begay, and Lynda Teller Pete. *Navajo Textiles: The Crane Collection at the Denver Museum of Nature & Science*. Boulder, CO: University Press of Colorado, 2017.

Wheat, Joe Ben, and Ann Lane Hedlund. *Blanket Weaving in the Southwest*. Tucson: University of Arizona Press, 2003.

Whitaker, Kathleen. *Southwest Textiles: Weavings of the Pueblo and Navajo*. Seattle: University of Washington Press, 2002.

———. *Common Threads: Pueblo and Navajo Textiles in the Southwest Museum.* Los Angeles: The Southwest Museum, 1998.

Weisiger, Marsha. *Dreaming of Sheep in Navajo Country*. Seattle: University of Washington Press, 2009.

Wilkins, Teresa J. *Patterns of Exchange: Navajo Weavers and Traders*. Norman: University of Oklahoma Press, 2013.

Williams, Lucy Fowler, and TahNibaa Naataanii. "A Navajo 'Slave' Blanket." In *Water Wind Breath: Southwest Native Art in the Barnes Foundation*, 118–20. Exhibition catalogue. New Haven and London: Yale University Press, 2022.

Yohe, Jill Ahlberg, and Teri Greeves. *Hearts of Our People: Native Women Artists*. Edited by Laura Silver. Minneapolis: Minneapolis Institute of Art in association with the University of Washington Press, 2019.

Contributors

Kevin Aspaas (Diné) is of the Towering House People Clan and born for the Bitterwater People Clan. His maternal grandfathers are of the Many Goats People Clan and his paternal grandfather is of the Mud People Clan. He is a weaver and fiber artist from Shiprock, New Mexico. Aspaas utilizes the traditional Diné sheep-to-loom weaving process. He is best known for producing the old-style Navajo wedge weaving technique and for creating other traditional and contemporary Navajo textiles. Aspaas currently serves as a board member of Diné Bé'iíná, a Diné-led nonprofit organization whose mission is to promote and preserve Navajo lifeways through land, sheep, fiber, and food.

Rapheal Begay (Diné) is Hónágháahnii (One Who Walks Around) and born for Kinłichii'nii (Red House People). His maternal grandfather is Tábąąhá (Water's Edge) and his paternal grandfather is 'Áshįįhi (Salt People). He is a visual storyteller based in Window Rock, Arizona. His work activates cultural landscape photography and oral storytelling traditions to document and celebrate the Diné way of life. Begay's research and practice include curatorial collaboration and community organizing informed by visual sovereignty and land-based knowledge. Begay is co-curator, with Hadley Welch Jensen, of *Horizons: Weaving Between the Lines with Diné Textiles* (Museum of Indian Arts and Culture, Santa Fe, 2023–2025). Begay holds a BFA in Photography with a minor in Arts Management and a Certificate in Museum Studies from the University of New Mexico.

Wade Campbell (Diné) is of the Towering House People and born for German Americans. His maternal grandfather is of the Near the Water People and his paternal grandfather is of Scottish American descent. He is Assistant Professor of Archaeology and Anthropology at Boston University. His research explores the historical relationships between Diné communities and other groups in the US Southwest, including the Pueblos, Spanish, and Euro-Americans. Campbell's work examines long-term patterns of Diné settlement and economic activity across the greater Four Corners region, with a focus on the origins of the Diné sheepherding tradition and related shifts in land use, social organization, and diet and subsistence practices from AD 1600 to the present day.

Tony Chavarria (Santa Clara Pueblo) has over thirty years of experience collaborating with tribes and curating Native material culture. As Curator of Ethnology at the Museum of Indian Arts and Culture in Santa Fe, he has curated many exhibitions of historic and contemporary Native art including *Comic Art Indigène, A New Century: The Life and Legacy of Cherokee Artist and Educator Lloyd "Kiva" New,* and *Diego Romero vs. the End of Art.* He served as the community liaison and co-curator for *Our Universes*, the inaugural Pueblo exhibition at the National Museum of the American Indian, and was co-curator for *Creating Tradition: Innovation and Change in American Indian Art*, the first Native exhibition at Epcot Center. He has co-curated exhibitions at the Barnes Foundation in Philadelphia and Chicago's Field Museum and is part of the Pueblo Clay Collective, which curated the traveling exhibition *Grounded in Clay: The Spirit of Pueblo Pottery*. He continues to consult on matters of Native art and culture while occasionally making art.

Jennifer Nez Denetdale (Diné) is Professor of American Studies at the University of New Mexico, where she teaches courses in critical Indigenous studies, Indigenous gender and sexuality, Indigenous feminisms and gender, and Navajo studies. As the first Diné to earn a PhD in history, Denetdale is a strong advocate for Native peoples and the next generation of students interested in Indigenous studies. Her publications include *Reclaiming Diné History: The Legacies of Navajo Chief Manuelito and Juanita* and *The Long Walk: The Forced Exile of the Navajo.* A frequent consultant for Indigenous-based museum exhibitions and films, Denetdale is chair of the Navajo Nation Human Rights Commission-and has advocated for Navajo women and the LGBTQI2S community. Her many awards include the Rainbow Naatsiilid True Colors Award, the UNM Faculty of Color Award, and the UNM Presidential Award of Distinction. In 2023, she was selected as the Benedict Distinguished Visiting Professor at Carleton College in Northfield, Minnesota.

Hadley Welch Jensen is Curator of Collections and Research at the Wheelwright Museum in Santa Fe, New Mexico. Through an interdisciplinary and collaborative approach, her work explores the intersection of visual art, anthropology, and material culture. Jensen is curator of *Shaped by the Loom: Weaving Worlds in the American Southwest* (Bard Graduate Center Gallery, New York, 2023) and co-curator, with Rapheal Begay, of *Horizons: Weaving Between the Lines with Diné Textiles* (Museum of Indian Arts and Culture, Santa Fe, 2023–2025). From 2018 to 2021, she was a Postdoctoral Fellow in Museum Anthropology, a joint appointment between Bard Graduate Center and the Anthropology Division of the American Museum of Natural History. She holds an MA and PhD from Bard Graduate Center.

Lillia McEnaney is a museum anthropologist and independent curator living and working in Santa Fe, New Mexico. Previously an assistant curator at the Museum of Indian Arts and Culture/Laboratory of Anthropology, she was the exhibition project manager for *Horizons: Weaving Between the Lines with Diné Textiles*. She is currently an assistant curator at the Museum of International Folk Art and the director of the Hands-On Student Curatorial Program at the Ralph T. Coe Center for the Arts. Lillia holds an MA from New York University and a BA from Hamilton College.

Larissa Nez (Diné) is of the Mud People and born for the Mountain Cove People. Her maternal grandfather is of the Red Running into the Water People and her paternal grandfather is of the Big Water People. She is currently a PhD student in the Department of Ethnic Studies at the University of California, Berkeley. Centering critical Indigenous theory, decolonial theory, and the Black Radical Tradition, her research explores the relationship between Blackness and Indigeneity as political projects and social analytics. Focusing on the work of modern and contemporary Afro-Indigenous, Black, and Indigenous visual artists and filmmakers, Larissa seeks to articulate the ways resistance and survival, kinship and belonging, memory and futurity are intrinsic to the world-making that comes about due to, and in spite of, the world-breaking of colonial and imperial violence. Her research shows how Afro-Indigenous, Black, and Indigenous people are imagining and building worlds and futures that are dialectically and intimately connected to the past and present, land/water/sky and body, and the material and spiritual.

Lynda Teller Pete (Diné) is born into her mother's clan, Water's Edge Clan, Tábąąhá, and born for her father's clan, Water-Flows-Together Clan, Tó'aheedlíinii. Her maternal grandfather's clan is Red Bottom People, Tł'ááshchí'í, and her paternal grandfather's clan is One-Walks-Around Clan, Honágháahnii. That is how she identifies herself as a Diné woman. Lynda is an award-winning fifth-generation weaver who is best known for using a traditional Two Grey Hills regional style. Instilled in her work from the age of six, when she was formally introduced to weaving, is the belief that beauty and harmony should be woven into every rug. Pete collaborates with art centers, guilds, museums, universities, and other venues to educate the public about Diné history and the preservation of Navajo weaving traditions. With her sister Barbara Teller Ornelas, she co-authored *Spider Woman's Children: Navajo Weavers Today*, the first book written by Diné weavers about Diné weavers, as well as *How to Weave a Navajo Rug and Other Lessons from Spider Woman*. Pete is a Luce Indigenous Knowledge Fellow (2022–2023) and the Board Director of Equity and Inclusion at the Textile Society of America.

Darby Raymond-Overstreet (Diné) is Many Hogans and born for White Americans. Her maternal grandfather is Towering House Clan and her paternal grandfather is African American. She is an award-winning digital artist and printmaker. Born in Tuba City, Arizona, and raised in Flagstaff, Arizona, she received her BA with honors in Psychology and Studio Art from Dartmouth College in 2016. In her artistic practice she studies, incorporates, and creates Diné pattern designs that materialize through portraits, landscapes, and abstract forms. Raymond-Overstreet's work is heavily inspired by and derived from traditional Diné textiles, in particular pieces woven from the late 1800s to the 1950s. She currently resides and works in Chimayó, New Mexico.

Tyrrell Tapaha (Diné) is of the Many Goats Clan and born for the Folded Arms People. Their maternal grandfather is of the Water's Edge People and their paternal grandfather is of the Mexican People. Tyrrell is a weaver and fiber artist from Goat Springs, Arizona. Their work encompasses the intergenerational pastoral living handed down through Tapaha's grandfather, great-grandmother, and other relatives. Tapaha produces woven textiles and felted objects for both aesthetic and utilitarian uses, made with raw natural fibers predominantly grown on the Navajo Nation and hand-dyed with local flora from the Four Corners area. Tapaha has worked as an apprentice with master weaver Roy Kady (Diné). In addition to their fiber and textile practice, Tapaha also works as a full-time sheepherder in the Four Corners region of the Navajo Nation.

Laura Tohe (Diné/Laguna Pueblo) is Sleepy Rock People Clan born for the Bitter Water People Clan. She grew up listening to and watching the women in her family create wonderous textiles with wool, color, and designs that grew upward on their looms. They inspired her poems about weaving. A librettist and an award-winning poet, Tohe has written three books of poetry, edited two books, and authored an oral history on the Navajo Code Talkers. Her commissioned libretto *Enemy Slayer, A Navajo Oratorio* world-premiered for the Phoenix Symphony, and her most recent libretto, *Nahasdzaan in the Glittering World*, was performed in France in 2019 and 2021. Many of her poems have also been translated into musical compositions and foreign languages. Among her awards are the 2020 Academy of American Poetry Fellowship, the 2019 American Indian Festival of Writers Award, and the Arizona Book Association's Glyph Award for Best Poetry. Tohe is Professor Emerita with Distinction at Arizona State University and Poet Laureate of the Navajo Nation.

Horizons: Weaving Between the Lines with Diné Textiles

An exhibition at the Museum of Indian Arts and Culture
Santa Fe, New Mexico
July 16, 2023–February 2, 2025

Exhibition Co-Curators

Rapheal Begay (Diné)
Hadley Welch Jensen

Exhibition Advisory Committee

Lynda Teller Pete (Diné, Chair)
Kevin Aspaas (Diné)
Larissa Nez (Diné)
Darby Raymond-Overstreet (Diné)
Tyrrell Tapaha (Diné)